The Archaeology of American Cities

THE AMERICAN EXPERIENCE IN ARCHAEOLOGICAL PERSPECTIVE

UNIVERSITY PRESS OF FLORIDA

Florida A&M University, Tallahassee
Florida Atlantic University, Boca Raton
Florida Gulf Coast University, Ft. Myers
Florida International University, Miami
Florida State University, Tallahassee
New College of Florida, Sarasota
University of Central Florida, Orlando
University of Florida, Gainesville
University of North Florida, Jacksonville
University of South Florida, Tampa
University of West Florida, Pensacola

The Archaeology
of American Cities

Nan A. Rothschild and Diana diZerega Wall

FOREWORD BY MICHAEL S. NASSANEY

UNIVERSITY PRESS OF FLORIDA

Gainesville Tallahassee Tampa Boca Raton

Pensacola Orlando Miami Jacksonville Ft. Myers Sarasota

This book may be available in an electronic edition.

First cloth printing, 2014
First paperback printing, 2015

Library of Congress Control Number: 2014934213
ISBN 978-0-8130-4972-4 (cloth)
ISBN 978-0-8130-6194-8 (pbk.)

University Press of Florida
15 Northwest 15th Street
Gainesville, FL 32611-2079
http://www.upf.com

Dedicated to our students

And to Bert Salwen, who taught us how

Contents

Figures

Foreword

HAVING SPENT MOST OF MY LIFE in the residential suburbs of moderate-sized cities, I was admittedly overwhelmed at the prospect of attending the Graduate Center at the City University of New York in the early 1980s. During my campus visit to Fifth Avenue in the heart of Manhattan, I spent considerably more time gawking at the towers that loomed overhead than thinking about what could possibly lie beneath my feet. As someone who was unaccustomed to the surroundings of a megalopolis, I chose the more rural setting of the University of Massachusetts–Amherst in the tranquil Connecticut River valley to earn my doctoral degree. While in residence my urban experiences were limited to regular archaeology conference venues, occasional trips to Boston to take in a Red Sox game, and visits to my hometown, the "city" of Central Falls, Rhode Island (pop. 20,000), located some seven miles north of Providence. To this day I admire cities from a distance and have approached them with some (perhaps unnecessary) trepidation.

Yet I have always returned from cities intellectually and emotionally invigorated, knowing that cities are centers of innovation, glamour, and excitement. Indeed, they are "central places" in the words of geographers—locales that harbored functions that could only be supported by large numbers of people, such as concert halls, stadiums, government offices, and marketplaces. American cities that were established as part of the process of European colonization have served these functions among numerous others for the past four hundred years. It would be trite to say that they were formative in the American experience and literally contain the materials from which our national history can be written.

Given their significance, prevalence, and time depth, it should come as no surprise that cities are an increasingly important context for archaeological study, especially of the recent past. Archaeologists have repeatedly demonstrated that stratum upon stratum of cultural deposits often exist below asphalt roads, concrete sidewalks, and even deep basements—hidden from view but relatively pristine. While urban development certainly destroyed traces of past city life, surprisingly untold circumstances and serendipity have often spared long forgotten building remains, privies, cemeteries, and other archaeological features that constitute a treasure trove of information about previous occupants in all their social, political, and economic complexity.

In *The Archaeology of American Cities*, Nan A. Rothschild and Diana diZerega Wall use their considerable expertise to showcase how archaeologists have begun to disentangle the complexity of our urban heritage. Initiated under the historical preservation movement and expanded by cultural resource management mandates, investigation of the materiality of America's cities has intensified in the last three decades. Rothschild and Wall, pioneers in the field of urban archaeology, provide an important and useful synthesis that demonstrates that the accelerating process of urban growth and renewal has not disturbed all vestiges of previous activities. Moreover, careful archaeological study can provide anthropological information on the people who have built, occupied, and abandoned cities since colonial times.

Archaeological deposits in urban settings can be daunting in their horizontal and vertical extent and regularly yield far more data than archaeologists are often prepared to handle. At the least, investigations of urban contexts can require a specialized set of discovery and recovery techniques, often beginning with a backhoe and involving sometimes costly safety precautions. The authors provide a reasoned approach to the investigation of America's cities grounded in the strengths of archaeological inquiry. First, they employ macro and micro scales. At the macro scale they focus on the city as artifact and link the features that archaeologists encounter (e.g., landfill, wharves, canals, railroads, and water and waste disposal systems) to the economic growth of the city. Analysis at the micro scale allows for close contextual examination of the intersections of race, ethnicity, class, and gender and the ways in which material culture was mobilized to assert and challenge social identities in urban settings. Next, they combine documentary and material evidence as complementary data sources that are seldom redundant. For example, while documents may suggest locations of interest, only archaeology can identify extant remains. Careful observation in the ground can also provide evidence of vernacular building traditions that went unrecorded in documents. Finally, archaeology is well suited to examine long-term history by peeling away layers and documenting settlement expansion as cities grew and annexed adjoining areas.

To compile this comprehensive synthesis, Rothschild and Wall have reviewed an enormous literature in urban archaeology, including CRM reports and other less accessible source materials, to highlight salient themes that reflect some distinctive characteristics of America's cities. They are also careful to note a broad range of factors that account for variation in their origins, construction, and organization as expressed in material remains. For example, while the grid was a common framework for the layout of cities, it was subject to modification where political and practical contingencies held sway. The authors provide useful definitions of the city and underscore its significance for understanding American life. They boldly suggest that the city is possibly one of the most important inventions in human history. It certainly is becoming an increasingly attractive residential option—some 82 percent of Americans are now urban dwellers. This changing demographic pattern underscores the relevance of urban archaeology to an increasing population that aims to connect with the past.

The city has been the site of political contestation and continues to be so. Beginning in the eighteenth century, urban growth was influenced by elites who could monopolize preferred locations to reinforce their positions of power. For example, they limited access to necessities like foodstuffs by placing markets away from consumers. The production, distribution, and consumption of goods and services in cities reflect changes in political economy that led to ethnic enclaves. These forces created a distinctive social geography in which newcomers to cities generally settled where there were others like them. Once they assimilated (provided they met the criteria, particularly whiteness), they, in turn, moved to other locations consonant with their class position.

This is the legacy of many industrial cities in the Northeast like Central Falls. Until immigration policies changed in 1965, most residents were attracted there to work in the textile mills. Working-class ethnics who migrated in the late nineteenth and early twentieth centuries, particularly Irish, Polish, French Canadian, and Syrian, dominated the city. Well-defined neighborhoods were clustered around their churches, integrating institutions that were scattered within the 1.3-square-mile municipality. The factories were located along the river on the eastern side of town. They were owned by outside interests and supervised by managers who lived nearby. Many immigrants toiled in the mills to ensure an education for their children, who were able to become socioeconomically and spatially mobile. In some cities, those who chose to remain were forcibly displaced in the process of urban renewal, which has ironically created opportunities to study these populations and begin to tell their story.

Control over the histories of cities has also triggered political struggles. Archaeological remains beneath city streets and blocks led to public outcries in at least two high-profile cases that have received national and international attention. Insofar as archaeology can challenge contemporary myths that serve the dominant society, the discipline and its findings will become relevant to communities that aim to expose injustices and rewrite history. Marginalized groups can have a voice through archaeology, and their voices can be amplified in urban settings where concentrated media channels can be used to galvanize public opinion. In the well-known African Burial Ground in New York City, the most glaring message was that slavery once existed in the North—an inconvenient truth that had long been ignored in favor of emphasizing the atrocities of Southern plantation slavery. At the President's House in Philadelphia, slavery also came under scrutiny when developments there led to the archaeological investigation of quarters used by people enslaved by our founding father, George Washington—just steps away from our most hallowed symbol of freedom, the Liberty Bell. Archaeology provided the literal space to entertain a dialogue on race, participated in by thousands of visitors. Urban sites that relate to historically disenfranchised groups have become a flashpoint to incite community engagement in archaeology. Archaeology is effective, to paraphrase one practitioner, at revealing the process of forgetting what has occurred in the construction of our national history. Much of that history took place in cities, where powerful figures congregated to legislate, regulate, contemplate, placate, negotiate, and emancipate. These same buildings, public squares, and back alleys were occupied by the relatively powerless who strived to forge their own view of what it meant to be an American, often alongside and sometimes in opposition to dominant ideals.

The myriad and prosaic threads of the past deeply buried in cities must be woven into the tapestry of our American experience. By presenting a historical overview of the archaeology of cities, drawing on examples from throughout the country since the colonial era, and highlighting distinctively American themes, Rothschild and Wall bring the texture of American life into better focus and help us to understand the importance of the materiality of past urban life for the present.

Michael S. Nassaney
Series Editor

Preface

WHEN MICHAEL NASSANEY first proposed the idea of writing this book to one of us (Rothschild), it was immediately apparent that it should be done by us both. We began our urban archaeological experience together over three decades ago, as students of Bert Salwen, by co-directing one of the first large-scale urban excavations in the country. So it was only appropriate that we should undertake this writing project together, too.

That early excavation took place at the Stadt Huys Block, in the heart of the Wall Street district in Manhattan. Before we started, we were afraid we would find nothing that was coherent or archaeologically interesting. However, the problem, as many of us who have done urban projects now know, is not that these projects produce too little but that they produce too much, literally tons of material. The success of these excavations was instrumental in incorporating archaeological study into New York City's environmental review process. Since that time there have been hundreds of excavations in cities all over the United States and many more in cities across the globe.

We felt qualified to write this book for two reasons. First, as we mentioned, we have long experience in the field. Second, we have experience in different kinds of urban projects, both those mandated by the Cultural Resource Management (CRM) process and large- and small-scale non-CRM projects, so we know that good archaeology is not restricted to one or another of these forms of funding and regulation.

What has proved so exciting about this writing project was that it allowed us to learn about the discoveries made by our colleagues throughout the country over the last three and a half decades. Prior to the 1970s, it did not occur to most archaeologists that fieldwork in cities could be productive, but the environmental legislation that requires the work has led to an awareness of how significant it can be.

When we began the book we were concerned about the nature of the findings—whether after all those years and all that money, the profession had discovered anything beyond the trivial—but fortunately that concern turned out to be unwarranted. We now know that these projects have archaeological value and that the archaeological approach is in a particularly strong position to consider cities and their growth and development because of its focus on space and materiality, seen stratigraphically.

Here, we summarize some of the discoveries that have been made about the American experience in the course of the archaeological study of urban sites over the last three decades. We have used two scales of analysis, both very appropriate for archaeology: the macro, where we examine the whole city, its spatial array and dimensions; and the micro, where we look at the consumption patterns found in urban areas as they are cross-cut by race, ethnicity, class, and gender. We also consider sites of manufacturing and trade as well as the archaeological evidence of service providers. We rely for interpretation on the materiality of urban lives, where excavation reveals the complex and often unpredictable ways that people mobilize objects in their homes and construct their cuisines.

Urban fieldwork is especially challenging. It may involve the use of big machines and small samples painstakingly recovered from complex sites, or it can take place in areas which have been protected from disturbance over the centuries. Sites can be preserved under the basement floors of modern buildings, or they are found in backyards, or under streets, or in city parks where the stratigraphy can be surprisingly straightforward. The data recovered from these contexts can be used to answer questions about the nature of The City, or the nature and development of a specific city, and of the people who lived in it, and that is what we have attempted to do here.

The writing of this book, more than most others, depended on the generosity and goodwill of our colleagues and fellow urban archaeologists. Although there has been some outstanding urban research done as part of the CRM process, most of it is part of the gray literature and is thus often little known and hard to find out about. We are heavily indebted to those who sent us URLs, files, CDs, and hard copies of site reports and to others who answered frequent and probably seemingly endless and boring queries. We could not have written this book without them. And for all those whose material we relied upon, there were many others who sent us reports or information that we could not use, as this was meant to be a short book. But we are grateful to them as well.

We particularly thank Thomas Beaman, Diane Dallal, Glenda Deyloff, Jean Howson, Meta Janowitz, Terry Klein, Cheryl La Roche, Mark Leone, Jed Levin,

Barbara Magid, Elizabeth Meade, Michael Meyer, Doug Mooney, Steve Post, Patricia Samford, Cherie Scheick, Jay Stottman, and Homer Thiel for all of their assistance with site information. We are also grateful to others whom we contacted frequently, including Linda Cordell, Dedie Snow, Steve Tull, Barb Voss, Rebecca Yamin, and Anne Yentsch. We also relied greatly on having online access to the Praetzellises' excellent site reports at Sonoma State University. We appreciate all those who helped with the images: Mark Leone, Elizabeth Meade, Arnold Pickman, Adrian Praetzellis, Emily Rothschild, Sarah Ruch, Molly Scofield, and Rebecca Yamin. Meredith Linn read and commented on chapters 3 and 5, which are better for her suggestions. Courtney Singleton took on the bibliography, which was more complicated than any of us realized. We are grateful to Sonia Dickey of the University Press of Florida for her help and support throughout the process and Elaine Otto for her excellent copyediting. We appreciate the comments of Mary Beaudry and Adrian Praetzellis on an earlier draft. Michael Cooper and Murray Wall helped in many ways. Last, but by no means least, we thank Michael Nassaney for inviting Rothschild to write the volume and for commenting on that earlier draft. We are grateful to them all, but take full responsibility for any errors. We hope you enjoy the book.

1

Studying Cities

CITIES ATTRACT ATTENTION as well as people; they are both appealing and elusive. They are crucibles of social movements and technological innovation and are arguably the most significant of human inventions. Archaeologists have been attracted to urban places since the earliest days of the discipline, although it was the large size and antiquity of the ruins that initially drew attention rather than the fact that they were urban places. Schliemann's excavations at Troy, Sir Mortimer Wheeler's work at ancient Ur, or the discovery of lost cities hidden in the jungles of Mesoamerica immediately come to mind. In a sense, cities and archaeologists created each other; urban excavations were dramatic and made the reputations of archaeologists as well as of the cities they examined.

This book is about the archaeological study of modern American cities, what they are like, and how people have lived in them. We consider how they have developed and how they have changed. And we are especially interested in how our understanding of these cities has been enhanced by archaeological research. We believe that archaeology has contributed to the story of all cities, pre-Columbian as well as modern ones, their commonalities and variability. Archaeology's strength in studying cities lies in a combination of factors that include macro and micro scales of analysis, scales that we use in this book. At the macro level we look at the city as a whole, as an artifact in its own right, and at the micro level we examine the people who lived in them. The discipline of historical archaeology has the advantage of integrating materiality with historic documentation, allowing us to create a richly nuanced picture of urban lives and places.

One of our primary concerns is the link between spatial and social aspects of cities. How does the changing geographical landscape of the city interrelate with the sociocultural characteristics of its inhabitants and the movement of people who are characterized by different attributes of ethnicity, race, class, and gender? Urban archaeology allows us to observe the formation and re-formation of spatially visible elements of the city in relation to these changes.

Modern cities today are increasingly important as places where people live. In 1950, 30 percent of the world's population lived in cities, while by 2000, that figure had increased to almost 50 percent. Today it is estimated that the urban population is about 80 percent (Abbott 2007). Modern American cities are similar to cities everywhere, although of course much younger than the world's famous early urban entities—Catalhoyuk (6000 BCE) in Turkey, Ur (3800–2000 BCE) in Iraq, Luoyang (2070 BCE–first century CE) in China, Harappa (3300–1300 BCE) in Pakistan, and Teotihuacan in Mexico (200 BCE–600 CE), not to mention the European cities of London, Paris, and Rome. However, even in the relatively short time since the European colonization of the Americas, a diverse array of cities has developed, ranging from those formed in a late medieval mold to those formed under postindustrial capitalism. We believe that the most significant differences among these urban places are those between preindustrial and industrial cities, in part because the elites relentlessly assumed greater control of space and its allocations in the latter cities (Harvey 1973; Smith 2008).

Because American cities are relatively recent, observers are able to examine elements such as their planning and landscape transformation. Urban form is critical, but so are urban processes, and archaeology's ability to record temporal change allows us to observe cities as they evolve. Urban processes are similar everywhere. Settlements begin with a core, either planned or formed organically around core functions. Urbanization (the growth of cities in size and population) expands the original settlement for particular reasons.

Early archaeologists working in the United States avoided doing fieldwork in its modern cities because it was assumed that there would be few undisturbed deposits left in them due to the intense development and redevelopment of the same piece of land. Archaeological priorities focused on non-urban, frequently undeveloped places. But ironically development has been the primary force behind doing urban archaeology in modern cities. Environmental compliance legislation in the United States, beginning in the 1970s, mandates the archaeological examination of urban places in some cases when development is planned (see chapter 2). Although most doubted that there would be intact or meaningful archaeological deposits and information extracted from excavations in places like New York, San Francisco, and New Orleans, those doubts were ill-founded. Archaeology's focus on stratigraphic analysis is particularly suited to the nature of urban construction as buildings can be layered one on top of another in the urban core. Although portions of prior deposits are often destroyed, enough frequently remain to clarify and amplify the sequence and nature of changing land use and ways of life through excavation and the examination of documents.

In this book, we present a singular story: how the practice and perspective of historical archaeology contributes unique insights to our understanding of urban development in the United States. Using an archaeological perspective, we hope to convey how and why cities appeared in the United States; under what cultural conditions they developed, persisted, changed, and disappeared; and how they were formative in the American experience. An archaeological viewpoint is grounded in spatial reality and materiality; it uses information recovered from excavations and from documents to examine questions of urban development and decline. Urbanization is particularly accessible to the archaeological observer; it involves the reworking and reinvention of the landscape in consort with changes in social organization and the political economy.

What Is a City?

Before we discuss the kinds of information that archaeologists have discovered from urban excavations in the United States, we need to address a number of questions related to our consideration of cities, including their characteristics. Brendan Behan offered a lighthearted definition of a city in regard to New York: "[It] is my Lourdes, where I go for spiritual refreshment . . . a place where you're least likely to be bitten by a wild goat" (Slattery 2008, note 1). More seriously, cities today are clearly increasingly important as homes and workplaces for people, so it is worth trying to explain what we understand by the term. How do we define those entities that we call "cities"? How can we characterize them? And finally, how can we study them archaeologically? (See chapter 2.)

The first two questions are related, of course. We can all recognize a city, but its definition eludes us. There is no absolute set of criteria which we can check off to ascertain that a place is a city. Louis Wirth (1938), an early urban scholar, offered what has become a classic set of criteria to characterize a contemporary city: size, density, permanence, and heterogeneity. We would also add to those attributes extraordinary variability in form and structural complexity. However, we will see that these do not necessarily work all the time and in all places. Cities contain most human activities and practices and many ethnic, racial, and class groups; for the most part they superimpose the cultural world on the natural, and they give the illusion of isolating humans from nature. They incorporate the future and the past, express hope and fear, wishes and anxieties; they connect and fragment their populations. Cities may arise from deep sociality, but points of contestation reveal tensions in the social fabric.

The first entities recognized as urban appeared relatively recently, given the sweep of human existence. The earliest we know of is Catalhoyuk in Turkey, where around 8,000 to 9,400 years ago between 3,500 and 8,000 people lived in tightly clustered residences. The community was unusual in that its houses contained burials and many works of art (previously interpreted as shrines). But it was unlike later urban centers in its lack of public buildings (Hodder 2010, 3). Just a few thousand years later (from 4500 BCE onward), cities began to appear in Mesopotamia and then throughout much of the world, prompting V. Gordon Childe (1950) to coin the term "urban revolution." While we cannot say what contributed to the process of urbanization initially, we can isolate the characteristics that these early cities shared. Subsistence was based on intensive agriculture and required a climate conducive to farming, often with the help of irrigation and access to varied econiches. Food production provided a surplus, and access to land and water was regulated by the state. Most cities either embodied states or were part of them and had relatively large and sedentary populations, with diverse and specialized occupations and activities, and were socially stratified by occupation and wealth.

One of their key attributes was the creation of iconic structures such as temples and pyramids that persisted for many generations (Hayden 1995) and that are often identified through archaeology. Cities, like states, exert economic control over their populations, regulating long-distance trade to restrict access to imported goods or those produced in limited quantities. They were sometimes multiethnic and often included "others," such as servants or slaves who did not enjoy the rights of citizenship. These entities included a municipal political structure (government and officials) and the ability to make laws and field an internal army or police force (Sjoberg 1960). Urban occupations included administrators, religious and military practitioners, specialized craftspeople, merchants and shopkeepers, educators, those who provided services for travelers (running inns for pilgrims and traders), and landlords (people making money through ownership of land).

One of the conditions under which cities arose was when urban specialists were needed to serve a large group of people, including those in the hinterland; as these specialists increased in number, the reach of the city and its size did, too. Cities came to be identified by the presence of specific institutions that dominated the landscape, expressing the power of the state in symbolic form. Samford (1996, 65), in considering towns in eighteenth-century Virginia, described them as "an accumulation of people in a locus which serves political, social and/or economic functions." Rural people came to towns and cities to perform specific tasks that could be done only there and brought resources needed by urban dwellers, establishing a consistently symbiotic relationship between city and hinterland. In a sense, urban settlements were created from demand and issues of convenience. Visitors could take advantage of economies of scale if they could go to the same place to consult a seer, pay taxes, and bring produce or animals to market. Local markets provided some foods, and local priests performed some functions, but less-frequently-performed tasks required greater distances: court visits, pilgrimages, or paying taxes. Thus a hierarchy of towns and cities with specific institutions developed; the same phenomenon is evident in today's American towns and cities (Berry 1967).

Quantitative Measures

As we mentioned above, two obvious urban criteria are size and density. One recent definition of an urban area suggests that it is the result of the spatial accumulation of productive activities (Baumont et al. 1998, 3:15). The evaluation of urban size and density must use relative measures, as both derive from particular conditions: the type of environment, the economic base and its carrying capacity, and occupational structure. In considering population size, there is a question as to what is being recorded: modern American census data take account of where people sleep and not where they work. However, contemporary cities often have relatively small residential populations and large numbers of commuters, raising issues of how to count and whom to count. The population growth of cities can derive from three factors: a rising birth rate, a falling death rate, and immigration, while their spatial growth results from the annexation of surrounding areas. If annexation occurs, the added areas are sometimes less "urban" in terms of density than the older core portion of the urban place (Gibson 1998, 5). In considering quantitative definitions it is also worth considering who makes the definitions and why. Government agencies create them as part of a mechanism to control their citizens: in the United States, communities of different sizes get different proportions of money distributed by state and federal governments. And tax rates vary for those who live in cities as opposed to non-urban communities. Nations also use their urban statistics to boast of development.

Historical archaeologists can evaluate the changing size and density of a city over time relatively easily, either through structural remains or old maps, although density can be difficult to use as a defining attribute because there are densely settled areas that do not meet other urban criteria. A contemporary definition of city that relies on density uses it quite loosely: "We use the term city to mean any human settlement that is functionally coherent and denser than its surroundings" (Decker et al. 2007, 2). Another criterion of urban life is the presence of special-purpose structures. For example, mining towns are dense but might not be described as urban because their population and architecture are fairly homogeneous and lack specialized occupations or structures. Virginia City, Nevada, is one such example of a community that has been described as urban in its heyday (Hattori 2008), but other observers might not consider it as such. Founded in the 1850s on the basis of gold and silver mining, it began as a tent city, but grew in importance during the Civil War, when the Union needed metals for its army. It was the most important settlement between San Francisco and Denver at that time, and after the railroad was established it got even bigger, with 30,000 residents at its peak in the 1870s and 1880s. However, the Comstock Mine there was depleted by 1898 and most people left. Now it is a historic district, housing about 1,000 people. If we use the attribute of density to consider Virginia City an urban place, we would have to define it as a "special purpose" city with a temporary and unbalanced population (by gender, age, and occupation), as at its largest it contained mostly men who hoped to generate wealth through mining and then return home. This example underlines the fact that urban places were not necessarily stable; populations shifted in response to changes in the political economy, disputes or war, natural disasters, and changes in the economic base; they were also extremely variable and contingent on historical circumstance. Many of today's major U.S. cities grew in the late nineteenth century as industrialization was taking hold and immigration increased (Rothschild 2006). David Harvey (1973) explains the structure of contemporary cities, noting that they are magnets for surpluses (of labor, resources, and capital). As labor is mobilized, production and capital increase and the concentration of services, producers, and transport facilitates production and consumption. Accompanying these processes is the development of social injustice in the uneven provision of infrastructure to varying parts of the city. Since our goal is to gain some understanding of cities, we accept that they exist on a continuum and are not all the same; as noted above, they are often easier to recognize than define.

Nonquantitative Factors

Numbers are important in characterizing cities but not sufficient, as they do not consider diversity, the quality of city life, and urban processes. One of Wirth's criteria is that of heterogeneity. He was writing about Chicago in the 1930s, and for him heterogeneity meant that individuals in a city belonged to many different groups, defined by ethnicity, class, occupation, and other parameters. He suggested that immigration to cities increased heterogeneity and led to specialization of people and occupations and superficial, transitory relationships. He noted the psychological effects of living in crowded, impersonal places where residents knew each other only in highly segmented roles, where contacts were secondary, impersonal, superficial, and transitory (1938, 22). Since his time, scholars have discovered that people form meaningful communities within these megalopolises, and in any case, these criteria only apply to large modern cities, and not to preindustrial ones—the eighteenth-century walking cities like Boston, New York, and Philadelphia (Blackmar 1979).

Archaeologists may find evidence of heterogeneity in urban architecture in traits such as differences in house style, size, or décor, usually taken to imply socioeconomic or ethnic distinctions among residents; Tell Brak, in Syria, is an early example of such a site (B. Bower 2008). The physical appearance of pre-Columbian as well as modern cities is an important element of their definition. They are crowded, buildings are close together, or dense, and their central portions often contain special-purpose structures representing different economic, political, or ceremonial functions, services, and institutions. Some cities are walled, and many were planned and have orderly layouts. The labor required to build large structures and walls is a manifestation of political power. Some institutions, such as theaters or performance spaces, are distinctively urban. (One of these has been investigated archaeologically in Charleston, South Carolina, by Martha Zierden and Elizabeth Reitz [2007]). City architecture expresses society's values symbolically, whether religious in preindustrial times or commercial in more recent urban centers (Harvey, in Smith 2008). Thus there is a set of characteristics by which we can identify an urban place, even though it does not apply in all cases.

Spatial Elements

Perhaps the simplest definition of a city is that it is a central place in a region where settlements have become differentiated in size and function. The centrality of cities in their regions can be seen from the air or on transportation maps, as roads, trains, and bus routes all emanate from and converge on cities and towns. The idea of a central place is relative and situationally flexible as well as cross-culturally valid. A central place in ancient southwest Asia would look very different from Boston or Shanghai, but each would have the "attractive" qualities that drew others to visit, work, worship, trade, and perform acts of citizenship. Central place theory, developed by geographers, suggests that there is a predictable relationship between towns and cities of specific sizes in a particular cultural unit, once a state system is in place (Berry 1967). Cities are centers of power, and in the colonial and postcolonial worlds they are the initial sources of modernization. They serve to integrate the surrounding areas through their markets and other functions, creating a magnet for trade or industry as they develop.

From an archaeological viewpoint, the organization of a community's space is as important in manifesting its urban quality as its material remains. Space is much more than an organizing device; it is a powerful force creating urban life (see Lefebvre 1991; Soja 1989). The spatial envelope defines the urban form, but spatial form and social process are inextricably and recursively connected. One of the earliest strategies that colonial governments employed was to appropriate and regulate space (the Spanish in Santa Fe, the Dutch in New Amsterdam) as they turned it into place. Those in power controlled and apportioned land and determined the "look" of the incipient city and its spatial order. Planning is a form of social control, and city governments instituted rules regulating spatial use by different groups at different times. Many American towns, established as part of the colonial process, had a grid layout (derived from the original Roman town plan as imported by the Spanish, French, and British) in which a political structure, a church, and a market were centrally located and the hub of a transportation network. Some, however, grew in a less controlled manner. Depending on the particular colonial ideology, residential areas in these early settlements were allocated on an egalitarian basis (as in New England) or settled by socioeconomic rank or power (in Spanish colonies). We discuss planning and urban landscapes further in chapter 3.

As noted, architecture and spatial order provide important insights into social order. For example, social and spatial centrality and marginality are often conjoined, so that economically and politically powerful people live in central places or wherever they want, and the poor and less powerful live in less valued settings or wherever they are compelled to be. Elites live in larger or more elaborate buildings, in desirable areas, however defined, and poorer people live in smaller, simpler homes. One of the important aspects of many cities is the reuse of areas of settlement and structures as the society and economy change. Descriptions of a city at a specific moment in time neglect transformations and re-formations of cities, which are among their most intriguing aspects. Cities remodel some of their important neighborhoods and buildings, but ignore others. And new residents often occupy the housing left behind until a government agency decides to do "urban renewal." Although this practice began in the late nineteenth century and continues to this day, in the United States its heyday extended from the 1940s to the 1960s. Urban renewal (often correlated with "gentrification") is frequently a mechanism for displacing less desirable residents, particularly the poor (some of whom are immigrants) and African Americans.

This story of changing land use in American cities relates to immigration and industrialization. Edward Soja, a postmodern geographer, offers a capsule, simplified account of contemporary American urban transformations: people living in the country came to the city for economic opportunity afforded by the Industrial Revolution, then middle-class city residents left for the suburbs, and the city was refilled by the middle class, immigrants, the poor, and homeless who joined the elite who stayed there (2000).

The Contributions of Urban Archaeology

Urban archaeology contributes to our understanding of cities and their development through two unique aspects of its approach. One is the conjunction of the macro and micro scales, combining a sense of the overall cityscape, its components, and how they fit together and change when a new area is opened or expanded, with a detailed examination of individuals and their lives as seen in documentary records and the artifacts they left behind. The second is the combined analysis of the historic record with information revealed through excavation. Historical archaeology is particularly important in examining the lives of undocumented individuals (Deagan 1998), those whom government records tend to ignore because they owned no property, paid no taxes, and were frequently illiterate. Social historians are often interested in these people as well, but their focus is not on the materiality of people's lives.

How then can we learn about cities in order to understand them better? Cities are shaped by ideology, desire, economic forces, power, and social structural difference, including discrimination. The distinctive perspective of urban archaeology combines the *flaneur* (or stroller) of Baudelaire and Benjamin (representing the micro approach), who walks through the city to understand and portray it, but catches only glimpses of scenes or moments of interaction, with the macro perspective of Certeau, who views New York City from the top of a skyscraper. There, "before one's eyes," the elevation transforms what is below, making the plan of the city and the integration of its parts clear (1984:92). When cities become large, the landscape is too grand to comprehend on the ground. From above one can identify important places (with grander structures) and ordinary or even neglected places. Historic maps allow a similar "bird's-eye view" of cities and represent an important tool that all urban archaeologists rely on. These show the history of the layout of the settlement, when aspects of planning were introduced; we can correlate these with specific details of the past.

Archaeology of the city (discussed in chapter 2) views the city as an artifact—its physical construction and reworking—and examines the functions of its various parts, exploring how these relate to events and histories in the world and how they have changed with modern global processes. Urban archaeologists tell the stories of the development of American cities as revealed or amplified through their examination of variability in material culture (such as houses, ceramics, and food remains), and the interweaving of these elements with social attributes (such as race, class, ethnicity, and gender). Because early American cities almost always appeared as transport nodes (on a river, ocean, railroad, or road), city dwellers had early access to trade goods or other innovations, and many studies of urban sites compare them with rural areas using this evidence. Urban archaeologists make use of landscape analysis, a perspective that allows the study of similarities across regions: What constitutes the urban core, and how do subsequent forms emerge? When and where do special-purpose structures such as churches, courthouses and jails, or mills and factories appear? The subdiscipline can examine changes in one place over time or look at variability within a category of contemporary communities.

Urban places have several crucial components. There is a physical substrate consisting of the built environment (What kinds of buildings are there? Built of what materials? How large are they and how permanent?); street layout; the locations of central and marginal institutions; and essential infrastructure (which alters with time and technology), including landfill, wharves, and roads. While cities are not uniform, each has a center and periphery, and most of the attributes or features that make it recognizably urban are found in the center, formerly the central business district, although a recent decentering of such districts has become common. Many cities and towns shared a common fate: when the original function of the town diminished in the nineteenth or twentieth centuries as innovations in transport systems appeared (such as railroads or highways), some downtowns were recycled as historic attractions. In Sacramento, historic architecture remained and was ultimately preserved because the town moved on; in Lincoln, Nebraska, in the Haymarket area, a remnant of the early market square survives; and in San Francisco, a peach cannery, built in 1907 right on the water so ships could access the produce brought by rail from the orchards, persists as well. The cannery closed in 1937, during the Depression. It was slated for demolition in the 1960s, but was redesigned on the interior so that it functions today as a shopping mall. Some of these "adaptive reuses" are correlated with archaeological projects.

Studying Cities

In studying cities, our questions are similar to those from other branches of archaeology. We examine the spatial locations and movements of groups of people that can be defined according to socioeconomic, ethnic, or racial attributes and their correlated lifestyles. The changing ethnic and racial populations of neighborhoods in American cities reflect the status and economic health of those neighborhoods and are correlated with urban lifestyles that are quite different from rural ones, especially after the Industrial Revolution.

Each urban locale has its own social geography, expressing the social relations that make up the city and how they change, redefine themselves, and move around. The political economy affects much of the physical and social structure, expressing the power of dominant groups in its manipulation of the cityscape and provision of services (Harvey 1973), and offset by the differing cultural interests of subdominant groups who want to manage their own spatial and social lives. These latter often live in what some call "slums," a term that obscures a significant form of urban working-class community. Typically these are enclaves of working-class poor, perhaps of alienated ethnicities, who can offer windows into alternative or resistant lifestyles. One of the common phenomena reflected in American urban landscapes, no matter where they are found, is the creation of hidden places and locations—places that breach the grid or town plan—which create a safe place for socioeconomically marginal residents (Mayne and Murray 2001).

The questions focal to urban archaeology are similar to those of urban anthropology but are also particular to this subdiscipline: they concern the material traces of urban development and change. What factors stimulate growth? How do global processes appear on the local level, and how do they affect people's lives? Most early cities in America served specific initial functions: ports of trade, administrative centers (managing populations), economic nodes (processing goods, producing money, and distributing elite goods), and/or fortresses (Mumford 1961). Colonial entrepôts associated with missions combined trade with religious propagation and social control. Some later cities developed with industrialization (producing many kinds of goods, developing transport and infrastructure, building factories). The function of the town or

Figure 1.1. Overview of the Stadt Huys Block, New York City, while it was under excavation in 1979. (William Duncan Strong Museum, Columbia University.)

city and its access to transportation contributed to shaping its form and layout, some of which persisted through later changes in the political economy and society. The shape of a city also depended on which European nation-state determined its original settlement. In eastern North America, most towns were developed initially by the British, others by the French, Dutch, Spanish, and Swedes; in other parts of the country, Russians had a role to play as well.

Successful towns grow and modify their land use patterns over time. Once industrialization begins, urban formation accelerates and the specialized use of land becomes more marked. Conflicts emerge among the users of urban space, with elites dominating the manipulation of its form. The basic unit of modern urban space is private property (Smith 2008, 184). City government, seen in planning agencies, tries to control the use of space (and society) through design, but conflicts between landlords and tenants and between industrialists and workers develop; they negotiate land use until the state intervenes and imposes the "political logic of planning" on the land market (Smith 2008, 185). Apart from these regularities, cities differ from one another, sometimes in their domestic architecture, or the kinds of public services and features they have, or their infrastructure. The variable kinds of connections to hinterlands were equally significant as were the types of goods moving in and out. Sometimes administrators or residents modified their own space through landfilling and other practices. When cities expanded, it was often for more living space or to suit industrial demands. Alternatively, administrators wanted better control of indigenous people or wished to move socially marginal people away from the center. These differences are often best seen through historical archaeology, and they make urban projects, with their large budgets and sometimes difficult working conditions, exciting (see fig. 1.1).

This Book

We have outlined here a series of topics that we believe are significant in urban historical archaeology. We began with efforts to characterize cities, both objectively and qualitatively. And we discussed the best ways to study them, in part or as wholes, static or developing. We will next incorporate material from urban archaeological studies throughout the United States in order to address these topics. The available material comes especially from those cities with early or strong historic preservation laws, for most urban archaeological research has been done there. We look at many different kinds of projects and interpret many different kinds of information sent to us by colleagues: documentary study, survey, and excavation all yield distinctive forms of data. In some cases the documentary research done prior to excavation is as significant as the archaeological testing itself. The analysis of historic maps and documents done with an archaeological eye, we argue, is an important part of historical archaeology.

In the rest of this study we focus on what we have learned from the archaeological study of cities in the United States. Some chapters examine the whole city, or the city as an artifact, while others concentrate on artifacts found in cities. Chapter 2 sets the stage, providing context in the form of an overview of the history of urban America and the development of urban historical archaeology. It also outlines the process involved in the practice of this particular form of archaeology in the United States. Chapter 3 highlights the changing landscape of the city, and how planning (or the absence of planning) has impacted urban growth. It also looks at the complexities of urban infrastructure. Chapter 4 looks at the archaeology of manufacturing, commerce, and the service industries within the context of the development of urbanization and capitalism. Chapter 5 examines the experience of the members of different ethnic and racial groups in the city through their materiality. American cities are different from European cities in that most of their population was created de novo from immigration, both voluntary and involuntary, in the relatively recent past. Chapter 6 considers issues of gender relations and the development of the modern class structure in American cities, which often serve as crucibles of change in the construction and material expression of these important social categories. After the Industrial Revolution, class becomes especially relevant in shaping the urban landscape. Chapter 7 examines urban cemeteries and the ways of life and death of those who were buried in them as well as how cemetery locations relate to land use changes. In several cases over the past few decades, the archaeological study of cemeteries and other features has served as a catalyst in stimulating civic engagement and posing questions about memorialization within urban spaces. Archaeological discoveries have played an important role in the creation of identity and empowerment among many urban subaltern groups.

All in all, the book demonstrates how much we have learned about modern American cities through urban historical archaeology. It also shows the ways in which archaeology is positioned to shed light on the American experience by offering unique insights into the development of urban forms and processes. In the next chapter, we begin by providing a context for this story.

2

Urbanization and Its Archaeological Study in the United States

URBANIZATION IS A RELATIVELY NEW process in the United States, and urban archaeology is an even newer way to study it. Here we begin with a brief overview of the history of urbanization in the United States. Then we discuss the beginnings of urban archaeology. Finally we discuss the present state of urban archaeology—how archaeologists study America's cities today.

Urbanization in the United States

Europeans first settled in what was to become the United States during the early part of the colonial endeavor, when newly formed European nation-states began to appropriate resources around the world to enrich themselves in the nation-building process. The main European players in early colonial North America were, first, the Spanish (who arrived in the sixteenth century), and, then, the French and English, who, along with other powers such as the Dutch and Swedes (who played important but relatively short-lived roles), arrived in the seventeenth century. As part of the colonial enterprise, many of these powers established fortified settlements to protect their interests against other European countries and to serve as entrepôts in the Atlantic trade with Europe, Africa, and the Caribbean, as well as with other parts of coastal America. Some of these settlements went on to become the earliest modern cities in the United States.

There was only a handful of cities in the colonial United States, including (earliest of all of the continuously occupied cities) Spanish St. Augustine in Florida (1565); Santa Fe, New Mexico (1609); New York, founded as Dutch New Amsterdam in 1626; and the English cities of Boston (1630); Charleston,

South Carolina (1670); and Philadelphia (1682). Most of them were port cities, perched on the edge of the continent. During the early part of the colonial era, Boston was the largest port, but it was soon eclipsed by Philadelphia, which in turn was overtaken by New York in the 1790s. New York continued to fill that role until the mid-twentieth century (Wall 1994, 2). Almost from the beginning of the European settlements, the colonial powers brought in captive Africans to provide a labor force for the colonies. Although most lived on Southern plantations, there was a sizable African presence in the North and in several cities, particularly Charleston and New York, in the eighteenth century.

The extractive economy of the colonies was based on harvesting, processing, and exporting products from the interior—agricultural produce, of course, but also others, such as lumber and furs (which were obtained in trade with the Native Americans). Most of the population lived in small towns or rural areas. Before the 1820s, less than 8 percent of the European American population lived in cities (Abbott 2007, 853; Teaford 1998, 841). As might be expected, this figure is far below those for contemporary Europe, although the European figures vary widely by area. As early as 1622, for example, well over half of the population of the province of Holland in the Netherlands lived in cities, while as late as 1700 only a fifth to a quarter of the population of England could be said to be "urban" (Merwick 1980, 77).

The growth of colonial cities was extremely slow. But economic development accelerated over the century after the Revolutionary War, as the economy shifted from one based on merchant capitalism to one based on industrial capitalism. This change had a profound impact on urban growth as the Northeast particularly became more of a core and less of a peripheral area (see Paynter 1982). Whereas in 1820 only 7 percent of the American population lived in cities, a century later more than half of the population were city dwellers (Teaford 1998, 845; Abbott 2007, 853). Factors such as inter- and intra-city transportation systems and patterns of immigration influenced urban growth in the course of that century. Before the Civil War, the most important form of inter-city transportation was by water, first by sail along the rivers and the shore, and later by canal and steamboat. New cities began to appear along the waterways of the interior. For the first time, they grew up in the Midwest, on the Great Lakes and in the valleys of the Mississippi and its larger tributaries. Almost all were in the north (New Orleans and Charleston were the largest cities in the south) and east of the Rockies—San Francisco was the only large city on the Pacific (Teaford 1998).

After the Civil War, railroads became the most important way to transport goods from city to city, a factor that influenced the location of new cities. Some, like Albuquerque, Baltimore and Atlanta, eclipsed older ones like Santa Fe, Annapolis and Savannah when the latter were bypassed by the railroad. Chicago, which began as a lakeside city, grew enormously after it became a rail hub. Manufacturing replaced commerce as the principal source of urban prosperity (Teaford 1998, 843), and many cities specialized in producing particular kinds of goods: clothing and shoes in the eastern cities, meat and meat products in Chicago, flour in Minneapolis, and steel in Pittsburgh (Abbott 2007, 853).

Industrialization called for a large urban labor force, and immigration helped swell urban populations, leading to the unprecedented growth of industrial cities in the Northeast and Midwest. During the 1830s and 1840s, most of the immigrants came from Ireland and Germany. Many of the former had little money and settled in the eastern cities of Boston and New York, while many of the latter, somewhat better off, either bought land in rural areas or migrated to interior cities like Cincinnati, Milwaukee, and St. Louis. Later in the century, most of the immigrants came from southern and eastern Europe. These newcomers, many of whom were Catholic or Jewish and some of whom were politically radical, did not fit in well with the native-born middle class, who were predominantly Protestant and descended from northern Europeans, and class and ethnic tensions intensified. These tensions erupted in strikes and other forms of political action, some of which, like the Haymarket Riot in Chicago in 1886, were extremely violent. By century's end, 40 percent of the population was foreign born and the same percentage of the population was urban.

The changing economic and social structure of the city was expressed in its changing landscape. The English colonial cities of the eastern seaboard had been walking cities, integrated across class, with employers living at their workplaces where they also housed their journeymen, apprentices, and slaves. But with the hardening of class lines in the early nineteenth century, employers and employees alike began to move their homes away from the workplace and establish new residential neighborhoods that were becoming segregated by class and structured by changing gender relations. Working class neighborhoods, regarded by the middle class as "slums" (Mayne 1993), were located close to the workplaces of the urban core, where their residents were subjected to the sights, sounds, and smells of industry but could walk to work. Many of these neighborhoods included ethnic and racial enclaves and were home to African Americans, who were gradually being emancipated throughout the North, with most becoming members of the urban working class. Richer folk moved their homes out to the edge of the city, away from disease and the poor, and the middle class settled somewhere in between (Wall 1994).

Horse-drawn omnibuses began to appear in the eastern cities in the 1830s. Catering first to the wealthy as seen by their high fares, they were replaced in the 1860s by horse-drawn street cars which ran on iron tracks, enabling horses to draw many more cars at once, and these in turn were replaced in the 1890s by electric streetcars. Fares became relatively cheaper over time, allowing access to the working class, and these transportation innovations allowed cities to grow spatially and people to live farther and farther from the urban core and still commute to work there. The phenomenal growth of cities in the nineteenth century exacerbated urban problems. Disease and hygiene became important issues, and cities began to institute public health measures along with a clean water supply and adequate drainage and sewerage. Indoor plumbing arrived gradually, beginning with the rich and only later appearing in poorer homes.

By the 1920s, urban dwellers in the United States outnumbered those who lived in small towns or the country. And between then and the 1970s, the process of urbanization was transformed again. First of all, the automobile allowed a new, individual means of transportation (Abbott 2007, 853) for all except the poor, and this enabled a new wave of suburbanization, drawing the rich and members of the middle class farther away from the central parts of cities. (Teaford 1998, 1847) Fueled by the development of air conditioning, people began to build cities in new places, in the South and the Southwest. Miami, Los Angeles, Oklahoma City, Houston, and Phoenix all grew enormously, anticipating the term *sunbelt* that would become common parlance in the 1970s.

The people who moved to cities also changed. In the 1920s laws were passed restricting immigration from overseas, so most of the new arrivals in urban areas were migrants from rural parts of the United States. Some European Americans left the plains for California, while others moved from Appalachia to the cities of the Midwest. Many African Americans, in an effort to find jobs for themselves and educational opportunities for their children and to escape the Jim Crow laws of the South, moved from south to north between World War I and 1970, a movement often referred to as the Great Migration. First, they flocked to the cities of the Northeast and Midwest, where they founded African American centers such as Harlem in New York and the South Side of Chicago. Then, they went to western cities for jobs in the defense industry. Many Puerto Ricans, too, began their own migration to New York, particularly with the growth of inexpensive air travel in the middle of the century. They had become American citizens in the 1920s. Later, in 1965, new immigration legislation removed restrictions on the national origin of immigrants, and since then cities have seen the arrival of many more newcomers from Latin America, Asia, and Africa.

Several scholars have pointed out that since 1970, the growth of urbanization has slowed enormously (Teaford 1998; Abbott 2007). In 1970, a total of 74 percent of the population was "urban," while at century's end only 79 percent were so designated, a mere 5 percent increase (Abbott 2007). And not only was that increase small; the experience of these so-called city dwellers was very different from that of their predecessors. Most were not living in core urban areas, but instead in the outer parts of greater metropolitan areas, and many worked there as well. There has been phenomenal growth in these decentralized areas; most residents of today's metropolitan areas do not experience life in truly urban cores like Manhattan and San Francisco (Teaford 1998). Furthermore, many of these cities have to compete globally for their economies to thrive. New York and Los Angeles vie with London and Tokyo for their places as investment and information capitals. Many smaller towns have become weekend and summer retreats for rich city-folk. Today, only a tiny portion of the population of the United States lives in rural areas, a transition that coincides with the decline in the number of people engaged in agriculture (see Groover 2008).

Urban Archaeology in the United States

In 1973, when urban archaeology was barely in its infancy, Bert Salwen (often referred to as the "father of urban archaeology" in the United States) made a distinction between two different kinds of urban archaeology: archaeology *in* the city and archaeology *of* the city. He defined archaeology *in* the city as the excavation of sites that are located in modern cities today, but which may or may not reflect the development of those urban centers. Port Mobil, a 10,000 year old Native American Paleo-Indian site located in what is now New York City, is an example of an important urban site that does not reflect the history of its city (Cantwell and Wall 2001, 40–42).

Archaeology *of* the city, in contrast, is the study of sites that relate to the development of the city in which they are located. It examines the city as an artifact and looks at how it developed and the functions of its various parts, and it explores how these relate to each other, to the city's history, and to the events that took place within it, and how it has changed with the development of modern global processes. Until relatively recently, most archaeological studies *of* the city focused either on ancient cities—like Teotihuacan or Ur—or on the deep history of modern cities—such as the Roman, Viking, or medieval periods of London's history. Cities with deep histories that continue into the present do not exist within the United States, although some indigenous settlements such as Cahokia or Pueblo Bonito might have been considered urban in their time. It is only within the last few decades that urban archaeologists have turned their attention to the study of the history of modern cities, in other words, the last four or five hundred years of urban history. Our focus in this book is on the archaeology of these modern cities in the United States.

Much of the history of the archaeological study of America's modern cities is part of the larger history of historical archaeology in the United States. Historical archaeology has been defined in many ways, but basically these definitions include two components. One concerns method, and requires that to be considered "historical archaeology," a study must include the analysis of written historical records as well as of material culture. The written records may have been made either by or simply about the people under study and might include studies of Europeans using material culture and written records left by European colonists in the United States, or studies of Native Americans based in part on written records left by European observers. Historical archaeologists use records such as maps, census returns, diaries, and tax records in planning their excavations as well as in contextualizing their finds and interpreting their results. The other component of the definition of historical archaeology concerns the discipline's subject matter, which might be described as the study of the archaeology of the development of the modern world and its impact on peoples everywhere, including colonists, indigenes, and enslaved laborers along with those living in the metropole (adapted from Orser 2004a).

Historical archaeology as a discipline grew out of the historic preservation movement, which began in the nineteenth century. In the buildup to the Civil War, many Americans feared for the future of the country and looked to celebrating its past as a way of strengthening the Union (Wallace 1986, 138). The first building that was ever purchased in order to preserve it was the Hasbrouck House in Newburgh, New York, which served as Washington's headquarters during the last two years of the Revolutionary War. It was bought by the State of New York in 1850. Soon after that, in 1859, the Mount Vernon's Ladies Association of the Union was successful in buying Mount Vernon, Washington's home in Virginia, also to preserve it (Hosmer 1965). To this day the purchase of Mount Vernon is unusual in that it was bought by a private organization as the result of a national (as opposed to a local) movement. Most historic sites that have been preserved have had appeal at the local or at most the regional level.

After the Civil War, as the United States began to change enormously in terms of the economy and the growth and makeup of its population (discussed above), many members of the European American, old-stock elite were threatened and looked to an idealized past. They needed a past in which they felt they had a stake, when life, they thought, was simpler, to shore up their position in their new world. Some focused their efforts on founding genealogical and historical societies, and it was often as part of that latter activity that they began to preserve the historic structures that embodied that history (either real or imagined). Most of these historic structures were associated with elites and tended to be located in small towns or rural areas, referencing an idealized agrarian past—the kinds of places where the large majority of Americans had lived at the turn of the nineteenth century. Many of those who organized these campaigns aimed at saving and maintaining historic structures were women of the old elite, who thought that the American history and values embedded in these buildings would help to Americanize immigrant children.

The horrors of World War I—called the war to end all wars—and the threats of radicalism that followed it attracted other interest groups to historic preservation as well, particularly businessmen like John D. Rockefeller Jr. and the federal government. It was then, in the 1920s and 1930s, that some preservation projects began to use archaeological study as a tool to provide information about the buildings that were being preserved and reconstructed. The most ambitious of these projects actually took place in a city, albeit a small colonial one, when Rockefeller bought up properties in Williamsburg, Virginia, in order to recreate it in its glory days of the eighteenth century, when it was the capital of that colony. This project was truly innovative. It was the first time a preservation effort focused not on a single structure associated with a single person or historical event, but on an entire community, made up of many structures and many people—in fact, a whole, albeit imagined, way of life. Furthermore, it was unique because of its enormous scale—it included tearing down over 700 buildings that had been built after its focus period in the eighteenth century, restoring more than 80 standing structures that dated to that period, and reconstructing almost 350 that had been built in the eighteenth century but had since been demolished (Wallace 1986). It was particularly during the reconstruction phase of the project that archaeology became important. Rockefeller was a stickler for architectural accuracy, and archaeological study was used to discover the fabrics and footprints of the buildings that had been demolished so that this information could be used in their reconstruction.[1] Initially much of this archaeological work was done by architects, but in the 1950s, the Williamsburg Foundation hired archaeologist Moreau Chambers, followed by Ivor Noel Hume. Noel Hume, a British archaeologist who had explored sites in London that had been bombed in the Blitz, continued at Williamsburg until the 1990s, and became one of the founders of historical archaeology in the United States. Williamsburg provided the first systematic, institutionalized use of historical archaeology in the country, and although the Foundation used archaeology to conduct research on questions related not to the study of urbanization but to architectural reconstruction and restoration, it was within an urban context.

Shortly thereafter, the National Park Service became an important player in the development of historical archaeology, particularly after the passage of the Historic Sites Act of 1935. This act empowered the Park Service to acquire historic properties "of national historical or archaeological significance" for the government "for the inspiration and benefit of the people of the United States" and to "restore, reconstruct, [and] rehabilitate [them] . . . and where deemed desirable establish and maintain museums in connection therewith" (quoted in King, Hickman, and Berg 1977, 202). So part of the charge to the Park Service was to make the properties accessible to the public by reconstructing them and establishing museums to interpret them. The Park Service began to use archaeology as a tool to achieve both goals: to discover information to be used in reconstructing and restoring historic structures and to acquire objects to use in museums—three-dimensional artifacts were perfect for exhibits.

During this early period, the Park Service as well as a couple of other entities sponsored a few excavations in modern cities, although most of these excavations took place in less densely settled areas. Most of them involved the study of forts. In the 1930s, archaeologist Verne Chatelaine of the Carnegie Institute of Washington conducted excavations at the Castillo de San Marcos in Saint Augustine, Florida. This was the fort that the Spanish had built in the late seventeenth century to protect the sea route between their New World claims and their homeland across the Atlantic (Deagan 1983, 48). Later, in the 1950s, James Swauger directed excavations for Carnegie Mellon at British-built Fort Pitt in Pittsburgh, Pennsylvania, constructed in 1759 for the French and Indian War. And in the early 1960s, Arnold Pilling of Wayne State University led excavations at the Revolutionary War Fort Lernoult in Detroit, which had been built in 1779 (Mason and Brown 1964). The goal of all of these excavations was to provide information for restoring the forts and interpreting them for the public.

But most important in terms of the development of urban archaeology in the United States were the excavations the National Park Service conducted in Independence Park in Philadelphia beginning in the 1950s (and which, as we shall see, continue to this day). Having observed the results of the fire-bombing in Europe during World War II, with the beginnings of the Cold War some Philadelphians became concerned about the safety of several historic buildings, including Independence Hall, the shrine so important in the nation's birth (see chapter 7). They proposed to reduce the threat of destruction by fire or enemy attack by removing the buildings described as dilapidated that surrounded the historic structures and creating a park. Independence National Historical Park was created by an act of Congress in 1948, and the National Park Service was charged with its development and maintenance. As part of the development, Park Service personnel conducted research on the historic structures and the eighteenth-century historic landscape there and made plans to interpret them for the public. To do this, they initiated the multidisciplinary team approach that has become the signature of National Park Service projects, using architects, historians, and archaeologists working together (Cotter et al. 1992). The development led to the revitalization of the historic downtown part of the city.

As part of the study, archaeologists uncovered the foundations of houses torn down centuries ago, the pits from old privies, cisterns, and wells as well as other landscape features. The centerpiece of this archaeological project was the excavation at Franklin Court, where in 1953 archaeologist John Schumacher discovered the foundation wall of Benjamin Franklin's home and the shaft from one of the family's privies; subsequent excavations uncovered a number of other features there as well (Cotter et al. 1992). As part of the interpretation of the history of the area, the Park Service arranged for architect Robert Venturi to design a steel-framed "ghost structure" outlining the Franklin home as informed by the excavations and by historical research (Yamin 2008, 158–59). This structure remains on the site today.

While the goals of these National Park Service excavations were somewhat limited—to help with the restoration and the interpretation of the landscape in the Park—their legacy proved to be extremely important because they showed American archaeologists that remnants of the relatively recent historical past could survive in heavily urbanized areas like downtown Philadelphia. This knowledge proved to be crucial when the federal government as well as state and municipal governments across the country began to draft and enact environmental legislation in the 1960s. But basically through the 1960s the primary role of historical archaeology was to provide information for historic sites restoration and interpretation. In fact, some wanted to call the field "historic-sites archaeology" instead of "historical archaeology," and saw it as merely a "supplemental technique in the service of architecture" (see Schuyler 1978, 1).

Before the archaeological study of modern cities could begin on a large scale, though, a few other elements had to be in place. For one thing, although the Philadelphia excavations showed that archaeological sites might be preserved in heavily urbanized areas, they did not show why, beyond the goal of site interpretation, archaeologists should bother to excavate them. Neither the public nor the archaeological community was ready to support urban excavations because it was not clear that people could learn relevant information from them. But this changed with the cultural revolution of the 1960s.

The social ferment of 1960s and 1970s had a profound effect on American culture. The new ideologies that gave rise to the civil rights, feminist, and environmental movements inspired academicians (including archaeologists) to expand their definitions of "relevant" subjects for study. Historical archaeologists began to realize that their discipline could go beyond merely providing information about how buildings had been built or supplying artifacts for museum displays. Instead, it could provide a powerful approach for understanding the past of the more recent, post-European settlement. Some who had formerly concentrated on the Native American past before the arrivals of the Europeans began to expand their study to Native American life during the period after those arrivals—called the Contact Period by archaeologists who study the Pre-Columbian past (see Silliman 2005 for a discussion of some of the ramifications of this periodization). Others began to explore the lifeways of the Europeans and Africans who came into contact with the Indians as well as those who came later (e.g., Deetz 1977). Inspired in part by their colleagues in the new field of social history, these archaeologists became interested in studying the everyday lives of ordinary people. Their thought was that they could use the archaeological record as a primary source to find out about the lives of the members of social groups that had previously tended to be neglected in the historical records: women; Africans and African Americans; the poor and working class; and members of immigrant groups, such as the Chinese, Irish, Italian, and Japanese. And not only were people who had lived in rural areas and small towns worthy of their interest—people who had lived in cities were too, regardless of whether they had lived there hundreds of years ago during the colonial period, or as recently as the nineteenth and even the twentieth centuries.

But there was still one other element missing for urban archaeology to become a field of study in its own right. Digging in heavily urbanized areas in downtown America can be very expensive, much more expensive than digging in rural areas. Because sites are often deeply buried under the modern city and because they can require the movement of literally tons of debris just to expose them, urban excavations require the use of expensive construction equipment, such as backhoes and front-end loaders, to remove the overburden and to truck it off site. Additionally, cities by definition have dense populations and have undergone intensive use of the land. These factors make them stratigraphically very complex, and of course sites with complex stratigraphy take longer and cost more to excavate. Furthermore, whether they lived in urban or rural areas, the people of modern times lived during or after the industrial and consumer revolutions, and therefore they had many more "things"—a much denser material culture—than the people of earlier eras. This in turn means that archaeological collections from urban sites are extremely large, and they are expensive not only to excavate, but to process, analyze, store, and curate (Rothschild and Rockman 1982). And research foundations have limited funds—they could not afford to support urban projects that might cost millions of dollars. So for urban archaeology to take off one other factor had to be dealt with—figuring out how to pay for the projects. This problem was resolved through the success of the environmental movement.

During the 1960s, many Americans (along with others around the world) became very concerned about the environment. They realized that most natural resources—whether oil or animal species—were finite and non-renewable, and that once they were gone, they were gone forever. They also realized that the same principle applied to the cultural resources, the archaeological sites and historic structures that make up our landscape. Once they are destroyed, they are gone—one cannot make more of them. As a result of this concern, environmentalists lobbied for the passage of legislation in the 1960s and 1970s to protect the environment. In many cases they were successful, and some of this legislation covered the protection of historic sites as part of the environment. Federal legislation, including the National Historic Preservation Act of 1966 and the National Environmental Policy Act of 1970, led the way, ensuring that if the federal government was involved in a development project, care would be taken so that that development would not wantonly destroy an important historical site, whether a historic house or an archaeological site, which was eligible for inclusion on the National Register of Historic Places. If an important site was threatened by development, one of several things might happen to mitigate the impact of the development project on the site. The project might be canceled, or it might be modified so as to avoid the site. But if the development project proposed for the site was very important, the overseeing government agency might require the archaeological study of the property, including, if appropriate, excavation, analysis, and the production of a report. And most important for urban archaeology, the regulations required that the developer (be it a private entity or a government agency) pay for the archaeological study. Over subsequent decades, these laws have been supplemented by others on the federal, state, and local levels.

Urban Archaeology Today

The effectiveness of these regulations varies from place to place and time to time. Decisions concerning preservation as a whole can be very political. In many cities, the mayor appoints agency heads, who in turn control agency decisions. Some mayors in New York City, for example, have appointed heads of the Landmarks Preservation Commission (the entity which oversees many of the projects there) who appear to be more in sympathy with developers than with preservationists. But as might be expected, cities that value their history—cities where historic sites are important tourist destinations, for example—tend to have city archaeologists and effective local regulations aimed at protecting archaeological sites. Cities such as Alexandria, Virginia, and Pensacola, Florida, have been extremely successful in protecting their archaeological sites, in part because they had visionary leaders (Pamela Cressey in Alexandria and Judith Bense in Pensacola) who had the foresight to build a constituency by developing archaeology programs that included the public's involvement in the archaeological process. Archaeological projects have proved to be tourist attractions in many places. But these are the archaeological winners. There are other cities which have only achieved protection for their archaeological sites very recently, and others that still have no protection at all. Albuquerque, New Mexico, for example, only passed a historic preservation law in 2007, and it applies mostly to the area to the west of the current city, which is less developed than older parts of the city. But whether or not they have their own regulations and programs in place, all of America's cities, like its rural areas, are obliged to abide by state and federal regulations regarding such sites.

This subfield of archaeology that specializes in projects mandated by the government is variously called "contract archaeology" (because of the written contracts that define the projects) or "cultural resource management" (or CRM, stressing the goal of the projects). There are several different ways that these projects can be structured in management terms. For some of the early projects, the structure was quite informal; for example, archaeologists working on early projects in New York City were sometimes simply put on the payroll of the construction firm that the developer had hired to build a building. Today, small projects and some phases of larger projects may be conducted by independent consultants or small firms hired by developers. But larger projects requiring full-blown excavation often require large outlays of capital that smaller firms cannot afford, so larger companies tend to run these projects. These firms range from relatively small corporations that specialize in historic preservation projects (such as John Milner Associates, with headquarters in West Chester, Pennsylvania) to huge engineering firms that have divisions that specialize in historic preservation and which offer their clients archaeological expertise as part of a menu of engineering and construction services (such as the URS Corporation,[2] headquartered in San Francisco and with a staff of more than 57,000 and offices in over 50 countries). There are also colleges and universities that have divisions that undertake CRM projects (for example, SUNY Stony Brook on Long Island, Sonoma State University in California, and the University of New Mexico all have arms that conduct these projects).

Finally, although virtually all of the large-scale and most of the small-scale urban excavations are CRM projects, some of the smaller projects done in American cities are not CRM projects at all. Occasionally university professors or non-profit groups pursue their own research interests by running field schools or conducting research projects in urban areas. Although for the most part these research projects tend to be on a small scale and conducted in less urbanized parts of the city, there is one major exception: Archaeology in Annapolis. This is a partnership formed by the City of Annapolis and the Department of Anthropology at the University of Maryland at College Park. Since 1981, Mark Leone of the University of Maryland has led Archaeology in Annapolis in annual summer excavations, working at over forty sites in all.[3] Several of these sites have become icons in the field of historical archaeology, and many of the students who were trained on the project (including Barbara Little, Christopher Matthews, Paul Mullins, Paul Shackel, and Mark Warner) have gone on to become figures in the field in their own right. Many of these excavations were carried out because of proposed construction projects.

But however a project might be organized—whether by a large corporation or a small mom-and-pop firm—urban archaeology is unusual in that there is a high proportion of women practitioners in the field. This may be due in part to the fact that women-owned businesses have a leg up in getting contracts from federal, state, and municipal agencies and also because many women find it more convenient for family reasons to work close to their homes, rather than in the exotic locales that we usually associate with archaeology. But in any case, in New York City, for example, a good majority of the reports submitted to the

New York City Landmarks Preservation Commission for review in a recent year were written by women (Sutphin 2012).

Since the 1970s, environmental legislation has required archaeologists to undertake literally thousands of projects in the nation's cities, areas where they might not have chosen to dig otherwise. At the beginning, they thought that there would be virtually nothing left in heavily urbanized areas, or if there was something, that the assemblages uncovered would not be intellectually relevant to their discipline of historical archaeology. But what they discovered was that the problem was not that there was too little preserved, but too much, and that today projects conducted in urban places are among the most stimulating and important in historical archaeology. The results of the archaeological projects in some cities have been synthesized into books, including studies of Albany (James Bradley [2007], who concentrated on Dutch and Native relations there during the Dutch colonial period), Denver (Nelson et al. 2001), New York (Cantwell and Wall 2001; Rothschild 1990, 2008; Wall 1994; Wall and Cantwell 2004), Philadelphia (Cotter et al. 1992; Yamin 2008), and St. Augustine, Florida (Deagan 1983). But most are described only in the so-called gray literature—the unpublished site reports that languish in government libraries or on the shelves of government bureaucrats. We draw on all of these different kinds of studies for the present work.

From the perspective of the archaeologists who work in cities, some "urban" projects are similar to those conducted in rural areas while others are very different. This is because cities are not homogenous in terms of their level of urbanization, and we mean this in two different senses. First, there is an enormous range among cities in terms of their degree of development—digging in Saint Augustine (with a population of around 13,000) for the most part is very different from digging in downtown Chicago (with a population of almost 3 million). Second, there can also be enormous variation in levels of development in different parts of the same city. For archaeologists who dig in New York City, for example, some parts, like its parklands or parts of its outer boroughs, are quite open and suburban in terms of development, while other parts, like the Wall Street District, are heavily urbanized. The methods that archaeologists use differ depending on the degree of urbanization in the area where they are working, including the level of past population density and the intensity of land use on the site, as well as the sheer quantity of administrative records that record the history of the project area.

In one way or another, the urban factor can have an impact on most phases of a project: the initial assessment of the site using historical sources; testing the site to see if there are in fact important archaeological deposits still in the ground; excavating the site if it is an important one and there is no way for the proposed development project to avoid it; processing the artifacts and ana-lyzing the records from the excavation; writing the site report; and finding a repository for the artifacts. We consider each of these project phases below, comparing the methods archaeologists use in heavily urbanized areas as op-posed to those used in less developed, more rural ones. Since most projects in heavily urbanized areas in the United States today are CRM projects, we use CRM projects as our model.

Digging in America's Cities Today

All CRM projects begin with a project area—the area which is under consid-eration for development. The first step of the project—referred to as Phase 1—involves assessing the archaeological potential of that area. This phase has two parts. The first part—Phase 1A—is often referred to as background or documentary research by archaeologists, and consists of researching the site through the study of written sources. It is geared toward answering two differ-ent kinds of questions about the site which have to do with different aspects of its history. One set has to do with determining the kind(s) of site(s) the area could contain: Who lived or worked there? Whose past could be recorded there? Native American? European? African? Chinese? Were there buildings there? If so, were they homes or workplaces or other kinds of structures? Where were the buildings and other features (such as privies, cisterns, and outbuild-ings) located on the site? To answer these questions, archaeologists consult many different kinds of records in the archives and libraries, including local histories, maps and atlases, deeds, census and tax records, and city directories. The second question is: If in fact there had been an archaeological site there, how likely is it that the site still survives in the ground? In addition to using some of the same records mentioned above to explore whether the site has been destroyed, archaeologists rely heavily on other government documents such as road and building records to explore this question. Was the project area built over with new buildings with very deep basements, so deep that they would have destroyed any archaeological site that might have been there? Was the project area graded, with soil being removed in order to put in roads or to level the ground? Grading might have destroyed an archaeological site. Was it a low-lying area to which landfill was added, thus possibly protecting an underlying archaeological site? The African Burial Ground in lower Manhattan (discussed below in chapter 7) was preserved in just this way. Or is the site located on landfill that was added along the shore very recently, thus indicating that the area was under water and that no one lived there in the recent past?

The big difference between doing a background study in a heavily urbanized area as opposed to a more suburban or rural one directly relates to the factors associated with urbanization. With the increased density of population, intensity of land use, and the development of city government, there are many, many more records to consult in heavily urbanized areas. For example, a two-hectare project area in a rural setting might have been occupied by only one or two farms and perhaps a half a dozen families since the time of the European arrivals. Researching such properties is a relatively simple proposition. But in a heavily urbanized setting, a project area of the same size might be made up of a myriad of smaller properties, each with its own history, and each of which must be considered an archaeological site in its own right with its own sequence of land use and owners and occupants, the latter of whom might total in the thousands. The Stadt Huys Block site in lower Manhattan, for example, consisted of a small single block, but over a 350-year period it was the site of over fifty separate buildings which in the nineteenth century were located on as many as twenty-one separate lots (Rothschild and Rockman 1982). Each of these twenty-one separate lots in effect constitutes a separate archaeological site. Researching each of these properties thoroughly would be an endless task that might not be warranted at this early stage of the project.

Instead, archaeologists studying urban areas have to learn how to focus their research narrowly to discover what they need to know. They might begin by first determining the properties that have not been subject to disturbance and then researching the history of those properties only. In addition, they might only sample the historical records. For example, they might check the tax records on the properties at ten year intervals, instead of every year, to see who was paying taxes on the property and whether the property had been redeveloped.

Once the archaeologists know that there likely are archaeological traces in at least part of the site, they will begin Phase 1B—"peeking" under the ground to confirm that such traces really exist. The degree of urbanization in the site area affects how this is done. When working in the relatively undisturbed parts of urban areas or in rural areas, archaeologists have a whole menu of techniques that they can use to see whether or not archaeological remains are present and if so, to define their extent. Some of these techniques are invasive, like shovel tests, auger tests, and soil corings, while others are noninvasive, and include geophysical techniques such as ground penetrating radar, electrical resistivity, or proton magnetometry. But most of these methods cannot be used in heavily urbanized areas, where there have been numerous episodes of building and rebuilding and the archaeological site might be buried under the basements of later buildings. In the latter situation the site is too deep for shovel tests to reach, and there is simply too much "noise" near the ground surface to be able to use the geophysical techniques reliably. One way that it is possible to "peek" into these heavily urbanized sites is to use soil corings. In this case, archaeologists working with coring specialists and a coring rig take a series of continuous samples down to the depth of the underlying natural, non-cultural deposits, in order to see the stratigraphy of the site—the layers of soil and debris that show where there has been modern disturbance and where there could be intact archaeological remains.

If based on the findings of the background research and possibly corings or other preliminary testing techniques it appears that there is a potentially important archaeological site in the area slated for development, a decision has to be made about what to do next. If the site seems to be both important and relatively intact, field testing might be required. This step—Phase II of the process—is done to determine the extent and importance of the resources in the ground, evaluate site integrity, and to guide the development of research questions for a full-fledged excavation (Phase III), if warranted. So the archaeologists working with the government agency that is overseeing the project develop a testing plan for the site area. The field work that they undertake in this phase of the project is very similar to their procedures in a Phase III, so we discuss them together here.

If the site is located in a lightly urbanized area, such as a park or a backyard, the archaeologists approach it just as they would a site in a rural area—they bring out their shovels and screens, lay out their testing units, and begin excavating. But in heavily urbanized areas they first have to expose the site, which, as we mentioned above, may be deeply buried in the ground. In this case, they work with backhoes and front-end loaders and their operators to remove the demolition debris from the most recent buildings on the site and expose the basement floors of those buildings as well as any undeveloped backyards that might have survived urban development (Figure 2.1). Using the backhoe, they then lift the basement floors and begin to look under them and in the backyards for "features," like the shafts from old privies and wells, cisterns, basement floors, or ancient ground surfaces. They often look for shaft features by scraping the ground with a special smooth backhoe blade, so that the outlines of these

Figure 2.1. A backhoe clearing rubble from an old basement floor at the Stadt Huys Block. (William Duncan Strong Museum, Columbia University.)

features are exposed against the surrounding subsoil. Archaeologists tend to concentrate on excavating shaft features because they often provide large assemblages of artifacts in sealed deposits, bearing information about the lives of the people who lived or worked on the site in the past. While privies were in use, for example, people often disposed of trash in them, and occasionally they accidentally dropped things in wells. Then, when people stopped using these features, usually with the advent of indoor plumbing, they often filled them up to grade with garbage. And of course garbage provides the information about the past the archaeologists are looking for.

Archaeologists have to be much more careful in looking for early buried ground surfaces because they are so fragile they can easily be scraped away by the backhoe blade. Old ground surfaces tell a different story than shaft features. Here, archaeologists might find not only the things that people threw away but also the things they lost accidentally, like coins or buttons. Furthermore, buried ground surfaces can provide pollen and phytoliths and other kinds of ecofacts that specialists can use to reconstruct the environment of the area when that ground surface was exposed and in use.

Working in urban areas can be much more complicated logistically than working in most rural areas and can be dangerous as well. Uncovering the site and digging with the backhoe have to be carefully planned because once the backhoe has revealed a sensitive archaeological area, it cannot pass over that area again to be able to reach somewhere else on the site—that would destroy the deposits and features in the uncovered area. Furthermore, because urban sites can be buried so deeply in the ground, care has to be taken that the walls of the excavation do not cave in on crew members and crush them. The excavation has to be in compliance with OSHA standards, with the walls being either shored or sloped at angles that are appropriate for the depth of the excavation. Finally, archaeologists working on urban sites often discover contaminated soil there. Such soil either has to be neutralized or removed from the site, or its location has to be removed from the excavation plan because it would be too dangerous for a crew to excavate it. Archaeologists working at the Metropolitan Detention Center site in Philadelphia confronted the presence of lead, PCBs, and asbestos in different parts of the site; the archaeologists worked around these areas (Louis Berger and Associates 1997, iv–1).

The digging process is also different in heavily urbanized neighborhoods because the intensity of land use that defines urban areas has an archaeological correlate: complex stratigraphy. Every time anyone—be it a dog, workman, gardener, or child—digs a hole into the soil, it leaves a trace in the layers (or strata) of soil in the ground. And each of these strata has to be excavated separately, so that the artifacts from each layer can be analyzed separately later in the lab, because if they come from different layers of soil, they were deposited in the ground at different times and as part of different events. Excavating sites with complex stratigraphy is painstaking work that can be difficult and take a long time. And, of course, as in all excavations, everything the archaeologists do at an urban site has to be recorded on maps and provenience sheets, and in photographs and section and plan drawings. Because of the sheer number of artifacts that archaeologists find on urban sites, they usually sample some of the artifacts in the field. For example, they might count and weigh the brick, mortar, and coal in the field and then discard them there, saving only a small sample for the collection.

Based on the results of their Phase II field testing, the archaeologists decide whether or not to recommend a Phase III for the project—full-fledged excavation. If they decide to go ahead, they use the results of both the documentary research and the field testing to design research questions that they can explore with the information learned from the excavations. They then use the research design to help make decisions about where to excavate. Sometimes, for example, there are so many shaft features that the overseeing agency decides that because of time and money only some of them can be excavated. So the archaeologists have to sample. Using all the information they have, they make the tough decisions about which features to excavate and which to leave unexplored, to be destroyed by development.[4] They might look back at their historical research to see the ethnicity and/or the class of the different people whose features they have found, and design their research questions around one of those topics. They may choose to excavate the features from, for example, an equal number of German and Irish immigrant households, so that they will be able to compare the lifeways of the members of these two groups. Or it may be that archaeologists working at another nearby site had recently excavated features associated with the homes of several German families from the same social class and period; in that case, the archaeologists might choose to excavate the features associated with the Irish homes, so that they could be compared with the sites associated with the German families. At the Metropolitan Detention Center, the archaeologists discovered a total of twenty-five shaft features; they ended up excavating only five of them. There, they took the feature's date of deposition and the occupations of the residents of the associated properties into account in choosing which features to excavate (Louis Berger and Associates 1997, iv–65). Some archaeologists look to see if a property had a long-term occupant, so that they might be able to link an archaeological assemblage to a particular household, although concentrating only on long-term residents biases the study toward the less transient and therefore more stable households on the block.

Having made their sampling decisions, the archaeologists go back into the field and begin their Phase III excavations, excavating the features that they chose in writing their research design. Usually Phase IIIs are fairly straightforward—the archaeologists simply follow their research design. But sometimes the unexpected happens, and the archaeologists make a discovery that was completely unforeseen. And this often happens at the end of the field phase, during the last week or even on the last scheduled excavation day of the project. One example of this in New York City was the discovery in 1981 of a sunken eighteenth-century ship at the 175 Water Street site during the last week of the excavations. There, the archaeologists were digging in landfill that had been put in place in the eighteenth century, and the ship had been scuttled and positioned so as to help hold the landfill in place. The archaeologists had to add an extra month to their excavation phase in order to record the ship.

After the field phase comes the laboratory phase of the project—when the archaeologists wash and catalogue the artifacts and analyze them along with the stratigraphy. And the laboratory phases of urban projects again tend to be much greater undertakings than those of their country cousins. As we mentioned, the artifact collections from urban projects are often enormous—some include well over a million artifacts. Furthermore, analyzing complex stratigraphy is much more difficult than analyzing the simpler stratigraphy that tends to characterize sites found in rural areas. So all in all, this means that analyzing the results of an excavation in an urban area is much more complex and takes much more time than analyzing the results of the excavation of most sites in rural areas.

Whether excavating an urban site or a rural one, the last phase of a project is writing the final report. And of course because of the complexity of urban sites and the large number of artifacts found, reports on these excavations tend to be much longer than those on rural excavations. The site report on the excavation of the Five Points site in New York City, for example, fills seven volumes (Yamin 2000a).

With the completion of the final report, the formal archaeological project is finished, but there are still two other tasks that need to be done. One is something for the public—be it a report on the project geared to an audience with no archaeological background or an exhibit at the site or somewhere else that interprets the excavation and its findings. The other task involves one of the biggest problems that confronts urban archaeologists today—finding a repository that is willing and able to take the often huge collections from these sites and to take care of them in perpetuity. Real estate in urban areas is very expensive and the collections take up a lot of space. Furthermore, curators have to be hired to look after the collections and conservators have to check on them to be sure the artifacts are stable and not disintegrating in their storage boxes. All of this, of course, costs money. In 2004, archaeologists working in New York City had the unfortunate experience of having their primary repository, the South Street Seaport Museum, redefine its mission, fire its staff archaeologist, and deaccession all of its archaeological collections. Fortunately, the New York State Museum in Albany took the collections, but it was a shock for many of the city's archaeologists to see that there was no repository in the city that was prepared to look after the collections.

Conclusion

Over the last four decades, archaeological study has made an important contribution to our understanding of how the cities of the modern world came into being. The strength of this study is that it allows us to examine the components that make up abstract processes like urbanization in the development of the modern world and to explore them on both a micro and a macro level, revealing the experiences of the people who lived through these processes on the ground. Next, we look at the city on the macro level, as one enormous artifact.

3

Landscape, Planning, and Infrastructure

City as Artifact

ONE OF THE WAYS that archaeologists study modern American cities is through the approach of looking at the city itself as an artifact, examining it either as a whole or in part. They might look at the city's plan or landscape or at the ways that the city has grown and the infrastructure that was developed to help it expand. In this chapter, we first look at studies of urban landscapes and plans, and then we examine some of the ways that archaeologists have examined different factors important in the development of cities, including the landfill and wharves that formed the waterfronts of the older cities, the materiality of utilities and transportation systems, and the shift from privatization to government control.

Urban Plans and Landscapes

Urban places develop landscapes which reflect the activities they contain and the administrative functions they perform and which in turn affect the experience of the people who live or work in them. Sometimes these landscapes are planned, but even if unplanned, some regularities in configuration appear because of similar functions and activities. An archaeological approach is uniquely able to use the perspective of landscape to uncover its stratified layers as land is reconfigured to suit new demands and purposes. It may also reveal the disparity between urban plan and urban reality. Archaeologists play a crucial role in discussing urban landscapes because of the discipline's comparative framework and its ability to consider time depth. The significance of urban communities as they developed was rooted in the novel ways they transformed space into place, connecting global and local, city and country, core and periphery (Harvey in Lefebvre 1991). Urban form was and is a function of the ways space, energy, and time were linked and made concrete (Lefebvre 1991, 12). Such forms define order and establish public spaces, such as pathways and multipurpose centers where important institutions are clustered. Residential, commercial, and other areas were designated within the city, some in close proximity to the urban core and some more marginal. European colonizers in the United States, with their varying concepts of the urban, imposed specific formal attributes on urban design and city dwellers, manipulating the landscape and prioritizing specific institutions.

Archaeologists' use of the landscape concept is effective in understanding the meaning of any spatially based data, including data on cities. We may define a landscape "as a set of relationships between people and places which provide the context for everyday conduct" (Thomas 2001, 181); it also includes the perceived settings that frame a person's sense of place and community (Stewart and Strathern 2003, 4). A landscape is a construct and thus may be experienced differently by its inhabitants, depending on their cultural perspective as molded by membership in different class, ethnic, racial, gender, and age groups (Upton 1988). Urban landscapes are particularly complex and are always in process; they change in accord with circumstances. Landscapes include places which are socially meaningful and identifiable—spaces with histories (Ingold 2000). Place helps to define community—a set of people who identify themselves by their connection to a place—and communities define and transform place (Low 1999; Hayden 1995). A continuing, reiterative interaction develops over time between landscape and populations. Landscapes once established are populated. The characteristics of those who live in specific spaces are shaped in part by those spaces. Social and spatial attributes are recursively linked so that an alteration in one yields consequences in the other. Thus as the population is reorganized either culturally or spatially, altering the landscape, changes occur in other elements as well, as shown below in St. Louis, Missouri, and Bowling Green, Kentucky.

Archaeological studies of cities as artifacts first gather data on the geographical layout of the community under investigation. Historical archaeology has the advantage of historical documents, including maps and plans from earlier periods, census and tax records, and construction and destruction records for a specific community. These documents provide detailed information about urban settlement and growth, as noted in chapter 2, and about the significance of economic priorities in commodifying land. Subsequent field research offers details of the city and urban life at particular moments in time or discovers unrecorded aspects of the city's development. The combination of these elements offers both macro- and micro-scale analyses of urban entities. Macro-scale changes are seen in changing land use, as in the shift from domestic to industrial spaces; this citywide perspective will be the focus of this chapter.

Many American cities were shaped from the beginning according to practical or ideological concerns. These macro-level ideas are visible in the initial germ of the town, particularly in its layout, including its streets, lots, and public open spaces, the location of important institutions, building styles, and major buildings (Burrows and Hunter 1996; Miller 1988). Settlers often sited communities in reference to a natural resource that had an important cultural meaning. American town plans were frequently based on a gridded model derived from Hippodamus more than two millennia ago and subsequently modified by Vitrivius (Crouch and Mundigo, cited in Tigges 1990), providing for a town center surrounded by units of equal size, evenly spaced. Significant religious and political institutions were located on the town square. It was seen as the ideal layout to foster a true community and was used successfully, especially in many walking cities.[1] This grid was used by colonists from places with roots in the Roman Empire (Spain, France, and Britain), and was sometimes laid out in spite of terrain (Zierden and Reitz 2007).

Any plan involves a theory of the ideal landscape, and the grid was no exception. On one level, with the gridded layout "[e]very location was provided equal access, and natural inequalities of topography were eliminated. The grid was perceived as neutral and non-hierarchical" (Nelson et al. 2001, 172), an appealing thought within the context of emerging democratic ideals in the United States. In reality, of course, not all portions of the grid are equal; properties at corners, or closer to the center, or in better topographic settings were more desirable (Zierden and Reitz 2007). In fact, as Chris Matthews notes, the grid is also one of the largest materializations of capitalist ideology ever constructed. The "rational organization of space and property led urban development to proceed predictably" (2010, 91) and also facilitated the commodification of land. Furthermore, straight streets enabled the movement of people and goods, and a central space at the city's center was useful for social control. The power of the center was enhanced by the siting of important political-economic structures there. The grid continued to be used after the colonial period because it "created order and unity by organizing individual selves" (Upton, quoted in Nelson et al. 2001). One of the important findings of archaeological research is the repeated breakdown of the grid plan as practical or financial considerations came to dominate ideological ones, especially in the early cities such as Santa Fe and New Orleans.

Modern urban landscapes bear traces of these early plans, and documentary research and excavation can reveal these origins. And regardless of theoretical designs, subsequent developments, particularly those associated with the growth of capitalism, inevitably altered some of these original plans. At the macro-level, transport changes (from ferries and canals to railroads and roads) or the establishment of local industries led to changes in land use (increasing subdivision of lots, or a shift from residential and commercial to industrial land use). Archaeological and historical research shows that as cities expanded, new residential neighborhoods based on class developed (Rothschild 1990; Wall 1994; Stottman and Stahlgren 2006, A149). Industrial growth in the nineteenth century drastically affected urban landscapes and made peri-industrial neighborhoods less appealing to residents, and those who could afford to move away did so. Architectural changes (in style and building materials) altered the look of the city. And later on, as noted elsewhere, urban renewal and gentrification involved the destruction and rebuilding of old neighborhoods, usually those inhabited by the poor, working-class immigrants, and African Americans. (See below and chapter 5).

We may speak of two types of landscape in discussing cities: those within the urban place and those outside it. The city had its own internal structure or landscape; some areas were perceived as more or less desirable, depending on the ideology of its inhabitants and the activities conducted there. Public spaces were multipurpose central places derived from the Roman piazza via the Spanish plaza or English commons, and they were important from their inception because significant political, economic, and religious buildings were located there. The landscapes surrounding these cities were equally important. In early days, some colonial cities were walled or fortified, leaving a clear distinction between urban (where Europeans and enslaved people, whether African or indigenous, were concentrated) and non-urban (often free indigenous locales). However, since the city relied on the hinterland for many things (provisions and traded goods), this separation was incomplete and somewhat illusory. Indigenous people were essential in providing access to the interior and its resources—labor and products.

Planning Early Urban Landscapes

The Spanish founded the earliest cities in what is now the United States, and one of the best-studied of them all is Santa Fe. Archaeology has proved particularly important there because nearly all the early Spanish records were burned in the Pueblo Revolt of 1680 (Scheick 2003, 27). A great number of archaeologists have conducted projects in Santa Fe,[2] and many of them have shown details of the ways in which this city exemplifies the tensions between a city as planned and a city as lived experience. The city was established around 1609–10 and functioned as the northernmost administrative center for Spanish America throughout the seventeenth and much of the eighteenth centuries (Sanchez 2010, 19). The settlement's location was chosen because it was defensible, close to a river, and afforded plentiful wood and fuel, and there were no Native Americans living there at the time (Hordes 2010, 131). The Spanish government was more involved in actual town planning than either the French or British (Hordes 2010, 130), and sixteenth-century laws were designed to allow unskilled builders to reproduce a familiar landscape in foreign climes (Crouch and Mundigo in Tigges 1990). In all Spanish towns the plaza was meant to be the physical, economic, social, and cultural center of the community, with government buildings and shops on the plaza, private dwellings on the streets leading to it, and the church on an elevation nearby. The Santa Fe plaza has been heavily disturbed since its early days, but documentary information suggests it served many functions over time: fiestas were celebrated, troops were mustered, gallows were constructed, and it was used for growing crops and possibly keeping domestic animals (Hordes 2010, 143; Cordelia Snow pers. comm. September 2012).

However, the most crucial element of planning in Santa Fe was part of the infrastructure—a system of acequias or water-delivery ditches that were built before any of the buildings (Plewa 2012, 58). They enabled the population to survive by irrigation, both for farming outside the town and gardening inside it. Acequia management also created low-level forms of community organization and a strong sense of place; users of the same ditches were connected to each other through kin-like ties (Plewa 2009). Archaeologists have recovered considerable information on acequia locations (D. Snow 1996), reinforcing their significance in defining settlement organization. These ditches were laid out hierarchically, with major ones leading to minor ones, so that correlating these with house locations provides insight into the social structure of the town.

In some ways the most significant aspect of urban development in Santa Fe from our perspective is that as it expanded it did not conform to the idea of the original Spanish plan: instead of settling in town, residents settled near their fields in order to protect them from local Native Americans (Dominguez 1956, cited in Rothschild 2003). The Urrutia map of 1766–68 shows houses spread in a linear fashion near the agricultural fields along the river (Tigges 1990, 234) with a few structures near the town plaza (Figure 3.1).

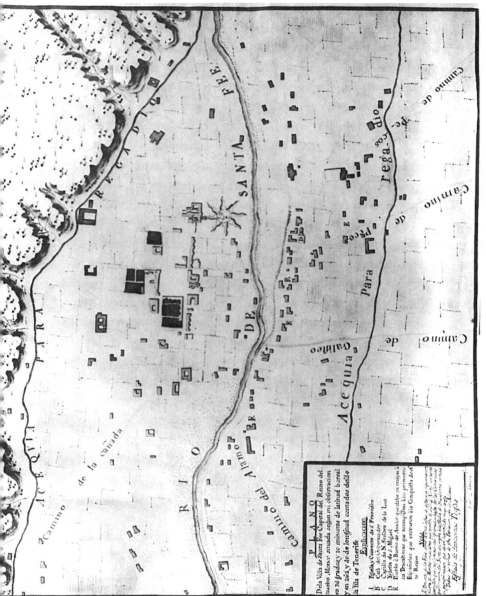

Figure 3.1. Town plan of Santa Fe. (Plano de la Villa de Santa Fe Capital del Reino del Nuevo Mexico, Jose de Urrutia 1766, Courtesy of Palace of the Governors Photo Archives NMHM/DCA], negative number 15048.)

French town planning was also initiated early in the colonial United States and has been studied in the settlements of Mobile, Alabama, and New Orleans. Mobile was planned as the military, political, and economic center of Louisiana before the capital was shifted to New Orleans. It was occupied by three colonial powers: the French (1711–63), the British (1763–80), and the Spanish (1780–1813). It became part of the United States in 1813. The town originally centered on a fort, but it expanded in the late 1830s after the fort had been abandoned. Mobile in the mid-nineteenth century was an important port from which cotton was shipped north to the New England mills or overseas to England, but open space was in short supply. Park designer Frederick Law Olmsted visited Mobile in 1856 and reported that "in its central business part, [it] is very compactly built, dirty, and noisy, with little elegance or evidence of taste. . . . A small central open square—the only public ground I observed—was used as a horse. . . . pasture, and clothes-drying yard" (quoted in Gums et al. 1998, 3).

In the early phase of the Spanish occupation in the late eighteenth century, Mobile's population consisted of about 1,500 people, a mixture of French Creoles, immigrants from Spain and the Spanish Caribbean, free and enslaved Africans, many mestizos and mulattos, and a few English residents remaining from the earlier period of British control. Creeks and Choctaws lived nearby and were involved in trade with Mobilers. The diversity in recovered artifacts shows the complex nature of colonial trade with a range of European countries and indigenous peoples. When excavating in downtown Mobile near the historic fort, archaeologists found Native American ceramics, eighteenth-century Spanish majolicas, French faiences, British pearlwares and creamwares, German stonewares, and Chinese and other porcelains, along with a variety of unglazed earthenwares. As more Americans arrived in Mobile after it was annexed by the United States as part of West Florida in 1813, some wealthier Spanish families left for Cuba (Gums et al. 1998, 76), and Mobile's ethnic diversity was gradually reduced, as was its ceramic variation; English imports came to dominate the tables of homes in Mobile as in other southern cities.

New Orleans, studied by Shannon Lee Dawdy, was another French colonial city, but quite different from Mobile. It is an example of an urban community whose landscape was altered by its successive colonizers: French (1721–1790), Spanish (1790–1803), and American (from 1803 on), as each re-created it into a new kind of city. In 1721, a French stock-based commercial enterprise, the Mississippi Company (which later became the Company of the Indies), sent a French military engineer to lay out New Orleans on a grid, albeit one influenced by Enlightenment ideas, planning an ordered city that they hoped would produce an "improved" society (Dawdy 2008, 67; Figure 3.2). As a site, the engineer chose the largest portion of more-or-less dry land within 100 miles of the mouth of the Mississippi River and laid out a city with a plaza in the center and four rows of square blocks around it, with a church on one side. Once having drawn the plan, the royal engineer had to assign building lots individually. Not surprisingly, the largest and driest lots went to company officials, military officers, and businessmen. A year later, although promotional materials published in French newspapers depicted 800 fine houses and five churches already in existence, Jesuit Father Charlevoix described the town as consisting of "about a hundred huts placed without much order, a large warehouse built of wood, two or three houses that would not grace a French village and half a wretched warehouse they had been good enough to lend to the Lord [as a church]" (Dawdy 2008, 66). As Dawdy notes, conflicts between the ideology of the *ancien regime* and immediate local interests ensued over the apportionment of lots, building styles, and pre-existing

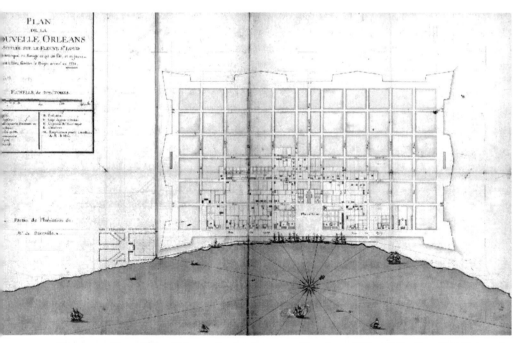

Figure 3.2. Plan of New Orleans, September 1723. (Courtesy of Map Collection, Yale University Library and Shannon Lee Dawdy, *Building the Devil's Empire: French Colonial New Orleans*. University of Chicago Press.)

buildings that did not conform to plan. As always, the theoretical equality implied by the grid gave way to considerations of power.

Dawdy notes that the French believed that the success of their empire depended on urban aesthetics and a formal plan. By laying out a symmetrical, attractive and organized space, they were trying to control both the social and natural aspects of town; however, the plan did not appear to establish either social order or political control. In the 1750s another visitor remarked, "The inhabitants, sailors, Indians, and slaves run around freely" (Wilson, cited in Dawdy 2008, 66). Taverns were seen as especially pernicious in New Orleans, because many different racial and social groups intermingled there. As in many other cities, they served as one of the few public institutions accessible to many.

The French began fortifications early in the town's development, and when the Spanish took control of the city in the 1790s, they completed and enlarged them, believing that the fortifications were an important symbol to impress local residents (Dawdy and Matthews 2010, 276, 279). At the same time, the Spanish didn't want to slow trade in their emerging crossroads market linked to Florida, Ohio, the Caribbean, and Africa, so they also built bridges that allowed traffic to flow freely in spite of the fortified walls. Much of what is thought of as French in New Orleans today was actually built by the Spanish, who rebuilt in brick after two big fires in 1788 and 1794. Dawdy and Christopher Matthews note that American transformations at the beginning of the nineteenth century tripled the city in size when they expanded the faubourgs (suburbs) created during an earlier economic boom (2010, 277). They suggest that combining a consideration of landscape alterations with changes in consumption practices provides the potential for allowing archaeologists access to wide-ranging phenomena such as creolization and colonization and other forms of both continuity and change.

A different European colonial model was established in Philadelphia in the late seventeenth century by Englishmen William Penn and Thomas Holme. The city was laid out on a grid between the Delaware and Schuylkill Rivers with five squares set aside as public spaces (Yamin 2007). British town planning concerns were somewhat different from those of the Spanish in that there was little governmental pressure on their application to the colonies. The Quakers, who founded Philadelphia, may have liked the egalitarian principles of the grid, and their vision of the city, as stipulated by Penn and Holme, persists today. The significance of the squares in Philadelphia as public spaces was understood by at least one resident named William Hudson, who in 1741 used his will to set aside some of his own land to be maintained as a square, as a form of posterity, although his descendants ultimately sold it (Yamin 2007, 7).

Less Formal Landscapes

Despite the frequent reliance on a grid, many cities grew organically, without comprehensive planning, starting from a perch on a riverbank or ocean shore. However, as towns expanded, elements of planning appeared as new municipal governments took control over land-use decisions, often in piecemeal fashion, resulting in irregular layouts. For example, Burrows and Hunter (1996) have shown that Trenton, New Jersey, was urban from early in the eighteenth century, with some streets laid out in a rectilinear plan in 1720 by William Trent. However, as the city grew, its layout was modified to suit expansion and topographic demands. In another early city, New Amsterdam (now New York), although there were some early plans, the 1620s town was centered on a fort with no clear strategy for growth. A series of early maps shows that later, in the eighteenth and nineteenth centuries, tracts of farmland were gridded individually as they were developed and incorporated into the city (Rothschild 1990).[3] But no overall grid was established in New York City until the 1807–11 Commissioners' Plan. This plan laid out a formal rectilinear plan over Manhattan up to 155th St, with 16 wide avenues running N–S, and 155 narrower streets going E–W, with wider E–W streets interspersed at about every ten blocks. The plan provided for small squares or parks as well, and established a new public market on the east side between 7th and 10th Streets and a site for a reservoir between 89th and 94th Streets (Bridges 1811b). It is interesting that the grid came late to New York City, and shows us that the concept retained significance in the planning of later American cities in the East and the West. The existence of the grid makes it easier to conduct archaeology in New York City as house locations are more predictable.

One of the important elements of the Commissioners' Plan was its concept of Republican simplicity, as the planners note:

One of the first objects that claimed their [the designers'] attention was . . . whether they should confine themselves to rectilinear streets, or whether they should adopt some of those supposed improvements by circles, ovals and stars, which certainly embellish a plan, . . . but a city is to be composed principally of the habitations of men, and that straight-sided and right-angled houses are the most cheap to build and the most convenient to live in. The effect of these plain and simple reflections was decisive. (Bridges 1811b)

An Alternative to the Grid: The Baroque City

A different theoretical model for urban development, the baroque plan, associated with the Enlightenment, was developed in Europe in the late sixteenth and seventeenth centuries (seen in Rome and Paris; Mumford 1961) and subsequently exported to the New World. It replaced the disorder of medieval towns and their early organic landscapes and grids with larger baroque centers, and organized and controlled space through the formality of straight, uniform streets and roof lines, centered on a new economic form (mercantile capitalism) that centralized power in the state. In contrast to earlier grid-based patterns, these cities included curvilinear areas and streets that were planned to be magnificent but also to enable fast movement of armies and goods in wheeled vehicles throughout the city (Mumford 1961). The most successful baroque cities in Europe, such as Paris, were dominated by bureaucracies and armies.

In North America, the early capitals of Maryland (St. Mary's City, studied by Henry Miller, and Annapolis, studied by Mark Leone) are intriguing examples of seventeenth century towns planned on the baroque model. Miller discovered the plan for St. Mary's City (which no longer exists above ground) through archaeological survey (1988). Annapolis began with a grid plan but was converted to a baroque plan at the end of the seventeenth century (Miller 1988, 58). Leone and colleagues have suggested that in both cases, as in other baroque cities, the convergence of streets "was organized to lead the viewer to the seats of civil and religious power" (Leone 2005, 8; Matthews et al. 2002), which were visible because of their size, architectural distinction, and sometimes topographic elevations. In St Mary's City, the dominant religion was Catholicism, but when Annapolis became the capital, those in power were Anglicans (Miller 1988, 59).

Washington, D.C., may be the best known baroque city in North America. It was laid out at a time when baroque planning had become popular, and was designed by Pierre Charles L'Enfant, a French engineer, who had the freedom to design the entire city from scratch, with broad avenues focusing on important buildings. The city, planned in 1791, incorporates a rectangular grid, but superimposes circles and diagonals in a truly baroque vision of the city, in which ceremonial spaces and wide avenues are as important as buildings. The avenues connected important sites on the landscape and were meant to impress the public with their monumental structures built of expensive materials; the President's House and the Capitol were two of those placed on natural elevations (Leach and Barthold, cited in Killion et al. 2001, 12). Apparently Washington and L'Enfant decided that the city plan should separate the various branches of government spatially (Zueblin 1905, 147), so that the demands of the Constitution could be met more easily. The symbolic and the practical were thus coordinated.

Such schemes often hid the poor and members of minority groups by housing them in unseen, out-of-the-way places. The poor are always present, but often their homes are hidden, and one of the ways that urban planners might hide them is in alleys that run behind the houses of the middle class and elites. Washington is one of the cities in which archaeologists have located and investigated alley communities (Little and Kassner 2001).

A Utopian Landscape

A town plan based on a distinctive religious landscape model is seen in the towns of Bethabara, Bethania, and Salem, North Carolina; the latter ultimately became Winston-Salem. Moravian immigrants who came in the mid-eighteenth century were pacifists seeking religious freedom. They settled on the North Carolina frontier with clear ideas about the best way to satisfy their needs (Hartley 2007). They imported a medieval European landscape (or landschaft) model and imposed it on a tract of 100,000 acres (called Wachovia), bisected by a river, separating natural from cultural areas. Salem was founded in 1766, at the center of the tract, and it became the dominant urban place in Wachovia. Winston, created as a secular county seat from fifty-one acres of the Salem town lot, was incorporated in 1856, and was consolidated with Salem in 1913 (Hartley 2007).

Bethabara, Bethania, and Old Salem are now National Historic Landmarks and open-air museums. As preservationists focus on their distinctive colonial elements, archaeology has been important in bringing knowledge of the original communities and their ideals to modern memory, identifying resources for exploring the past and emphasizing the significance of this landscape model for visitors and residents. Although Winston-Salem has become a modern city and has expanded in concert with industrialization, the older towns exemplify the Moravian vision of a sustainable community, designed for individual well-being through the maintenance of resources for the group as a whole (Hartley 2007).

Western Urban Landscapes

Most inland western towns had different stimuli and trajectories from those in the East; many of them arose because of a local need for transporting goods and often grew on the site of a fort or mining camp. Although not necessarily planned at their origins, consistent landscapes emerged centered on a gridded core, showing the dominance of the grid concept throughout the United States. Archaeological excavation reveals the layering of different landscapes within a community, and artifacts repeatedly demonstrate the impact of railroad construction, expanding local markets into national ones with American annexation in the late nineteenth century.

Tucson and Phoenix represent contrasting forms of urban development. Homer Thiel and his colleagues have studied both areas archaeologically. Tucson is an oasis community (Thiel and Mabry 2006, 1.1), and for centuries the Santa Cruz River offered a reliable water supply and an important focus for settlement. Archaeologists discovered the remains of thirteen agricultural canals from the pre-Columbian Hohokam culture (CE 650–1450) there (Thiel 2005). These early western Anglo-European settlements were organized to protect the oasis and its water and thus were always concentrated, territorially defensive, and quite self-sufficient. Some of these attributes are archaeologically visible in the clustering of residences and evidence of defense, and self-sufficiency can be seen in the primary use of local materials and objects, with relatively little evidence of trade until the arrival of the railroad in the 1880s (Thiel and Mabry 2006, 22.4).

Tucson's origins as a modern city derive from a Spanish mission and Presidio established there in the late seventeenth century to defend the area from the Apache to the north and also to keep other European powers from claiming it. As soldiers began to live near the Presidio, Native Americans moved away, but artifacts show the mixing of cultures. When the Presidio was in use (1775–1856), local residents used iron or brass pots; then they switched to Hispanic ceramic *ollas* and tortilla griddles (Thiel and Mabry 2006), local wares made by Native Americans, and majolicas from Mexico. By the late nineteenth century, the area was home to a diverse group of residents: people of Mexican descent (Thiel 2005), a few Native Americans, Anglos, and Chinese, among others (Thiel and Mabry 2006, 22.1). Many of these groups came to live in spatially distinct ethnic enclaves.

Tucson remained a community based on agriculture and ranching as well as trade until the end of the nineteenth century. When the United States took Arizona from Mexico in 1856, the railroad reorganized the landscape and starting in the 1880s brought access to American and other goods, as seen in domestic ceramics. The railroad also brought easterners and Californians and their goods; initially these newcomers were men who married indigenous women (Thiel and Mabry 2006), but soon European American women came to the area.

Phoenix, Arizona, on the other hand, was settled exclusively by European Americans in the 1860s. It provides a contrast with Tucson in period of settlement, trajectory, and the homogeneity of its population. It began as a mining supply town (Camp McDowell, in 1865) and was fully planned from its inception. It offers a model for how urban development occurs at a later time. Phoenix lies in a difficult environment; because of its intense summer heat, nothing in its location made it the obvious location for the core of an urban place although it offered agricultural potential (Thiel 1998, 3). It was subject to raiding by Apache and Yavapai who resented encroachment on their lands.

The town was settled as a speculative venture and established on the assumption it would become significant. When the site was laid out in 1870, it consisted of ninety-eight blocks, each with twelve lots on them (Thiel 1998, 6). The symmetrical grid had wide E–W and N–S streets. The pioneers created areas for businesses and residences, with the center of the grid (reminiscent of the plaza) set aside for government structures, including a courthouse.

The city grew because the town became a service center and delivered goods to army bases, Indian agencies, and miners. After the town was incorporated in 1881, it levied taxes, passed laws, and provided services, such as street and irrigation ditch cleaning, a fire company, streetcar line, and gas for lights. The railroad arrived in 1887, and the town was named the state capital in 1890, when Arizona became a state. Institutions such as the Territorial Insane Asylum and the U.S. Industrial Indian School (1889), designed to force the assimilation of Native American children from the Southwest and the Pacific coast into European American culture, stimulated the town's growth, as Phoenix's economy did not have a strong manufacturing component (Thiel 1998).

An archaeological examination of a two-block project area on two major streets just west of the business district shows that urban growth was slow. Phoenix was quite different from Tucson, as most residents were European American and ranged from working-class to upper-middle-class store owners and professionals.

Artifacts recovered during excavation provided information on a range of subjects, including the impact of changes in transportation networks and manufacturing centers on the use of objects in the home. For example, the shift from European to American ceramics is seen on these blocks between 1895 and 1900, as American production in places such as Ohio and on the East Coast increased (Thiel 1998). Native American water jars were in use in many households but were discarded when city water became available. European decorated ceramics also increased over time, as did the use of porcelain, suggesting both stylistic change and an increased ability to purchase more expensive items. Households associated with residents at higher socioeconomic levels also demonstrated different taste in home décor, the degree of landscaping in the yard, and more attention to innovations in home healthcare, such as thermometers (Thiel 1998, 347). The project offers an interesting insight into consistent late nineteenth- and early twentieth-century newspaper accounts about the "disorderly disposal of waste" and its relation to both epidemics and ground-water pollution. These accounts may have influenced new locations for, and the deeper construction of, privies. However, in spite of these concerns, none of the archaeologically excavated privy deposits demonstrated any evidence of parasites (Thiel 1998, 432).

Denver is another western city, similar to Phoenix, that emerged from the need to provision miners (here in the gold rush of the late 1850s)[4] and then transitioned to a hub for farming equipment, agricultural produce, and processed goods when the railroad arrived there in 1870. Denver provides an interesting example of "grid conflict." The older portion of the city was gridded to follow the Platte River, but when it was chosen as the state capital in 1881, the expanded part of the city was gridded to align with the cardinal directions (Nelson et al. 2001, 173). Sarah Nelson and her colleagues explain that, as part of the competition to have Denver selected as the capital, its promoters believed it was important to have it laid out in conformity with the conquest of nature and the imposition of order on the landscape, European and Enlightenment ideals associated with progress. The intriguing outcome of these two grids is seen in the variations in occupants and institutions: the new grid housed the elite and influential whereas the older grid retained more marginal residents and institutions.

Nineteenth-Century Concerns and the Ideal City

As American cities expanded and were modified during later periods, planning incorporated a new consciousness of topographical, aesthetic, and public health issues (Zueblin 1905). An awareness of the need for improved amenities like street paving, parks, sewers, and transport facilities was common.

The evidence of these services is seen through archaeology and utility planning maps (Graff 2011; Palus 2010). Chicago took advantage of the World's Fair of 1893 to develop a new portion of the city as an ideal model of a salubrious environment. "A complete city, equipped with all the public utilities caring for a temporary population of thousands . . . was built as a unit on a single architectural scale" (Zueblin 1905, 60); it was called the White City. Placed on the shore of Lake Michigan, it demonstrated a sharp contrast with the rest of Chicago, which was "bordered by ugly docks and warehouses, spanned by hideous bridges, and defiled by the city's foulness" (Zueblin 1905, 61). This project has been given credit for the City Beautiful movement (Graff 2011) at the turn of the twentieth century: a reform movement within architectural planning that relied on beauty and grandeur to increase the common good and create moral and civic virtue (Olmsted 1911). Frederick Law Olmsted was the landscape architect for the project, and Chicago's famous Louis Henry Sullivan was one of the architects. The fairground's thoughtful plan recognized the need both for appropriate transportation as cities expanded as well as for public spaces such as playgrounds and parks to enhance the health of city-dwellers.

Archaeological work at the site of the World's Fair in Chicago's Jackson Park by Rebecca Graff (2011) focused on the intersection of contemporary tourism with fantasies of past events, and the daily experiences of fairgoers in this utopian city were meant to privilege technological advances. The project recovered significant elements of infrastructure (water pipes, cisterns), architecture, and objects left by tourists (ceramics, bottles, and tobacco pipes). Graff notes that the Fair's infrastructure was closely planned with the advice of physicians who were concerned with garbage disposal, sewage, and cleanliness. Ironically it was the (invisible) infrastructure and its artifacts rather than the (visible) monumental architecture that persisted. The Fair served as an example of future urban planning mainly in its innovations in sewerage, water, trash disposal service, an internal elevated train, and electricity.

San Francisco is an example of city planning that ignored basic topography. It had a superb port, but planners laid out a grid on an impossibly steep set of hills that do not appear to offer any chance for reasonable traffic circulation through the streets (Horowitz 1982). Even at the time of its construction it seems that observers realized that the project, which required "cut and fill" on a massive scale because of the city's geomorphology, was expensive and impractical (Praetzellis and Praetzellis 2009, 366).

There has been a significant amount of archaeology conducted in San

Francisco, mostly in conjunction with Cultural Research Management (CRM), much of it under the leadership of Adrian and Mary Praetzellis and Barbara Voss. Some of this work is described in chapters 5 and 6. Here we briefly discuss one of the neighborhoods where the Praetzellises worked that shows the absence of thoughtful planning in its development. The project area, Tar Flats, is in the "South of Market" area. In the early 1850s, it was marginal to the more settled portions of the city and was used for cheap housing and for unpleasant-smelling industries. The area became the kind of working-class community found in many American cities of the time, in which groups without political and economic power were located in marginal areas in sub-standard and overcrowded housing. Archaeology was important in recording lifeways in this neighborhood, as many records were lost during a series of earthquakes that ultimately destroyed the neighborhood. The first one was in 1868 (Praetzellis and Praetzellis 2009, 115); a second in 1906 devastated the area, especially through associated fires; and, most recently, the Loma Prieta quake in 1989 led to the razing of the area for a new approach to the San Francisco–Oakland Bay Bridge. Ironically this last quake required the project that produced the archaeological reports documenting the early neighborhood.

Urban Expansion

Many of the features that archaeologists encounter in their study of the city as artifact have to do with the expansion of the urban center. Most are related to the economic growth of the city with its accompanying commodification of land and water and the increase in trade as the United States became a more and more important player in the global economic system. These features make up the city's infrastructure, its underlying foundation or basic framework, and constitute the materiality of the city itself. This infrastructure includes the physical features that underpin the landscape and form the fabric of the city: landfill and its associated structures, wharves and other waterfront features, particularly in the old eastern port cities. Landfilling brought engineering problems in modifying the waterfront and associated wharves through which goods were imported and exported. Infrastructure also includes the canals of the early nineteenth century and, after the Civil War, the railroads used for transporting goods that gave so many cities their reason for being. There are also other features that are related to urban expansion that resulted in the transformation of the system that provided basic services to the residents of the city—water and the disposal of waste, issues that became more and more important as cities grew. Initially these existed on the scale of the individual house lot—the back-yard privies, cisterns, and wells that brought water to the people and handled their waste—and then they were taken over on a citywide scale as municipal water and sewer systems.

Landfill

A number of cities, especially those on the East Coast, altered their landscapes through the process of landfilling, which added new acreage to expanding towns. Making land was an important component of urban development. Here we consider the contributions that urban archaeologists have made to our understanding of the landfill process and the wharves that were the focus of the earlier cities.

One of the correlates that accompanied the development of western capitalism is the commodification of land—turning land into real estate. To that end, developers in the United States have been making and remaking the urban landscape since the seventeenth century. These alterations have included leveling hills, filling in low-lying ground, regularizing shorelines so the land there can be easily developed and sold, and even "making land" by claiming it from adjacent waterways.

Landfill has been used to make land alongside urban shores, from marshes, rivers, lakes, and the sea. We tend to assume that this process is a modern one, one that is dependent on modern technology, but that is not true. Landfilling began in the colonial port cities along the eastern seaboard in the seventeenth and eighteenth centuries. Often, land was claimed from adjacent waterways to build dockage and to augment valuable waterside real estate, where ships docked and merchants' countinghouses and warehouses were located. Many of the projects that archaeologists have conducted in the eastern seaboard cities have been located on the landfill of the old ports; the excavations were done in conjunction with the redevelopment of the old waterfronts as modern tourist attractions in the 1980s and 1990s. Excavations in Boston (e.g., Balicki 1998; Seasholes 1998, 2003), New York (Cantwell and Wall 2001; Rothschild and Pickman 1990), Baltimore (Norman 1987), and Philadelphia (Cotter et al. 1992; Yamin 2008) have revealed a great deal about early landfill practices and waterfront technologies; similar excavations have taken place in smaller cities in other parts of the country as well (including Louisville and Mobile). These excavations are important because of what they can tell us about the nature of the fill, the artifacts the fill contains, and the lost technologies that were used to hold the fill in place or to build on unstable landfill. Examining the landfill itself can be important for several reasons. It can tell us where people were obtaining the fill—from dumping garbage, dredging waterways, or leveling hills and digging cellar holes. The nature of fill changed with our understandings of disease (Geismar 1987; Seasholes 2003, 16). In New York in the eighteenth century, for example, a relatively high percentage of landfill was made up of organic garbage. But after a series of yellow fever epidemics hit the city at the turn of the nineteenth century, regulations were enacted demanding that only clean fill be used in making land. These regulations were consistent with contemporary understanding of the cause of yellow fever: miasmas that emanated from decaying organic material. We know today that miasmas do not play a role in the spread of yellow fever; it is spread by mosquitos. However, by cleaning up the landfill, early New Yorkers did the right thing, because mosquitos bred in standing water in the organic material in the landfill. Joan Geismar's 1987 study of landfill in New York showed that while most New Yorkers apparently complied with the new regulations controlling the contents of the landfill, some did not—she discovered a deposit of cattle skulls and jaws, showing that some illegal dumpers, perhaps from a nearby market, had been at work, disposing of leftover remains from butchering.

The fill can also provide us with a sample of artifacts from the city dating to the periods both at and before the time the fill was put into place. These artifacts can be particularly important when the fill is very old, even if the material cannot be associated with a particular household (Pickman and Rothschild 1981). For example, if the fill was put into place in the seventeenth century, all of the artifacts that it contains are valuable because we have so few artifacts from that period (see, e.g., Rothschild and Pickman 1990).

The technology of building wharves and landfill-retaining structures is also important to record. People claiming land along the eastern seaboard used a technique different from that used in the Netherlands, where land is claimed from the sea by building dikes that enclose low-lying tracts of land called polders, to keep the water out. Instead, they used the technique of "wharfing out," whereby shoreline property owners had wharves built that extended out from the shore, forming slips or basins between them (Figures 3.3, 3.4). They subsequently filled in the slips, using the wharves to enclose the landfill (Seasholes 2003, 3).

Before the nineteenth century, vernacular building traditions, passed down from master craftsman to apprentice, were used to build these wharves, and they are not found in written records. Archaeologists have had trouble in recording them, however, because for the most part they are not trained in ver-

Figure 3.3. An exterior view of the log wharves uncovered at the Assay site, New York City. (Courtesy of the New York State Museum, Albany.)

Figure 3.4. An interior view of a log wharf uncovered at the Assay site, New York City. (Courtesy of the New York State Museum, Albany.)

nacular building traditions and cannot appreciate the finer points of their construction. Recently Molly McDonald, an archaeologist with training in architectural history, made a study of many of the wharves and landfill-retaining structures that have been explored archaeologically along the East Coast and in Europe in an effort to clarify the differences among them (2011). She has standardized the nomenclature for the various kinds of structures, the construction traditions that were used to make them, and the cultural context of these traditions. She also discovered something very interesting: although some carpenters in eastern North America made some of their waterfront structures (such as bulkheads) using the same techniques they used to build their houses (the English timber frame and plank tradition), they used log construction for building their wharves and quays. Log construction is a northern European tradition that was never used for building houses in the coastal cities at all. Instead, it was a legacy of northern Europeans from forested areas—the Swedes and Finns who settled New Sweden (the Swedish colony on the lower Delaware River) in the seventeenth century, and the Germans and Swiss who settled in Pennsylvania in the eighteenth century. They introduced the tradition, which was picked up by others and disseminated throughout the Middle Atlantic area. McDonald suggests it was the prevalence of wood in the mid-Atlantic colonies that contributed to the adoption of this tradition for building the waterfront.

But people did not use only log wharves to hold the landfill. Then, as now, they used whatever would most cheaply do the trick. Archaeologists have discovered that they often used scuttled ships to form part of their bulkhead lines. There have been several such ships unearthed in New York City, including an eighteenth-century merchantman that was discovered at 175 Water Street in 1982 (Cantwell and Wall 2001). Most recently, archaeologists working in the eighteenth-century landfill as part of the redevelopment of the World Trade Center area discovered the remains of a two-masted ship buried under twenty to thirty feet of landfill (Figure 3.5). Nautical archaeologist Warren Riess has noted that it was probably active in the coastal trade.[5] The discovery of an English military button suggests that the ship may have been used by the British for transporting troops.

Archaeologists have also shown us how people in the past have adapted their building construction techniques to the fact that landfill settles for a long period after it has been put into place, and therefore builders have to do something to prevent the structures that are built on it from settling, too. In New York in the eighteenth century, builders rested their structures on

Figure 3.5. The stern of the boat that archaeologists from AKRF discovered at the Southern Site of the World Trade Center redevelopment site, 2010. A year later they found a small segment of the boat's bow on the other side of the wall visible in the background. (AKRF, Inc., courtesy of the Lower Manhattan Development Corporation.)

spread-footer complexes (Figure 3.6). These were wooden structures made up, first, of a series of planks set perpendicular to the buildings' walls, overlain, in turn, by a large beam set parallel to the wall, on top of which the stone footing of the foundation wall rested (Cantwell and Wall 2001). This arrangement in effect floated the building on top of the landfill, preventing it from settling. Earlier, in the seventeenth century, when land was being made in New York along the natural shore, where water was shallow, builders lay the footings of their stone foundation walls directly on the riverbed and deposited the landfill around the walls, so the load of the building rested on the riverbed and not on the fill itself (Rothschild and Pickman 1990). Nineteenth-

Figure 3.6. A spread-footer complex from the Assay site, New York City. The stone foundation wall of the building sat atop the large wooden beam. (Courtesy of the New York State Museum, Albany.)

century Bostonians used a different technique to achieve the same purpose. There, masonry houses were set on foundations of wooden pilings that were driven down through the fill to the river bottom, so that the natural, stable soil of the river bottom (and not the unstable landfill) supported the load of the building (Seasholes 2003, 1; this technique was also discovered at the Assay site in New York City [Louis Berger 1987]).

Utilities

Archaeologists have also looked at another important component of infrastructure: the utilities that people have used to procure water and to remove waste
in their cities. Before the introduction of municipal water and sewer systems in
the nineteenth and twentieth centuries, people living in cities handled these
needs privately, on the level of the neighborhood or house lot. Behind almost
every house there was a privy or outhouse. And behind many houses there were
also cisterns or rain barrels, which held rainwater that was collected from roofs
and drained into these containers by way of gutter systems. There were also
wells, which were often located on street corners in urban areas, to be shared by
the people of the neighborhood, as well as, occasionally, in backyards. Then in
the later nineteenth and twentieth centuries, there was a switch in urban areas
to water that was piped in and sewage that was piped out.

But backyard utilities related to sanitation were prevalent throughout much
of the country's history, and archaeologists have basically three foci in studying
them: the artifacts found in them (see Warner and Genheimer 2008 for a study
of a privy with an unusual number of feline bones); construction technology;
and the definition of the role of government in the lives of its citizens. Features
such as privies, wells, and cisterns serve as repositories for artifacts—many of
the assemblages that we use to talk about consumption patterns and ethnicity,
race, gender, and class in this volume have been excavated from these features.
Artifacts were deposited when the feature was being built (in the builders'
trenches of privies, cisterns, and wells; these artifacts can be used to date the
feature), while it was in use (in the form of night soil for privies and for the
intentional or accidental disposal of waste and trash in privies and wells, and
after it was abandoned (in order to fill up the now-useless hole that was once a
privy, cistern, or well shaft).

Most of the artifacts found in wells and cisterns were deposited after the
features were abandoned. The fill might consist of household trash, coal ash,
architectural materials, and clean fill. Unless they were cleaned out before they
were filled, privies also contain a layer that resulted from their use—the fine,
dark organic layer of night soil resting at the bottom of the privy shaft. Night
soil can inform us about diet and health. For example, it often contains a large
quantity of small seeds, such as those from strawberries or raspberries, that
have passed through the digestive system, as well as parasites, which provide
evidence of some of the diseases suffered by some of the site's occupants. The
layers discovered on top of the night soil were placed in the privy to fill up the

shaft after it was no longer in use and are similar to the deposits found in cisterns and wells. These layers often include a thick deposit of domestic garbage, usually deposited in one episode, overlain by a cap of clay or some other clean fill like coal ash or architectural material.

The excavation of these features can also tell us about technology. Like the wharves discussed above, they were built in vernacular building traditions that were not recorded in writing (see Cantwell and Wall 2001 for a description of those found in New York City, and Benedict 2003 for a comparative discussion of the technology of privy building in other parts of the country). Most cisterns were made of brick and lined with plaster or mortar on the inside to seal them, while wells were usually lined with stones or brick. Both wells and cisterns were typically round in cross-section.

In most cases, privies or outhouses consisted of an above-ground structure—the outhouse—which contained a cabinet with an open seat atop. Below it was an underground shaft or vault which held the bodily waste. The big difference between privies in urban and rural areas was that because rural properties were usually much larger than urban ones, when a privy shaft filled up from use, it was capped with clean fill and a new shaft was dug, and the old outhouse was moved and placed on top of it. But in urban areas, where backyards were smaller, instead of moving the outhouse, both the outhouse and its vault were permanent structures, and the vaults were cleaned out rather than topped off and moved (see Wheeler 2000a for a collection of articles on privies, many of which are located in urban contexts). Therefore, in most cities, privy shafts were lined. But what they were lined with varied through both space and time. In some cities, such as Philadelphia, Pittsburgh, and Wheeling, West Virginia, they were usually lined with brick (Benedict 2003, 2004), and in others, local stone (with sandstone in Wheeling, schist in Manhattan, limestone in Zanesville and Cincinnati, Ohio, and shale in Harpers Ferry, West Virginia [Benedict 2003; Cantwell and Wall 2001]), and in others still, with wood (e.g., Manhattan in the seventeenth and eighteenth centuries, West Oakland in the nineteenth century, Portsmouth, New Hampshire, throughout its history [Cantwell and Wall 2001; Praetzellis and Praetzellis 2004; Wheeler 2000b, 5]). Outhouse shafts were variable in shape; they did not have solid floors, so that the liquid waste could leach out.

Most cities developed ordinances covering privy construction. In Boston, for example, a 1652 law required that privies could not be built within twelve feet of a neighboring house or street unless it was vaulted and at least six feet deep (Heck and Balicki 1998). In Louisville, an 1853 ordinance required that privy vaults be twelve to thirty feet deep and lined with brick (Stottman 2000). Archaeologists have shown that in general the city's residents complied with most of these regulations. However, excavations have also shown that there were other regulations that they usually ignored. For example, ordinances often specified the kinds of materials that could be used to fill up the vaults when they were no longer in use. By 1860, New York City's laws and ordinances prohibited using organic substances to fill a privy or cesspool (Geismar 1993, 65), while an 1881 ordinance enacted in Wheeling forbade the deposition of any "kitchen garbage or offal" in privy vaults or cesspits (Benedict 2003, 64). But urban archaeologists have shown (thankfully, from their perspective) that city dwellers often ignored these ordinances and dumped their garbage into the privy (e.g., Geismar 1993). And of course it is this garbage that provides the artifacts that the archaeologists are interested in studying (see chapters 4 through 6).

In cities where the water table was high, there were ordinances that prohibited the use of underground privy vaults or limited their depth so as not to contaminate the groundwater. Because of the high water table in parts of Washington, D.C., people used no underground privy vaults at all, but instead used self-contained, above-ground containers that could be emptied periodically (Chapin 1901; Crane 2000).[6] In Santa Fe before the nineteenth century, human waste was placed in fields, irrigation ditches, and even in the street. "Once tossed, scavengers in the form of dogs, pigs, and chickens consumed much of it aided by the strong sun and wind which quickly dried up any remaining filth" (Matthew J. Barbour pers. comm. 2012). And ethnicity could also be a factor in privy technology. In New Brooklyn, New York, a German neighborhood developed in the 1850s, archaeologist Joan Geismar was surprised to find very few stone-lined privy vaults. After a great deal of research, she discovered that the developers of the neighborhood came from Prussia and Bavaria, places where open sewers were common and stone-lined privy pits were unknown. Geismar surmised that when the new arrivals learned that there were no open sewers in their new home, they improvised and perhaps used outhouses with buckets that sat under the cabinets, on top of the ground, to catch the human waste (Geismar 1996; Wall and Cantwell 2004).

Archaeological and documentary study together have provided an unusually detailed history of privy vaults in Philadelphia, where archaeologists have examined over three hundred shaft features over the last half century. Most of the vaults there are lined with brick and are circular in cross-section. During the early colonial period (perhaps following an "out of sight, out of mind" [Stottman 2000] philosophy), these vaults extended deeply into the ground, often down to the water table. But later it became evident that the deep privy shafts were contaminating groundwater, and in 1763 regulations were put into place to ameliorate that problem by requiring that the bottoms of the shafts be well above the water table. This meant that since the water table was at different depths in different parts of the city, the depths of the shafts had to vary accordingly (Cotter et al. 1992, 46; Benedict 2004, 11; Yamin 2008). Apparently these regulations applied not only to new vaults but also to those already in existence, so that people who had privies with deep vaults were required to alter them so that they did not exceed the new limits. Archaeologists often find artifact-rich deposits at the bottom of the older privies in Philadelphia. They believe that these deposits were placed there either to fill the floor of the privy up to the depth permitted on that block in compliance with the 1763 code or to serve as "percolation fill" (a porous fill that facilitated the movement and filtering of human liquid waste out of the privy shaft and into the surrounding subsoil), or both (Yamin 2008, 217n9).[7]

Archaeologists have discovered that there was an innovation in privy design in Philadelphia in the early nineteenth century: the double-shaft privy. Here, a wide upper shaft with a floor of wooden planking rested on top of a narrower lower shaft. Some think that the upper shaft served as a receptacle for solid waste, which rested on the plank flooring, thus facilitating access for cleaning. Liquid waste, on the other hand, slowly traveled through the flooring and leached down into the lower shaft. More than twenty of these double-shaft privies have been excavated (Benedict 2004). To date, this construction design has been recorded only in Philadelphia.

Backyards as Mini-Landscapes

The study of backyard utilities can tell us not only about technology but also about changes in our attitudes toward privacy, sanitation and the causes of disease, and the definition of the appropriate role of government. Archaeologists have looked at the locations of these features in urban backyards in order to study the layout of the yards as mini-landscapes. For privies, there was a balance between being close enough to the house for comfort and convenience but far enough away to keep the odor and leaching liquids at bay. Cisterns, on the other hand, were close to the house, both for convenience in connecting them to the gutter system from the house's roof and for pumping water into the kitchen, and to keep them as far away from the privy and its leaching liquids as possible. Following these rules, in nineteenth-century single-family middle-class homes in New York City, privies were located near the back property line while cisterns were placed just outside the back door (Cantwell and Wall 2001).

Municipal Services

When urban areas expand, land becomes a commodity, and entrepreneurs often begin to speculate in real estate. The development of citywide utilities was often associated with this growth and spelled the demise of the private privy/cistern system. Inspired by fires and cholera epidemics, in the mid-nineteenth century cities began to install water and then sewer systems for the first time. The introduction of citywide water required finding a clean water source (usually outside the city), piping the water down from that source into a holding reservoir in the city, and laying water pipes under the streets. Individual property owners could then pay for the installation of water lines from their houses to the city water pipes. Later on, the city lay sewer pipes to remove sewage and developed the technology for disposing of it.

The transition period between the era of the privy and the introduction of the modern indoor toilet saw several innovations in outhouse design; some of these solutions have been documented archaeologically. At the Tenement Museum in New York City, archaeologist Joan Geismar was looking for a stone-lined vault of the privy that she thought should have been built behind the tenement when the latter was constructed in the early 1860s. Instead, she discovered the brick vault of a "water-cleansed privy," a transitional facility that was hooked up to the municipal water supply and sewer systems and included a row of compartments, each with a cabinet topped by a seat, underlain by a single, shallow common vault that was "flushed," ideally on a daily basis. This privy must have been installed when the tenement was built, years before they were first documented in the literature (Geismar 1999/2003).

Contrary to popular conception, the transition to citywide water and sewer systems began several decades before the general acceptance of germ theory in explaining the causes of disease. As mentioned above, before the late nineteenth century, western science understood that most diseases were caused by miasmas or vapors emanating from rotting organic wastes; diseases were not believed to be contagious, and there was no understanding of germs. The cholera epidemics that swept through European and American cities in the nineteenth century were seen through the prism of miasmic theory, and even though miasmas were not in fact the cause of this and other deadly diseases, this interpretation helped to build support for an environmental approach to public health that was effective in combating these diseases. So, fortuitously, the introduction of clean water and effective sewer systems removed not only the miasmas but also the bacteria that were unfamiliar to people then but which we now know cause cholera and so many other diseases. In city after city, inspired by public health concerns, governments began to install public water and sewer systems, and the private well/cistern and privy systems were gradually phased out (see Stottman 2000 for a discussion of Louisville).

But gaining access to these amenities was not an even process. It was expensive for individual house-lot owners to hook up to the system. In Louisville in the 1930s, for example, there was not only the outlay for plumbing fixtures; there were also hook-up fees that ranged from $100 to $125 (Stottman 2000, 45). Records often show when pipes for water and sewage were laid under streets, but they rarely show when individual houses were hooked up to these systems. Archaeologists can use the artifacts found in the fill of cisterns, privies, and wells to find out when the features were abandoned and thereby can infer when people got access to indoor plumbing. In many cases, they have shown that getting access to city water and waste removal was defined by class. On one block in New York City, for example, the upper-middle-class owner-occupants of the buildings that fronted on one side of the block installed indoor plumbing by the end of the 1840s, while a building that fronted on the other side and that housed members of the working class got indoor plumbing much later, around 1870 (Howson 1992–93, 139–40). Needless to say, this three-decade difference in access to public utilities resulted in gross inequities in the quality of life, particularly when we remember that people living on the upper floors of the tenement had to haul their water up and slops down many flights of stairs.

Another real difference in the transformation from the well/cistern–privy system to the citywide water and sewer system was the redefinition of the role of municipal government. In the early nineteenth century, like today, some Americans placed a high value on a limited role for government—this philosophy was one of the rationales behind the well/cistern–privy system, which was privately controlled and contained within each individual house lot. But as the century progressed, there was a growing awareness and acceptance of the idea that one of the main functions of municipal government was the delivery of services (Ogle 1996, 159; Melosi 2000, 1). It is only with this change in the definition of the role of government that city dwellers could begin to envision and implement citywide water and sewer systems.

Recently, some archaeologists have begun taking a Marxist approach in looking at this relationship between changing cultural values and the introduction of municipal water and sewer systems. Jared Barrett (2002), using the case study of the introduction of these services into a home in Battle Creek, Michigan, shows how elites imposed their notions of what they regarded as "proper etiquette" onto members of the middle and working classes. In so doing they were able to add to government coffers and ultimately their own pockets through the bonds that were sold to pay for the water and sewer lines and the fees that people paid to hook up to them. Even water, which formerly had been free, became a commodity that could be bought and sold. Those who did not buy into this new system (both literally and figuratively) were subject to exclusion, in that they were stigmatized as old-fashioned, uncivilized, and backward, as opposed to forward-looking and modern (Barrett 2002, 104). Ultimately, everyone who lived in the city and was subject to municipal regulations was forced to become part of this system, under the threat of the fines that these regulations imposed.

Matthew Palus has taken this argument one step further. Following Foucault, he has suggested that we look on the transformation of the well/cistern and privy system to the municipal service system and the introduction of a city-wide electrical system as part of the materiality of the growth of government, showing the intrusion of governmental power into the lives of its citizens (2010, 42–43). Looking at Eastport, an African American neighborhood in Annapolis, Maryland, he shows how the introduction of electricity and water and sewer lines in the late nineteenth and early twentieth centuries can be seen as part of the process of the consolidation of knowledge and power under the control of government. For some, being disconnected from municipal services may have reflected the lesser rights of citizenship afforded African Americans, with this infrastructure reifying class- and race-based privilege, underscoring the meaning of identities based on class and race (Palus 2010, 2012). But, as Palus points out, it is also possible that some African Americans chose to remain disconnected from municipal services so as to remain free from the apparatus of the state.

As cities expanded, a number of historical archaeologists have shown through documents how some citizens understood impending land use changes and hoped to profit from them by speculating, or investing in land in anticipation of future growth. Archaeologists demonstrate these changes through the reorganization of land use and through artifacts that show changing socioeconomic and ethnic composition (discussed in chapters 5 and 6). Basically residential areas come to be differentiated from one another by population density and by population composition, including elements of class, ethnicity, and race. Not all expansion is planned, and the urban poor, as they are priced out of their residences, may move into older areas as wealthier people move out, or they may settle in informal areas at the city's edge. Archaeologists have documented both kinds of movement. Although official records may portray growth as orderly, it often is not. Marginal spaces are often contested places as the city government tries to regularize and incorporate them (Gray and Yakubik 2010, 298).

Archaeologists have noted examples of this process throughout the country, in the Bowling Green section of Louisville (Stottman and Stahlgren 2006), on Walsh's Row in St. Louis (Meyer and Austin 2008), and in New Brunswick (Yamin 2007, 176). Louisville, for example, was first laid out in the late 1700s, and the Bowling Green area was developed in the 1810s, when town administrators added more sections just adjacent to the town and speculators acquired agricultural land anticipating urban growth (Stottman and Stahlgren 2006, 9, 145). Initial growth was slow, but as subdivisions were laid out in the 1850s, businesses began to appear and the area was incorporated into the town's commercial district. The nature of the residential population shifted from a relatively few richer families to a denser population of working-class wage earners. When large-scale industry moved in during the late 1800s, the rich moved out and their residences were converted into working-class rental units which then gradually deteriorated; the proximity of the railroad and associated structures further shaped the character of the neighborhood. By the early 1900s the area was almost completely industrial, and the remaining residents were mainly Irish and African American workers. Archaeological investigation recovered small outbuildings that were not recorded in documentary sources. Some of these could have housed the enslaved or servants in the Antebellum period, and they were demolished as land use changed (Stottman and Stahlgren 2006, 147–49). Unfortunately, they had no associated deposits, but archaeological study showed the way lots and structures were reconfigured, abandoned, and brick-robbed.

As archaeologists analyzed the documents, they highlighted the contrast between different kinds of strategies used by mid- to late nineteenth-century landowners, one of whom chose to develop his piece of land and live at a relatively comfortable level, whereas the second used his resources to purchase larger amounts of land. As it turned out here and in many similar situations, this second strategy was more economically beneficial, as that landowner rented his land out and lived on its income, whereas the former's land ultimately declined in value as the neighborhood changed, and he sold his property for less than he had paid for it (Stottman and Stahlgren 2006, 149).

In another midwestern city, St. Louis, some decades later, the same process was repeated: a formerly prominent residential area declined when industry moved into a neighborhood (Meyer and Austin 2008, 22). Then the railroad penetrated the area in the late 1870s, and once again wealthier residents moved away to other sections of the city and population density in the remaining houses increased. In the 1880s, as mills, factories, foundries, and warehouses joined tenements and boarding houses, the socioeconomic characteristics of residents shifted to include working-class immigrants from Europe (especially parts of Germany) as well as the native-born (Meyer and Austin 2008, 30, 40). By the 1930s, when this area was dominated by railroads, warehouses, and industry, the residential population decreased and came to consist of an underclass of American-born workers and the unemployed, undoubtedly affected by the Depression.

Urban Renewal

Another familiar, though relatively recent, component of the process of American urbanization is redevelopment, sometimes in association with highway construction (seen in St Louis's Lamar Terrace, for I-70), building housing for the middle class or wealthy, or park creation, and often described as "slum clearance" or "urban renewal." This common phenomenon, promoted particularly in the 1960s but still going on today, involved taking the land from members of the least powerful communities through the right of eminent domain and razing whole neighborhoods. The Reverend Calvin Butts, of the Abyssinian Baptist Church in New York City, has noted that "urban renewal" is synonymous with "Negro removal" (pers. comm. 2010).

Some of the more recent renewal projects have been associated with substantial archaeological endeavors and have been documented by archaeologists in several cities, including West Oakland (Solari 2001), St. Louis (Meyer and Austin 2008), and Bowling Green, Kentucky (Stottman and Stahlgren 2006). In West Oakland, Elaine Solari described a solid community that grew around the terminal for the ferry to San Francisco (2001, 22). Because West Oakland had convenient access to the railroad (which terminated in Oakland) and the port, it had developed as a transport node, and most of its residents worked for the railroad and related industries. By the turn of the twentieth century its population had become primarily African American. During World War II, the defense industry geared up in Oakland and provided a good deal of work, increasing the African American population there substantially. However, as the war ended, these jobs disappeared and the area declined economically. West Oakland was officially declared "blighted" in 1949, and hundreds of adequate, if old, homes were destroyed. "In the name of urban renewal, the government destroyed entire neighborhoods, including their churches and businesses. . . . [T]he irony of urban renewal in West Oakland is that it created the blight it sought to ameliorate" (Solari 2001, 32, 35). This process has been repeated in many cities, and the effects are still being felt today.

Conclusion

The archaeological projects described above indicate the commonalities in urban development as well as the distinctive attributes derived from particular historical and topographical circumstances. Using the framework of the city as artifact and considering the whole urban space, we have examined the frequent use of the grid as a base plan in many parts of the country, but we have also demonstrated the ways in which practicalities dominated abstract theory. Although many city administrators began with a plan, changes emerged because of many factors: issues of class, race, and ethnicity; environmental and topographical elements; political and socioeconomic conflict; transportation changes; population growth; industrial development; and natural disasters, just to mention a few. Urban archaeology has informed us about the materiality of public health, concerns which were paramount throughout the nineteenth and early twentieth centuries. All cities showed some interest in the creation of public spaces, although criteria for whom the "public" includes have altered over time. There are always reflexive relationships between people and the landscape, and changes in each produce alterations in the other.

The changes in infrastructure we have described also resulted in changes in the landscape. The use of landfill and the building of waterfront structures such as wharves and quays regularized the shorelines and turned what had been natural beaches and riverbanks, with ships moored out in deep water, into the valuable real estate that made up some of the best ports in the world. And the replacement of the well/cistern and privy system with municipal water and sewer systems transformed the private space of the backyard from a work area and the site of utilities like privies, wells and cisterns into (in many cases) a decorative space used for leisure activities. All in all, these changes were part of the larger process of commodification that accompanied the development of the modern world system: the commodification of land, water, and even of some bodily waste. Next, we discuss some of the insights that urban archaeologists have provided in regard to that process of commodification and the development of commercial and industrial capitalism of which it was a part.

4

Trade, Manufacture, and Services in the City

THE SUBJECT OF THIS BOOK—the development of America's cities as illuminated through archaeology—parallels the rise of capitalism as a modern worldwide system, and an understanding of capitalism informs our understanding of urbanization in the United States. Historical archaeologists have traditionally looked at aspects of the development of capitalism (e.g., M. Johnson 1996; Leone and Potter 1988, 2005; Matthews 2010). After all, one of the sets of definitions for the field of historical archaeology as a whole focuses on the study of the development of capitalism and the modern world (Orser 2004a). Under capitalism, private owners, whether individuals or corporations, control the state's economy, both its trade and its industry, for private profit. Although all of the sites that historical archaeologists have studied are linked at least indirectly to the development of capitalism, many are related more directly. Here we discuss what historical archaeologists have discovered in looking at American urban sites that are directly related to the economy and the rise of capitalism. Some are related to commerce, others to manufacturing, and still others to the service industry.

Modern capitalism began in Europe in the sixteenth and seventeenth centuries in the form of mercantilism, whereby European merchants, supported by state controls, subsidies, and monopolies, made most of their profits from buying and selling goods and resources. Proponents of mercantilism emphasized the power of the state and overseas conquest—colonialism—as the principal mechanisms of economic policy. If a state could not supply its own raw materials, according to mercantilist theory, it should acquire the colonies from which they could be extracted. This period was associated with geographic exploration and exploitation on the part of the European states, particularly Portugal, Spain, England, France, and the Netherlands, and the European colonization of the Americas as well as of other parts of the world.

Colonies constituted not only sources for raw materials but also markets for finished goods. Because it was not to its advantage for the state to allow competition, it protected its interests by prohibiting its colonies from engaging in manufacturing or trading with foreign states. This was the economic environment under which the European powers began to claim colonies in what became the United States and which guided colonial policy until the end of the American Revolution in the 1780s.

Colonial Cities

Many colonial urban sites are associated with commercial capitalism. One of the oldest is Fort Orange, built by the Dutch in 1624 on the site of today's Albany, New York, on the western bank of the Hudson River. The fort was built there for several reasons: for conducting the trade in furs with nearby Native Americans (particularly the Iroquois), for protecting that trade from other European powers, and as an entrepôt for shipping the furs down the river to New Amsterdam (today's New York), where they were loaded onto oceangoing vessels for the long trip to the Netherlands. Archaeologist Paul Huey discovered traces of the fort and of several of the buildings associated with it during the course of his excavations there in 1970–71, which he planned and implemented in anticipation of the construction of a highway interchange in the area of the site (Huey 1985, 1998). In addition to being important in terms of the significant finds that the archaeologists made, these excavations were among the earliest urban digs in the United States and were therefore also very important in underlining the fact that significant discoveries could be made in downtown America.

A related discovery was the warehouse which Joel Grossman (1985) uncovered in lower Manhattan in what had been Dutch New Amsterdam. Augustine Heermans had this warehouse built right next door to that of the Dutch West India Company in the late 1640s. Heermans, born in Prague, had come to the colony as an agent for a Dutch firm, and traded in furs, tobacco, provisions, and wines. He was also active in the trade in enslaved Africans (Stokes 1915–28, 1:129, 2:266–67; Cantwell and Wall 2001, 114; adapted from Cantwell and Wall 2010).

The excavations uncovered a floor paved with cobbles. On the floor, the archaeologists found a slate pencil and a jeton or casting counter (Figure 4.1), both artifacts associated with making calculations and keeping accounts. The jeton commemorated Prince Maurice of Nassau's election as Stadtholder in

Figure 4.1. Obverse and reverse sides of the jeton or token found on the floor of the Heermans warehouse, New York City. (Courtesy of the New York State Museum, Albany.)

the Netherlands in 1590. For centuries, European merchants had made their calculations in Roman numerals, using jetons or counters like this one and counting cloths or boards, a graphic technique similar to an abacus. But by the beginning of the seventeenth century, much of Europe had changed from Roman to Arabic numerals, which were easier to manipulate for the complicated computations needed in the new mercantile economy, and began using pens or pencils. So many jetons, which were no longer needed for making calculations, began to be used as medallions. But the use of jetons and counting boards was still important well into the eighteenth century, particularly for the illiterate, since it was a visual form of calculation. At Heermans's warehouse, both African and European workers may have made their calculations with counters. The jeton's presence and that of the pencil allow us "to consider this major change in reckoning that facilitated the growth of the modern economy, which was also manifested in the warehouse as well as in New Amsterdam itself" (Cantwell and Wall 2010, 204).

Wampum, beads made out of shell, played a fundamental role in the early colonial economy. The Dutch settled New Netherland, that colony which extended from the Delaware River to the Connecticut River, to control the fur trade. In order to "buy" the furs from the Native Americans who trapped them, they obtained wampum from the coastal Algonquian Indians, who made them from clam and whelk shells, and traded them with the Native Americans in the interior (particularly the Iroquois), who had access to the furs and for whom wampum held important social and spiritual value (Cantwell and Wall 2001, 133). By the end of the seventeenth century, when native populations in the East had been decimated by war, exodus, and disease, Europeans had begun to make the beads themselves (Lesniak 2003, 129). Excavations at the Key Corp site in Albany revealed thousands of fragments of cut clam and whelk shell, partially formed beads, and tools such as awls, drills, and whetstones, all in association with mid-eighteenth-century artifacts (Peña 2003, 122). At that time the Key Corp site was the location of the almshouse for the Dutch Reformed Church, and archaeologist Elizabeth Peña speculates that its residents were making the wampum. Other assemblages of wampum in the process of manufacture discovered at nearby military sites suggest that soldiers also may have been making it to supplement their incomes (2003, 125).

It is worth noting that this period was during the era of British rule and that the British had prohibited the use of wampum as legal tender early in the century. So the question remains as to why these Europeans were making these beads. Peña suggests that they may have been making wampum for an illegal trade with the French to the north, so that the latter could use the beads in negotiating with the Indians for furs (2003, 126).

The Early Service Industry: Tavern Sites

Taverns played many important roles in colonial life. They were often the only large buildings in a community where people could meet for secular purposes. There, people ate, smoked, and drank, learned the day's news, conducted business, and held political and other meetings, and tavern-keeping was one of the few occupations open to women. But one of their more important functions was to provide a place for merchants to meet and conduct their business—before the building of the stock exchange in New York City, for example, merchants met at taverns and coffeehouses to make their deals. Buildings that began life as taverns in colonial communities often went on to play other roles. For example, the Stadt Herbergh, or City Tavern, in Dutch New Amsterdam was transformed into the Stadt Huys, or Statehouse, when New Amsterdam became a municipality in 1653 and needed a place for the local government to meet (Rothschild et al. 1987; Wall and Cantwell 2013).

Archaeologists have worked at many colonial tavern sites. One, the Three Cranes Tavern in Charlestown, Massachusetts, was built in the early 1630s as the town's religious and administrative center and continued to serve as a meetinghouse even after many of the settlers moved across the river to what was to become Boston. In 1635, when the town was planning a new meetinghouse, the building was sold to Robert Long, who lived there with his wife and ten children and ran a tavern called Long's Ordinary. This tavern, whose name was later changed to the Three Cranes, was unusual in that it remained in business for almost a century and a half, until it was burned in the Battle of Bunker Hill in 1775 (Lewis 2001).

When archaeologists discovered traces of the tavern as part of Boston's "Big Dig," they were not only able to track the changes made to the building throughout its history, but they also discovered five privy shafts that were filled with objects dating to five different points in time. The privies' contents provided five snapshots of tavern life during the building's long history. The artifacts from the privy shafts recorded the transformation of colonial New England society from one stressing communal values, as expressed in shared drinking vessels such as posset pots that were passed around the table, and wooden dishes known as trenchers, to the individual drinking glasses, plates, cups, and forks that we know today (adapted from Lewis 2001, 18–20). Discoveries like these provide evidence for the growing importance of individuals and the materialization of "the means by which they distinguish themselves from their family and peers," a process whereby "the self is authenticated by capitalism" (Matthews 2010, 10).

Archaeologists have uncovered the traces of several taverns in colonial Williamsburg, Virginia (e.g., Noel Hume 1969; Brown et al. 1990).[1] When Ivor Noel Hume and his crew were excavating the Wetherburn Tavern in Williamsburg in the 1960s, they made an unusual discovery (Kelly Ladd Kostro pers. comm. 2013). During the course of their efforts to date the tavern's original construction and to record its alterations through time, they encountered over fifty English and French wine bottles along with a few wide-mouthed food storage bottles that had been buried in various places around the tavern property. Many of the bottles showed evidence of having contained cherries; in some cases the cherries were still intact, while in others only the pits remained, and in others still, while there were no physical traces of cherries inside them, it seems likely because they were found in a similar context that they had once contained cherries as well, but the fruit had completely decomposed. The intact cherries showed that their stems had been trimmed but retained, to ensure that the juice remained inside the fruit. The bottles had apparently been filled with the fruit and buried as part of the fruit-bottling process—researchers found an eighteenth-century English source that suggested burying bottles of fruit in the ground so that they would be kept at a constant temperature. But why did no one ever retrieve the bottles? Did the person who buried them die or leave the area? Either way one would think that the loss of over fifty bottles would have been noted in colonial Williamsburg, where bottles had to be imported from abroad.

Several decades ago, the present authors explored possible differences in the functions of taverns in rural and urban settings (Rockman and Rothschild 1984). We wondered if taverns in rural areas might have been used more for accommodating travelers, while those in urban areas might have been used more for socializing, information exchange, and conducting business. To explore this question, we analyzed the functions of taverns by looking at the artifacts that were discovered during the excavation of four roughly contemporary ones, sites that were located along a continuum from urban to rural. These late seventeenth- and early eighteenth-century taverns were the King's House, built in New York City in 1679; a tavern in Jamestown, which was Virginia's capital in the seventeenth century; John Earthy's tavern in the village of Pemaquid, Maine; and a tavern in Wellfleet, Massachusetts, which was a completely rural area. We used two kinds of artifacts, tobacco pipes and ceramic dishes, to look at the taverns' functions. We posited that a high frequency of tobacco pipes would correlate with the functions of socializing and information exchange, while high frequencies of ceramic dishes would underline the importance of

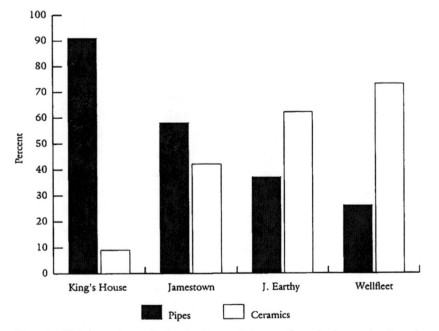

Figure 4.2. The percentages of tobacco pipes and ceramics from the four tavern sites, showing that the more rural sites have a higher percentage of ceramics, and the more urban ones have a higher percentage of tobacco pipe fragments. (Drafted by Arnold Pickman.)

providing food and accommodation for guests. We expected that there would be a regular, inverse relationship between the proportions of pipes and ceramics among the four sites as they moved along the continuum from urban (the King's House) to rural (the Wellfleet Tavern). And that is exactly what we found (Figure 4.2). To people in rural areas, taverns were multipurpose structures, providing room and board for travelers as well as meeting places for those who lived nearby. These activities were expressed in the higher proportion of ceramic dishes at the rural taverns. But for those in urban areas, taverns like the King's House were used primarily as meeting places, a function expressed in the higher proportion of tobacco pipes (as opposed to ceramics) at the urban taverns (Rockman and Rothschild 1984; Cantwell and Wall 2001, 157–58).

Building Ships for Trade

There were some exceptions to the manufacturing restrictions that England imposed on the American colonies, and most of them had to do with the West Indian trade. During the eighteenth century, the Atlantic seaboard cities became important entrepôts in this trade, whereby provisions grown on colonial farms and plantations were sent down to the islands to feed the captives on the sugar plantations there in exchange for sugar products that were sent back for processing into sugar and rum. Colonists built the single-masted sloops and double-masted brigs needed to carry these cargoes back and forth and the smaller boats that brought the produce in from the farms to the cities. They also provided the appurtenances such as barrels and rope to support this trade.

As mentioned in chapter 3, archaeologists have discovered ships incorporated into the landfill in several cities. The *Ronson*, the eighteenth-century merchant vessel discovered at the 175 Water Street site in New York City, was made in the Chesapeake area and showed evidence of teredo worms, tropical shipworms she probably picked up in the Caribbean, showing she was involved in the West Indian trade. The smaller boat found at the World Trade Center site was probably used in the coastal trade, perhaps to transport goods and provisions back and forth from the hinterland to the entrepôt (see Figure 3.6). Scientists at Columbia University conducted a tree-ring study of wood samples from the ship and discovered that the trees had been cut down no later than the 1770s and almost certainly came from the Philadelphia area (Dunlap 2011), suggesting that the boat was built at a Philadelphia shipyard.

Shipbuilding continued to be important in the seaboard cities until the mid-nineteenth century, when the high costs of urban real estate and labor forced them to move to more rural, less expensive areas. But archaeologists have uncovered traces of early shipyards along with the wharves and piers that made up the waterfront that we discussed in chapter 3. Carmen Weber, digging in Philadelphia in the 1980s, discovered an 83-foot stretch of a late eighteenth/ early nineteenth-century slipway on the bank of the Delaware. Slipways, precursers to marine railways, were shipyard structures that served to guide ships as they were lifted out of or slid into the water. This one was made up of two smooth and parallel wooden beams laid to form tracks (or "ways") between two bulkheads; it sloped down to the water at the angle of 1 vertical foot per 15.6 horizontal feet. Grooves in the beams indicated that they probably served as the base for the carriage or cradle that actually held the vessel. The narrowness of the slipway suggested to the excavators that it served small boats that plied the Delaware or sailed along the coast, perhaps picking up produce, rather than oceangoing vessels that transported goods or produce overseas. This slipway is particularly interesting in light of the contemporary technological literature, which called for the use of piles or a series of horizontal timbers like railroad ties in building slipways instead of the sleepers (or supports) that were uncovered in this excavation. The use of the sleepers made the slipway more similar to a contemporary wooden railway; one of these was also built by the man who owned the slipway. Constructed in 1809/10, this was one of the first wooden railways made in this country (Yamin 2008, 126–32).

An unusual aspect of ship construction, or rather deconstruction, was recovered in San Francisco. The *Candace* was a whaler built in Boston in 1818; it was discovered buried beneath the landfill in San Francisco by archaeologist Jim Allan of William Self Associates. Just back from a voyage to the Arctic, the *Candace* was leaking badly as it limped into San Francisco Bay, where it was condemned and never sailed again. The archaeological investigation revealed the *Candace* in a "ship breaking yard," where Chinese laborers (hired because they would work for low wages) dismantled vessels to recycle their component parts. Ship parts were sold to nearby shipbuilders, and the wood was sent to foundries. Although recycling did not have the cachet it has today, it was important in providing raw materials for the industrial growth of the city.[2]

Postrevolutionary Trade

With the end of the Revolutionary War, the American economy was no longer subject to British economic restrictions. Independence "unleashed a whole new set of . . . conditions to which merchants responded creatively by moving into new ventures, with new forms of organization and new credit mechanisms" (Foner 1976, 27). American bottoms began to carry cargos throughout much of the world.

One kind of cargo that is particularly evident in the archaeological record is ceramic dishes. Before the late nineteenth century, Americans used ceramic dishes imported from England for most of their meals. Archaeologists have encountered a number of assemblages of sherds from dishes, particularly earthenwares, that had broken, presumably in shipment, and that had been discarded in backyard features like privy shafts or in the landfill. They can tell that the dishes came from the stock of china dealers because of both the sheer quantity of vessels represented by the sherds in the assemblage and the fact that the dishes show none of the scratches and other marks of wear that indicate use. They can also often use historical records to see if a china dealer was on a particular property during the period when the sherds were discarded.

Archaeologists discovered one such ceramic dump in Albany. Pegeen McLaughlin (2003) analyzed this set of materials, which consisted primarily of hand-painted pearlware tea vessels and plain white plates and platters. She was particularly interested in the marks that the decorators in the Staffordshire potteries left on the vessels' bases. These decorators, mostly women, were paid by the piece, and they marked the vessels to keep track of their own work. The marks also provided insights into the work process. McLaughlin noted that vessels in the same pattern exhibited a variety of decorators' marks, showing that a number of decorators had painted the vessels and that therefore the decorators were simply copying the pattern rather than designing it themselves.

Another interesting ceramic dump was found at Whitehall Slip at the South Ferry site in New York City. Totaling over a hundred vessels made up of almost a thousand sherds, the dishes were made of pearlware with painted, slip-decorated, and other forms of decoration. During the period between about 1775 and 1830, pearlware, along with creamware, was the most common earthenware sold throughout the British commercial world, of which, ironically, the newly postcolonial United States was an important part (Yokota 2011). Ceramic analyst Meta Janowitz has proposed that these vessels may have broken in transit while crossing the Atlantic and were discarded directly from the ship into the slip while the ship was being unloaded. They date to the first decade of the nineteenth century and provide a window into the kinds of ceramic vessels that were being imported (Dallal et al. 2012 6–55–57).

All of the pottery dumps of goods broken in shipment that we are aware of are composed of sherds of refined earthenwares, be they painted pearlwares, monochrome creamwares, or transfer-printed whitewares. These earthenwares are more fragile than other imported wares such as the Chinese export porce-lains and granite wares that were also popular in the first half of the nineteenth century but that, perhaps because they were sturdier, were less likely to break in transit. They were also not imported in such large quantities as the earthenwares.

Merchants continued to constitute America's economic elite through the early nineteenth century. It was they who imported and exported goods. Many of them began to specialize in particular kinds of merchandise (such as groceries or hardware) on a scale unknown to their colonial predecessors. One example is provided by the groceries and other goods discovered on a basement floor located in downtown New York City, as that city's economy underwent its phe-nomenal growth after the completion of the Erie Canal in 1825. In 1835, a con-flagration known as the Great Fire swept through lower Manhattan, destroying almost 700 buildings, including the one at 93 Front Street, which housed the business of Anthony Winans. Winans was a grocer, a designation which at that time and in that place (near the docks, in the commercial heart of the city) meant that he was an importer of nonperishable groceries and other related items, rather than a retailer who sold quarts of milk to local customers (Dallal 2013).

In 1984, archaeologists working under the direction of Roselle Henn and Di-ana Wall discovered several inches of deposits containing the charred remains of goods that had been stored on the basement floor of Winans's business es-tablishment at the time of the fire. The artifacts show the kinds of goods that a merchant like Winans imported and stored in crates, baskets, and barrels there. These products, many of which had been melted by the fire's heat, not only provide physical testimony for one of the greatest fires in New York's history; they also constitute the materiality for the scope of international trade during this period of the city's growth. They include a variety of goods from all over the world and thus underline the international nature of the market. The ar-chaeologists found peppercorns embedded in the cloth bags they were stored in for their long voyage from Sumatra and coffee beans still in the barrels that had been used to ship them from either Turkey or Central or South America. In addition to bottle fragments whose shapes revealed that they had contained English wine and beer, there was an assemblage of wine bottles with sloping shoulders, indicating they had come from France. Some of the latter bore glass seals embossed with the word *Leoville* and a bunch of grapes. This seal indicated that the wine had come from the St. Julien estate of the Marquis de Las Cas in Bordeaux. Although Winans was wiped out by the fire, he was resilient, and a year later he had reestablished his business at another location on the same block (Cantwell and Wall 2001, 163–64; Dallal 2013, 328–29).

Provisioning the City

One of the perpetual problems that cities have had to confront is how to provision their residents. Up into the twentieth century in the eastern United States, most people living in urban areas bought much of their food in public markets, where farmers from nearby rural areas brought in their produce and meats for sale. European Americans living in the West bought staples in general stores that dealt in all kinds of products, only some of which were foodstuffs. Archaeologists have studied markets in several cities in the East as well as a general store in San Francisco.

Nan Rothschild and Martha Zierden and Elizabeth Reitz studied markets in New York (Rothschild 1990, 1992) and Charleston, South Carolina (Zierden and Reitz 2005). Rothschild, using the "city as artifact" approach (employed here in chapter 3), looked at the spatial distribution of markets throughout New York City from the seventeenth through the mid-nineteenth centuries, while Zierden and Reitz developed an in-depth biography of a single eighteenth-century marketplace in Charleston.

Rothschild discovered that it was only during the late seventeenth century that markets specialized in particular items. In 1695, for example, of the four markets that served the small colonial city, two were specialized—one was a meat market, while another sold fish (although they presumably sold other products as well). Later on, as the city grew, they became "general markets" and apparently sold a wide variety of goods (Rothschild 2008, 57).

Before the early nineteenth century, New York's markets were placed at fairly regular intervals along the city's shore, first along the East River and later along the Hudson. These markets were close to the docks where boats were tied up to unload the produce, fish, and meat that would be offered for sale that day. Household members shopped at these markets on a daily basis (refrigeration was not widespread), and before the mid-eighteenth century no one had to walk for more than a quarter of a mile to get provisions (Figure 4.3). But as the city grew in the eighteenth century, and even after the addition of an inland market on Broadway (the only inland market in place before the mid-nineteenth century), some shoppers had to walk as far as three-quarters of a mile for their food. Thus the city's growth was accompanied by inequality in terms of access to necessities such as foodstuffs. It was only in the early nineteenth century that the spatial distribution of markets began to mirror "rational" or central place behavior (Figure 4.4).

Rothschild notes that the "market experience" was vastly different in the

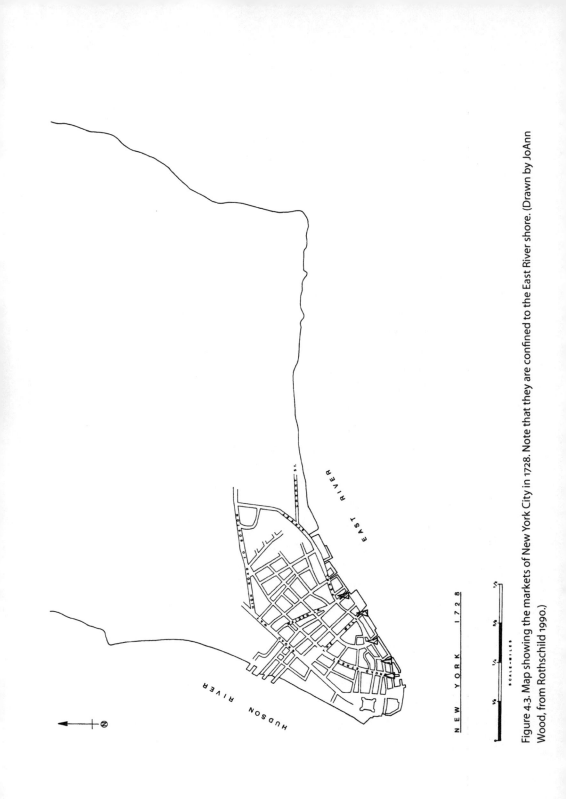

HUDSON RIVER

EAST RIVER

WALL ST.

N E W   Y O R K   1 7 2 8

SCALE—MILES

Figure 4.3. Map showing the markets of New York City in 1728. Note that they are confined to the East River shore. (Drawn by JoAnn Wood, from Rothschild 1990.)

NEW YORK 1808

SCALE—MILES

Figure 4.4. Map showing the markets of New York City in 1808. Note that most of them are aligned with the shores of the Hudson or East Rivers, while one is inland, on Broadway. (Drawn by JoAnn Wood, from Rothschild 1990.)

nineteenth as opposed to the eighteenth century. In 1755, the city had eight markets for 13,000 people (or one market for every 1,625 people), while in 1844 there were only thirteen markets for a whopping 370,000 people (or one market for every 28,500 people). It was during the mid-nineteenth century that the system changed from the old-style public markets where most people shopped to one where the markets were primarily wholesale, supplying neighborhood retail stores, with only the poor continuing to shop at them. The middle and upper classes purchased their food at local retail shops. These changes were related to economies of scale with population growth, the development of capitalist ideologies, and innovations in transportation which allowed for the faster movement of foodstuffs from the producer to the consumer. This market system has persisted into the twenty-first century with the modern addition of "green markets," which are supported for the most part by the middle and upper middle classes (Rothschild 1992).

Zierden and Reitz's study of the Charleston Beef Market (2005) was done in conjunction with the renovation of Charleston's City Hall, which was built in the early nineteenth century on a site which had served as a marketplace throughout the previous century. At first, it was an open air market, with no standing structures. But in 1739, a permanent structure was built; it in turn was succeeded by a new building in 1760. The Beef Market burned down in the 1790s.

Using both archaeological and written records, the archaeologists were able to construct a description of the 1760 market building. They discovered that it was a single-story brick building, around 100–105 feet long by 45–50 feet wide, supported by brick columns, with a tile roof and a portico. It had both a well and a drain, which together were probably used to wash down the market floor at the close of business every day. The archaeologists also uncovered a line of postmolds, revealing the presence of posts that were presumably used to support the hooks the butchers used for hanging meats and other products.

Archaeologists (most notably Zierden) have worked in Charleston and its hinterland for several decades and have developed comparative data sets for both rural sites and residential sites in Charleston. Comparing the faunal materials from the market with those from local homes allowed them to construct a broad picture of Charleston's food procurement system. As its name implies, meat, and particularly beef, was the principle product of the market, although other things were sold there as well. But the importance of beef declined as fish and small animals (including wild game, some of which was slaughtered on site) became more important (Zierden and Reitz 2005, 256). Although there are few traces of poultry in the market assemblage, domestic deposits show that poultry came to be more important through time. Its relatively low representation in the market deposits has two possible explanations—people could have raised poultry at home or they could have bought it live at market, a practice which would have left few archaeological traces there (Zierden and Reitz 2005, 114).

With the exception of the rich, the market brought people of many different backgrounds together. Most of the shoppers at the market were middle-class and poorer women. The rich tended to send their servants and captives to market, and they supplemented their purchases with their own livestock, which they slaughtered at home. Enslaved African Americans played important roles in this system. The men supplied fish for the market, and their wives often ran the stalls (Zierden and Reitz 2005, 252, 256). The gardens that the captives tended on the plantations were important sources of produce for the market, too. Interestingly, few fragments of colonoware pottery (the hand-built vessels believed to have been made by African and Native Americans and commonly found at African American domestic sites in South Carolina) were found at the market, indicating that it was probably not sold there or used as containers for food (Zierden and Reitz 2005, 252, 256).

The archaeological study revealed that people were engaged in many activities at the marketplace besides shopping. The archaeologists point out that aside from the animal bone, the assemblage is similar to those from tavern sites and suggest that, as at taverns, socializing was a very important market activity; artifacts recovered included a myriad of tobacco pipes and drinking vessels along with utilitarian cooking wares (Zierden and Reitz 2005, 253, 243, 255).

Provisioning was different in the frontier cities of the West. There, general stores offered merchandise for sale that for the most part had been brought in by ship or, later, rail. Throughout the nineteenth century, San Francisco was the primary port on the West Coast and the major depot for provisioning the miners in the gold fields. Ships traveling around the Horn brought manufactured goods from the East for the miners and picked up bulk goods, such as hides and tallow that had been brought up from Mexico, to carry to China, in another form of triangular trade. There, they picked up luxury goods (including teas, silks, and porcelains), which they brought back to their home ports. After the gold rush was over, ships picked up agricultural produce and timber in California in exchange for manufactured and luxury goods brought from the East. The primacy of San Francisco as a major city was affirmed by the designation of nearby Oakland as the westernmost terminal of the transcontinental railroad (adapted from Walker 2009, 325–26).

In 1985, archaeologists discovered the burned remains of the Hoff Store, a general store that operated in San Francisco during the gold rush (Pastron and Hattori 1990). This store, located in the heart of today's financial district, was located on Howison's Pier when the Fifth Great Fire struck San Francisco in May 1851. Then, the pier burned and the building collapsed and sank into the mud. The fire's charring combined with the anaerobic environment of the mud provided the perfect conditions for the preservation of organic material. Later, the site was covered with landfill and lay undisturbed until its discovery over 130 years later.

At the time of its destruction, the store was offering a wide array of products, including chandlers' goods supporting the sea trade that provisioned the gold rush town; construction hardware; military arms; consumer goods, such as bottles of preserved foods, alcoholic beverages, medicines, and toiletries (many of the bottles were sealed, with their contents intact); Chinese export porcelain toiletry sets (although this porcelain had gone out of fashion in the East, it was still popular in the West [Terrey and Pastron 1990, 75]); work shoes and boots; and foodstuffs, like commercially packed preserved pork (some still in its barrel), cakes, bread, rice, fruits, dried beans, peas, coffee, tea, tinned oysters and sardines, and even butter. All in all, the Hoff Store assemblage provides "a vivid image of a thriving San Francisco retail establishment on a single day at the height of the Gold Rush" (Pastron 1990, 3).

Manufacturing

Although merchants were quick to seize the new opportunities presented after the Revolutionary War, it took longer for manufacturers to adjust to these new conditions, in part because it was hard to attract investors as there was little confidence that American-made products could compete with British-made ones. So the development of industry in the United States was a slow, uneven process that occurred in different ways depending on the industry, place, and time. By midcentury, some trades were still traditionally organized under the artisan system (like Van Voorhis's silversmith shop, discussed below), while others had undergone industrialization. Here we provide a series of examples that shed light on various aspects of this process, including a traditionally organized shop, a pottery that had trouble competing with imported goods, and the clothing industry, which did not switch to the factory system until relatively late in the century, as well as several manufactures that did.

The Artisan System

Before the demise of the traditional artisan system that resulted from the reorganization of production and the development of industrialization, artisans both manufactured and sold the goods they produced (often along with other goods) from combined homes, manufactures, and shops. There have been several excavations that have uncovered information about these workplaces. One example is the shop of Daniel van Voorhis, a silversmith who was active in New York from the 1780s, just after the American Revolution, until the early 1800s (Wall 1994, 2008, 2013). He described himself as a "Jeweller, Gold and Silversmith" in newspaper advertisements (Gottesman 1954, 75), but there was not enough of a market to support a full-time silversmith in the small postcolonial city, so he supplemented his living. Excavations along with historical documents revealed that Van Voorhis also imported plated goods, hardware, and jewelry from England and bought ready-made jewelry from local merchants. He sold the latter along with sundry items such as fans to casual walk-in customers, including Martha Washington. He also performed mundane tasks such as replacing heavily worn faux gems with new ones. The archaeological assemblage from his shop included badly scratched glass gemstones that he had probably discarded when he replaced them in rings, for example, as well as a green glass rod that might have been used as a source of glass for making new stones (Wall 2013). The examination of census records shows that Van Voorhis was an artisan in the old tradition. In 1790, there were sixteen people in the Van Voorhis household, only eight of whom were members of the immediate family; the rest included five men and a boy, all of whom presumably worked as apprentices and journeymen in the trade (Wall 2008, 63; 2013, 219).

Somewhat surprisingly, Van Voorhis left the silversmithing trade in the early 1800s, when he was in his early fifties. Of course we do not know why he left, but we can speculate. Techniques of mass production and shop reorganization were penetrating the silversmithing trade, and many craftsmen who had been masters became jobbers, supplying finished pieces to retailers. Perhaps Van Voorhis could not raise the capital to become a retailer or perhaps, after his decades as an independent craftsman, he did not want to. But in any case, he became a weighmaster at the customs house in 1803, a position he continued to fill for a decade and a half (Wall 2008, 2013).

Archaeologists have looked at pottery production at the Lewis Pottery site in Louisville, Kentucky, which provides an example of some of the perils of manufacturing in the United States in the early nineteenth century (Westmont 2012).

In addition to making stoneware, these potters attempted to make the refined earthenwares that were so popular in American homes and which throughout much of the nineteenth century continued to be imported from England. The Zane and Lewis families began production when they moved to Louisville in 1815. Lewis had been an entrepreneur with a pottery factory in West Virginia. Shortly after purchasing the property in Louisville in 1817, he hired two potters and began circulating advertisements for Louisville's first stoneware pottery. This pottery was not successful because of the financial Panic of 1819, which caused many industrial projects to fail (Westmont 2012).

Then in the late 1820s Lewis found a clay source in Missouri that was based on kaolin and that burned white, free of oxides, and yet held a glaze—the primary attributes needed for producing refined earthenwares, a process which had proved elusive in the United States. He decided to produce an American version of queensware. English-made queensware (or what we now refer to as whiteware) had become the most popular of the refined earthenwares in the English commercial world, having replaced creamware and pearlware in popularity. However, imports from Staffordshire were costly because of shipping and a 20 percent tax that had been imposed on them in 1816. But Lewis's efforts were impeded by changing trade patterns following the introduction of a series of locks across the falls of the Ohio River. Easier transport for urban potteries led to increased production, and Lewis had difficulty competing with these firms (Westmont 2012, 10). In 1836 he moved to another firm with a Staffordshire potter in Indiana (which failed the subsequent year), and others took over his Kentucky pottery. The record for the latter business becomes unclear after the Panic of 1837 (Westmont 2012).

The excavations at Lewis's original factory in Kentucky revealed a large number of ceramic wasters and kiln furniture, used mostly for making American whiteware, along with some stoneware. They also showed the details of construction for a new type of kiln (called a glost kiln) that was built in 1832 and used specifically for whitewares. The recovery of some coal in the assemblage suggests that potters from England had introduced this fuel type from the Staffordshire potteries; it had not been previously recorded in American pottery production (Westmont 2012, 47).

One of the interesting aspects of this report is its discussion of the difficulties the potters faced, including competition with imports, problems with partners, and technological, transportation, and distribution issues. The study provides an excellent example of the problems encountered and proposed solutions that are probably characteristic of a number of early types of manufacture in the United States.

Apart from whitewares, other kinds of ceramic vessels were made locally from early on. These include the stonewares that potters make almost everywhere. Relatively cheap and bulky, heavy and fragile to transport, these are among the earliest manufactures in what became the United States. Meta Janowitz has analyzed the stoneware sherds, wasters, and kiln furniture from the eighteenth-century Crolius and Remmey potteries that were located next to and were roughly contemporary with the African Burial Ground (see chapter 7) in New York. In fact, the sherds were mixed in with the soil in the grave shafts as well as spread throughout the site. What was interesting about these wares is that although they were thrown in the United States with American clays in the eighteenth and early nineteenth centuries, they were made in the German medieval tradition. And although we tend to think of these vessels as being used almost exclusively for food preparation and storage, a relatively high proportion of the vessels were tablewares made for food consumption: the assemblage includes stoneware plates, porringers, decorated tankards, and even teacups and saucers, marking the transition of tablewares from metal to ceramic in the eighteenth century. This was before the refined earthenwares had been developed and became the ware of choice for setting the table. Furthermore, they also showed that many of the sherds and vessels that archaeologists had assumed had been made in Germany could in fact have been made here in the United States. Some of the design elements showed that potters moved from pottery to pottery, taking their design traditions with them: It had previously been thought that pots with the spiral/watch spring motif, for example, were made exclusively at a New Jersey pottery, but that motif was also discovered on pots found in the Crolius/Remmey dump (Janowitz 2008;

Figure 4.5. A jar fragment with the spiral motif, made by the Crolius/Remmey families, from the African Burial Ground site, New York City, c. 1720–65. (African Burial Ground Collection: photo, John Milner Associates.)

Figure 4.5). Their discovery at the New York pottery shows that they were made at other potteries as well.

Cloth and Clothing

The urban poor and working classes have deep roots in the production of cloth, clothing, and their components in both colonial times and the nineteenth century. One example of the use of the poor as a labor force comes from Philadelphia, where Mara Katkins describes the production of cloth, spinning, weaving, and knitting, and the picking of oakum (or unwinding ropes to use for ship caulking) in the mid-eighteenth century in the first Philadelphia City Almshouse. Few written records remain of these activities, but there is ample evidence in the form of fabric, tools, ribbon, rope, wool, and thread to demonstrate the tasks done there. Fabric remains recovered suggest that they may also have made clothing. Although most fabrics were not of high quality, some were silk (Katkins n.d., 11). Sherene Baugher (2001) has noted a similar use of the poor for manufacturing in New York City in an eighteenth-century almshouse.

Several studies have shed light on the manufacture of clothing in the nineteenth century. Although members of the working class actually made the clothes, the way their work was organized varied enormously within the trade. The associated archaeological material is often recovered from privies, because the conditions for preservation, particularly for textiles, were relatively good in such environments (LaRoche and McGowan 2000).

While clothing for wealthier customers tended to be custom-made by tailors and dressmakers throughout most of the century, clothing for the middle class and poor (including seamen and captives on the plantations in the South) was mass-produced as a sweated trade and tended to be made by de-skilled workers under the out-work system. But as Heather Griggs (2001) has noted for the Five Points site in New York, the nature of this work varied by the gender and ethnicity of the workers involved. Among the Irish, the workers were mostly unmarried women, either young or widowed, many of whom had immigrated on their own. There were fewer Irish men than women in the cities because many of the men found work in the hinterland, digging canals or building railroads, dangerous work that often resulted in injury or death. So these women were on their own to construct a strategy made up of several components to support themselves and, often, their children. For many, their primary work was sewing together the clothing pieces that had been cut by skilled cutters, work which they did either in their own homes as part of the out-work system or in massive inside shops.

Archaeologists working at the Five Points site uncovered evidence of other activities that the women performed to add to their incomes. In one privy associated with a tenement whose residents were primarily Irish they found a large number of rags without cut or selvage edges, suggesting that the women collected rags. Once collected, they probably sold some of them for recycling: cotton rags to make paper and woolen rags for "shoddy," the low-quality material made from chopped up woolen rags. They could also have gathered rags to recycle them themselves, into rag or punched rugs either for their own homes or to sell.

Several Jewish families who lived around the corner were active in a different branch of the garment trade. Many of them had immigrated in young family units, and they worked as families, pooling their labor. Some started businesses in secondhand clothes, which they altered and mended for resale. These more stable families did better financially than their Irish neighbors. But the archaeological record shows that they did not spend their discretionary income on more expensive consumer goods like fancy dishes—their dishes matched those of the poorer Irish who lived nearby. Instead, they spent their disposable income on real estate (Griggs 2001).

Artifacts from several features at the Five Points revealed many types of fabric, mostly woolens, along with some shoddy cloth (made of scraps), as well as sewing artifacts: pins, hooks and eyes, part of a darning egg, a thimble, and embroidery materials (Griggs 2001). Another feature yielded jet glass and copper buttons, thousands of pins, and black damask, perhaps all for making clothes for mourning.

The clothing industry was important in San Francisco, too, where it served as a source of income for women, work that was often not documented because it was performed in the home. Sunshine Psota and Mary Beaudry (2009) have analyzed the clothing and sewing-related artifacts from a set of household privies along with associated documents to study the different contexts in which clothing was made. In San Francisco, as in New York, many ethnic groups were involved in this kind of production: Jews, Irish, and Scots were often employed in the craft there. A hierarchy from tailor to seamstress spanned a number of skill levels. At first work was done by hand, but by the 1850s garment workers were increasingly using sewing machines. These machines were expensive, but the resulting savings in time meant goods were produced at lower cost and profits for capitalists were greater. The ability to produce more goods at a faster rate is correlated with growing markets, one of the tenets central to capitalism.

Archaeological examination of several shops and households uncovered a variety of models, with seamstresses working in their own homes and dressmakers going to their clients' houses. A lot of "refashioning" of clothing was apparent, as was work done to repair and maintain clothes. Some of the clothing remnants exhibited machine-stitched seams alongside buttonholes that were hand-sewn, showing the use of various skills. The features also yielded the appurtenances of sewing: pins, darning eggs, thimbles, a crochet hook, spools for thread, and an occasional container for sewing machine oil (Psota and Beaudry 2009).

The Factory System

Industrial capitalism came into its own with the development of the factory system, which was characterized by complex changes in the social relations of production between management and labor, as work was de-skilled and routinized, resulting in the creation of a permanent working class. These changes had sweeping social and political implications (Nassaney and Abel 1993) and resulted in the reorganization of the social geography of urban life (see Blackmar 1989 for New York City). Rather than living in the master craftsman's home as was common under the artisan system, workers moved into separate quarters, in boardinghouses or tenements in different parts of the city. Rather than working for a number of years as a journeyman or an apprentice with the possibility of becoming a master himself, the status of laborer was permanent. And cash was the nexus of relationships. Additionally, the demands of capitalism meant that there was continual pressure for greater production; work was measured by the clock, and there were specific expectations for output (Leone and Schackel 1987).

Industrial archaeologists have made an enormous contribution to our understanding of the industrial process. They record, study, interpret, and often attempt to preserve the material remnants of industrial features, whether architecture, artifacts, or sites, within their social and historical contexts. The field began to develop after World War II when old systems of industrial production were being replaced. Typical projects focus on bridges, railroads, factories, and canals; there is less concern with domestic life in workers' homes. Here, we discuss projects that have focused on recording both the technology of factories and the ways of life of factory workers.

Between the Revolutionary War and 1830, Baltimore became the major port in the middle Atlantic states for importing raw sugar. Maryland merchants sent provisions down to the West Indies to feed the captives on the plantations there and often received raw sugar in exchange. By 1825, there were eleven refineries in Baltimore. The technique used for refining sugar then was one that was discontinued later in the century. This method required workers to heat the raw sugar in lime water to which they added some raw eggs to absorb the impurities in the mixture. Then they skimmed off the impurities from the top of the mixture. Next, the mixture was poured into conical earthenware molds placed upside down in earthenware crocks that would catch the draining molasses liquid (Williams et al. 2000, 173–74).

Archaeologists from R. Christopher Goodwin & Associates explored traces of one of these Baltimore refineries, which advertised itself as "Shutt and Tool, sugar bakers" and was in existence from around 1804 until 1829 (Williams et al. 2000, 174). They discovered two artifact-rich features associated with the refinery: a square shaft from either a privy or a well and the basement of the refinery itself. The artifacts recovered included many fragments from the conical molds and also some from the earthenware jars. Their discovery revealed the method that had been used to refine the sugar there (Williams et al. 2000, 274–80).

Water power was a crucial energy source for many of the factories that were developed during the nineteenth century, and many cities grew around the waterfalls that could supply that power. Paterson, New Jersey, was one such city. It was founded as the site of what was possibly the earliest American industrial complex, when Alexander Hamilton established the Society for the Establishment of Useful Manufactures there in 1791. He chose that area because of the Great Falls, which fell seventy-seven feet, and then hired Pierre l'Enfant to design a system of three tiers of raceways (open channels for water) for water-powered factories, each capturing a third of that long drop. Hamilton thought industrial production was an important part of the new nation's independence. Over the years Paterson's factories produced many things, including textiles, revolvers, paper, and locomotives. In the 1860s, it became known as the Silk City after what had become its major product.

In the 1970s, industrial archaeologists, under the leadership of Edward Rutsch and supported by determined preservationists at the Great Falls Development Project, conducted a study of the site after the New Jersey Department of Transportation (NJDOT) made plans for Route 20 to intersect with Interstate 80 on the site of the Rogers Locomotive Works. The site was nominated to the National Register of Historic Places in 1970 and began to get national attention; it became a National Historic Landmark in 1976.

The Paterson locomotive works study was one of the earliest projects in industrial archaeology ever done in the United States (Rutsch 1975). It was conducted in 1973–75 under less-than-ideal circumstances because the study was not incorporated into the planning process. Instead, NJDOT hired an archaeologist to monitor the construction work and to call a halt when anything interesting was found, thus inevitably delaying construction. The archaeologists discovered (and the *Historic American Engineering Record* recorded) many structural features associated with the works: machine shops, a blacksmith shop, forge foundations, various kinds of equipment, a boat for the Morris Canal, along with workers' housing (a neighborhood called "Dublin" [De Cunzo 1983; Yamin 1999]) where the mostly Irish factory workers lived. The tools most commonly recovered were hand files, which, Rutsch tellingly notes, were supplied by the employers (1975, 7), suggesting that workers may have "lost" them as acts of defiance. Tools owned by employees were recovered less frequently.

The textile mills of New England also provided foci for urban development in the nineteenth century. The Boott Mills of Lowell, Massachusetts, hired young women to run the machines that processed the cotton grown on the plantations of the South into finished cloth. In an effort not to replicate the working-class conditions that horrified observers in industrial England, mill owner Francis Cabot Lowell was determined not to use child labor when he established the mills in 1812. Instead, he thought that because intelligence was necessary for the work but strength was not, women would be the ideal labor force. More than a generation of young women left their family farms to work in the mills for twelve hours a day, six days a week. The company established boardinghouses for the women that had strict rules governing their moral behavior. The young women organized themselves into the Factory Girls Association, an early labor union formed to protest salary and housing cost issues. They were ultimately unsuccessful. Finally, their effectiveness was further reduced at midcentury, when immigrant families, willing to work for less money, moved into the Lowell labor force.

Archaeological excavations at the Boott Mills boardinghouses conducted by Stephen Mrozowski and Mary Beaudry revealed how much alteration the landscape needed to support the factories. The mill was water-powered and located at the confluence of the Merrimack and Concord Rivers. The land was floodplain and had to be extensively filled, so archaeologists encountered artifact-rich landfill instead of sterile glacial soils under the Boott deposits. Many other landscape alterations were made as well, including canals to bring in water for power (Mrozowski et al. 1996).

Archaeologists Michael Nassaney and Marjorie Abel discuss the relationship between the organization of labor and technology, using the Russell Cutlery factory in Greenfield, Massachusetts, located in the Connecticut River valley, as a case study. They note that the changes in labor practices accompanying the Industrial Revolution were not accepted readily (1993, 249) and that the control of workers, "de-skilling," and technological changes did not fit smoothly together. From management's perspective, industrialization was meant to improve production efficiency, and factories arranged floor space to that end. However, workers' interests were not taken into account, and they could and did resist "efficiency" by various means, including slowdowns that reduced the profits anticipated from changes in the organization of production, such as the introduction of piecework (Nassaney and Abel 1993, 252).

The Russell Cutlery, founded in the 1830s, was known for its excellent chisels and knives. Traditionally, making these knives was a labor-intensive process, but in the 1850s management introduced a mechanized process using dies and heavy presses, which increased the factory's output twentyfold and decreased the need for some of the skilled labor. In 1870, Russell relocated his factory to Turner's Falls to take advantage of the water power there. It became the largest factory in the area, attracting immigrants from many European countries into the area. Management organized its space scientifically and divided the work process into a series of standardized tasks. The factory was successful for a while, but then profits declined, other producers began to compete, and there were labor difficulties, including worker dissatisfaction with safety precautions and wages. The plant closed early in the twentieth century (Nassaney and Abel 1993).

The archaeological part of the project included an examination of the river bank. There, the archaeologists found, along with structural remains from the factory, more than two hundred objects, many of them cutlery rejects or wasters. The authors wondered why these imperfect objects had been discarded along the river. Former employees said in interviews that they might throw imperfect objects out the window and into the river in order to avoid having to correct their mistakes. The authors intriguingly suggest the possibility that these manufacturing mistakes represent proletarian acts of defiance against management and that because many of the workers were related to each other, they would not have reported this act (Nassaney and Abel 1993).

Minneapolis is one city that has engaged in the celebratory study of its nineteenth-century heyday as an industrial site: it was the largest direct-drive water-powered facility in the world. Its power was based on the St Anthony

Falls, the highest falls on the Mississippi, at the confluence of the Mississippi and Minnesota Rivers. As a major center for milling the wheat of the Great Plains, it became one of the largest producers of flour in the world. Its flour was shipped internationally and led to the formation of corporations such as Pillsbury and General Mills, household names even today. The same power sources were used to mill lumber, make beer, and create electric power. Twenty industrial sites there have been examined over the past dozen years.

Services: The Commodification of Domestic Life in the Nineteenth Century

The service sector of the economy deals with the selling of intangible services rather than the tangible products provided by manufacturing. As in many other countries, this sector of the American economy has become more and more important with time, particularly with the decline in American manufacturing in recent decades. But the service industry has a deep history in the United States, just as it does elsewhere, and it has provided archaeologists with a multitude of sites in both urban and rural contexts. Here we discuss some of the entities that provided the domestic services that became common in urban areas in the nineteenth century, including boardinghouses and commercial laundries.

Boarding and Lodging

As we mentioned above, under the old artisan system, workplaces and manufactories in urban areas were geographically integrated by class, with masters, journeymen, apprentices, and the enslaved all tending to live under one roof. That settlement pattern changed in most cities in the nineteenth century, with the separation of homes and workplaces as masters and their male employees moved away from their workplaces, creating residential neighborhoods that were relatively segregated by class. Many people, particularly those who were "unattached," or living away from their nuclear families, lived in boardinghouses and hotels, which provided the appurtenances of domestic life without the labor and expense needed to establish and maintain a household, and some of the activities that had traditionally been performed in private homes began to be commodified.

Marta Gutman (2004) has done a study of living arrangements and their material correlates in West Oakland, California, during the last decades of the nineteenth century. She discovered that the residential building stock of the area consisted of private homes, hotels, saloons, boardinghouses, and lodging houses. She also learned that throughout the country at around this time there was a transition in the kind of services provided in private homes, as accommodation switched from "boarding," whereby patrons received their meals along with a place to sleep, to "lodging" or "rooming," whereby they received no meals but just a room to sleep in. In West Oakland, most of the clientele for these establishments were white (although some were also African American; see chapter 5) men who worked for the railroad, although "unattached" white women lived in them, too. These accommodations provided services for the clientele and income for the women who ran them. Many of these women (who were often single or widowed) were members of the working class, but it was also one of the few ways that respectable middle-class women could make money at that time. Gutman discovered that boarders and the other members of the households that they lived with apparently ate together, consuming the same foods from the same dishes, and the butchering patterns on the faunal remains from these sites revealed that households with boarders ate roasts for family-style meals, rather than individual portions of steaks and chops. This suggests that boarders were partially incorporated into a community along with those they lived with (Gutman 2004, 264).

West Oaklanders also found accommodation in commercial establishments, such as hotels and saloons. Corner saloons often offered rooms for rent above them. Hotels were structured by class. The Railroad Exchange Hotel, geared toward a respectable working-class clientele, was run as a boardinghouse. Family-style meals, which included both steaks and roasts, were served on plain white "hotelware." But the later (and more expensive) Pullman Hotel served meals not only on hotelware but also on plates decorated with gilt and/or painted or transfer-printed designs. Glassware, too, was decorated, and meat was served in individual portions. At the turn of the twentieth century, this hotel had made the switch from boarding to rooming—meals were no longer included as part of hotel accommodation—and the hotel's restaurant was renovated so that it was accessible from the street, and not from the hotel itself, so that the general public could frequent it more easily. As Gutman points out, these studies are important in that they remind us of a way of life that is gone—in the United States today, travelers stay in hotels, but very few people actually live in them. And needless to say, this way of life encouraged the associated development of the laundries, restaurants, etc., of the service sector. All in all, they were "harbingers of great changes to come as middle-class women entered the labor force in greater and greater numbers and thus depended on commercial services to meet family needs" (Gutman 2004, 276).

The classic archaeological study of the Boott Mills boardinghouses in Lowell gives us an idea of what boarders got for their money in workers' housing in one of the New England mill towns. There, the farm girls who came to work in the mills in the early nineteenth century were replaced by immigrant workers who often lived in family groups. All of these workers lived in boardinghouses that were run by the company.

On average, the workers received from $1.50 to $2.00 a week on top of the $1.25 to $1.50 that was withheld from their salaries for room and board (Mrozowski et al. 1996, 4). This sum gave them a room that they shared with five other people and a bed that they might share as well. Three meals a day were included. They sat at long tables where they were served on large platters and ate their meals from plates. The dishes were usually undecorated china. The food itself included meat, particularly beef, and not only the less expensive cuts, as might be expected, but more expensive cuts as well (Mrozowski et al. 1996, 61, 63). In fact, the meat eaten in the boardinghouses was on a par with that eaten by the Company's agent and his family, who lived nearby, although the dishes and other appurtenances used for serving the food in the agent's house were fancier.

Although the excavations revealed the constant presence of rats in the backyard of the boardinghouse (as most of the animal bones found there showed rat bite marks, unlike those found in the agent's yard), management maintained the boardinghouses much better during the girls' tenure than they did while the immigrants lived there. This could be seen particularly in the ambience of the backyard. During the early period, while the mill girls were there, pollen and archaeological studies show that the backyard was relatively clean and covered in grass, whereas it was trash-strewn and covered with weeds after the immigrants arrived (Mrozowski et al. 1996, 48). And the artifacts also showed the failure of management to comply with city sanitary rules requiring the closing of privies and replacing them with water closets and piped water. Although this law went into effect in 1890, as late as 1910 the boardinghouse privies were still in use. Needless to say, disease was a constant threat for all workers. Although archaeological remains are very revealing, there is also a wonderfully evocative set of documents, including letters and diaries, which provide rich detail on the workers' lives.

The Praetzellises' research on the Golden Eagle Tavern in Sacramento (Praetzellis et al. 1980) provides insight into the transformation of a frontier community from a supply center servicing nearby mines to a Victorian city. Looking at the contents of several features, including a cellar hole from an oyster saloon and a privy from the Golden Eagle Hotel, the archaeologists examined a number of factors. One concerned patterns of meat consumption, with food sources changing from native species to domestic ones, with, for example, domestic chickens and turkeys replacing game birds. They also recorded changes in architecture. The hotel began as a wooden-framed structure covered with canvas, but it was rebuilt several times, first as a wood frame building, then as a brick structure to which an Italianate façade was later added—that is, it had become a hotel in the style of its eastern counterparts. Furthermore, dining patterns changed in the hotel, which switched from serving meals at long communal tables to using smaller tables for smaller groups, supporting the trend from communalism to individualism seen so often in the late eighteenth and nineteenth centuries. This study is particularly important because it is one of the earliest CRM studies of an urban area in the United States—it took place in 1979–80.

Chinese Laundries

The discovery of gold in California in 1848 inspired a gold rush there that lasted until the mid-1850s. More than 300,000 people from all over the world, including immigrants from China, responded to the promise of wealth. When they first began to arrive, the Chinese were tolerated at the mines, but after gold became scarce they were forced to leave. Subsequently, many of them worked on building the railroads; then they flocked to western cities and towns (see chapter 5), where they tended to live in Chinatowns. With hard economic times, European Americans blamed the Chinese for lowering wages and contributing to the bad state of the economy, and the Chinese began to be subjected to official discrimination that included legislation on the local, state, and federal levels as well as unofficial repression manifested in day-to-day harassment and physical assaults. Between 1850 and 1908 in the United States, over 10,000 acts of violence were committed against the Chinese and almost 150 people were killed (M. Praetzellis 2004b, 245). The capstone of the legislation was the federal Chinese Exclusion Act of 1882, which placed severe restrictions on the immigration of Chinese laborers. This is the only American immigration act aimed at one particular immigrant group and was the first to be based on race; it was not repealed until 1943.

Although gold-rush society was by no means made up exclusively of men, a large majority of the population (both European and Chinese) was male. In western cities and towns, the Chinese, who were kept out of many industries, filled a niche that European (and Chinese) women filled elsewhere—providing domestic services, including cooking in restaurants and laundering clothes. By 1870, there were more than 2,000 Chinese laundries in San Francisco alone, and in 1920, 30 percent of the Chinese in the West worked in laundries (M. Praetzellis 2004b, 244, 245). Although in the nineteenth century Chinese laundrymen tended to live in Chinatowns (M. Praetzellis 2004b, 251), their laundries were dispersed throughout the city, in the neighborhoods where their predominantly European American customers resided. This isolated workplace pattern left them and their laundries vulnerable to the vandalism and harassment of anti-Chinese demonstrators.

The laundry trade was attractive to Chinese immigrants for many reasons. First of all, because it was a line of work that was looked down on by most European men, there was little competition. But equally important was the fact that in being a laundryman, a Chinese man could either own his own business or work for a Chinese boss alongside Chinese co-workers—he did not have to work for or with European Americans and endure their harassment. Furthermore, one did not need much training or a large capital investment to open a laundry. All one needed (in the early period) was an abacus, a sink, a boiler for heating water, irons and a stove for heating them, and drying racks (M. Praetzellis 2004b, 245).

Archaeologists have excavated many sites associated with the Chinese (often referred to as the Overseas Chinese) in the western United States (see M. Praetzellis 2004b, 239–40 for references to studies of Chinese sites in the United States prior to that year of publication). The excavations and the scrutiny to which the sites and their occupants have been subjected have helped to overcome many of the modern-day stereotypes about these immigrants. First of all, the laundry workers had been looked on as sojourners who were isolated from American culture and who planned to return to China once they had made their fortunes. The material traces of this experience show that this was in fact not true, in that they used American products as well as Chinese ones. In examining the artifacts from a laundry in Stockton, California, for example, every artifact category showed a mixture of Asian and non-Asian materials, indicating that the Chinese were not as isolated as believed. For example, the artifacts suggest that the laundry workers at the site used both American and Chinese medicines (Orser 2007, 170). Another stereotype is that the Chinese immigrants were primarily illiterate peasants. However, data from both the census records and the artifacts recovered from the laundries confirm that this was not the case. Artifacts retrieved from Chinese laundry sites include ink stones, pencils,

pens, ink bottles, and even newspapers in both Chinese and English (M. Praetzellis 2004b, 252). So archaeology has revealed a great deal about the lives of
Chinese laundry workers.

Conclusion

It seems that urban archaeologists have devoted less time and energy to the
excavation of sites associated with production, commerce, and the provision of
services than they have to domestic sites. However, these studies of manufacture, trade, and the service industries are particularly useful in demonstrating
the materiality associated with economic and historical change. Although most
of American history, whether colonial or postrevolutionary, was characterized
by a form of capitalism, the impact of industrial capitalism is particularly pro-
nounced in social behavior and on the landscape.

Obviously, capitalism is not going to work without the presence of consumers to buy the goods and services that are being produced. Next we discuss
those consumers and their consumption patterns—a topic that has received a
great deal of attention from archaeologists. First we look at the patterns related
to different ethnic and racial groups, and then we explore patterns related to
class and gender.

5

Race and Ethnicity in the City

AMERICAN CITIES WERE UNIQUE from their inception in their complex, global mixtures of residents: Native Americans—the original inhabitants of the continent—along with Europeans and enslaved Africans from many different cultural backgrounds were found in most seventeenth- and eighteenth-century cities. East Asians began to arrive in the 1840s, first in coastal areas (especially on the West Coast and in New York City), and then gradually in the middle of the country as well. In the mid-nineteenth century the numbers of European immigrants increased dramatically, and most spent at least some time in the eastern seaboard cities.

Historical archaeology, perhaps more than any other discipline, offers a glimpse of the ways people clustered together by race and ethnicity. Sometimes and for some groups this clustering was by choice, while at other times and for other groups, it was not. This chapter investigates the insights that historical archaeologists have gained by examining the association of different forms of material culture (be they landscapes on the macro level or artifacts on the micro level) with the members of different racial and ethnic groups. It also shows the ways that the social geography of cities has changed over time as these factors intersected with class. This chapter investigates the insights that historical archaeology has revealed through landscape and its rearrangement (on the macro level) and the association of artifacts (on the micro level) with members of different racial and ethnic groups.

We begin with a brief discussion of material culture on both the macro and micro levels of landscapes and artifacts, respectively, and how archaeologists have approached its analysis in regard to the social categories of race and ethnicity. We then move on to definitions of both race and ethnicity. Finally, we survey the studies that historical archaeologists have made of the members of different ethnic and racial groups in American cities.

Material Culture and Group Identity

Archaeologists have observed how material culture is mobilized, often in complex and inconsistent ways, to make statements about the affiliation of individuals and groups with the categories to which they have been assigned and/or with which they identify. Initially, objects were seen as simply communicating these affiliations (Meskell 2005, 2). But since the 1980s, works by Ian Hodder (1982), Lynn Meskell (2004), Julian Thomas (2007), and Tim Ingold (2012) in particular have all considered the ways in which people, ideas, and things are interconnected and the agency associated with each component of this triad. The adoption of Bourdieu's concept of *habitus* (1977) has shown that "the physicality of the artifact is enmeshed in the work of praxis: cultural construction is achieved through action rather than simply conceptualization" (Meskell 2005, 2).

North American historical archaeologists have adopted some of the ideas put forth by Daniel Miller (1987), Paul Mullins (2011), and others, to consider the different kinds of statements expressed about affiliation and identity in looking on particular kinds of objects (or artifacts) as consumer goods with specific symbolic referents. Although it is clear that consumption has an economic component, not all of consumption is rational, and many people use material goods to shape their definitions of themselves, others, and the social order (Mullins 1999, 3). Archaeologists' interpretations of the meanings of these material associations vary. Some see adoption of the dominant group's material culture as the emulation of that group; others see forms of resistance in similar data; and still others see creative uses of materiality adopted from others' subcultures. What is clear is that an archaeological perspective on consumption practice and the social geography of the city is essential in order to understand such phenomena.

But although material culture plays a crucial role here, we must emphasize that it is hard to find easily identifiable or consistent practices. "Consumers use material culture to imagine new social possibilities. . . . Objects embody relationships between producers and consumers, future and past, and Black and White, but they are not mirrors for 'real' identities. . . . [I]t is infeasible . . . to reduce objects simply to reflective or mimetic mechanisms or . . . to accord them absolute power to forge identity" (Mullins 1999, 29). Furthermore, the analysis of race and ethnicity intersects in complex ways with aspects of class and gender, intersections which we discuss in chapter 6.

Definitions: Race

In the United States, many people think that human races are real, in the sense that they are scientifically legitimate, natural or biological divisions within the human species. However, scientific research shows that that concept of "race" cannot be applied meaningfully to humans. The analysis of DNA and other data has revealed that more physical variation exists within every so-called racial group than between them and that there are no biologically valid differences among them. Throughout history, whenever groups have come into contact with one another, they have interbred, promoting all humans as one species with a shared gene pool.

But the fact that "race" has no biological meaning does not mean that the concept has no meaning at all. Instead, it is a powerful cultural concept which is socially constructed. Culturally constructed races are not scientific units but folk taxonomies defined in particular historical settings by and about people subject to various economic and social forces, and these categories are then naturalized (Williams 1990).

We cannot be certain when people first began to classify others into races by their physical and other attributes, but by the time of recorded history (and well before the concerns of this book), it was a well-established practice throughout the world. We also do not know when slavery—the ownership of one human being by another and the passing down of that status of "property" from generation to generation—began, although it too was an ancient practice. But we do know that these two concepts coalesced in North America in the late seventeenth and eighteenth centuries, when enslavement became racialized and inextricably linked with peoples of sub-Saharan African descent (see, e.g., Epperson 1990). The system of enslaved labor both relied on and was validated by these racial constructs, generating power and wealth for slave owners. Whereas slavery was legally ended at different times in the eighteenth and nineteenth centuries in various parts of the United States, the oppression and discrimination associated with its practice still persist today. Ideas about race continue to intersect with economic and political concerns, defining attitudes projected onto members of racial groupings so that they have unequal access to significant resources. Dominant groups maintain the trope of race in order to protect their own economic and political interests (Orser 2004b, 2007). Several scholars note the intersection of economic status with the spatial separation of class and "racial" attributes; they suggest that for African Americans, race and poverty are inextricably linked and mutually reinforcing (Davis 2002; Soja 2000; Orser 2004b, 31; see also Dawdy 2006).

Racism involves the practice of using some arbitrarily chosen genetic and physically observable differences between people to assign individuals to categories (races) whose members are believed to differ in meaningful ways from other such groups (Appiah 1990, 4). Once defined, these groups are assigned relative worth based subjectively on what are thought to be moral and intellectual differences as well as physical ones. Attitudes toward race and racism are contested and politicized (Mullins 1999, xi–xii). Those in dominant cultural positions (usually in the fabricated racial category of whites) defend their status by marginalizing nonwhites in order to protect their own power and affluence (Ignatiev 1995). Racism exists throughout the world, and in the United States, as well as in other societies, legal regulations and/or cultural attitudes have been used to structure and justify socioeconomic inequality and cultural, social, and class difference by claiming race as the primary source of all variability.

Our modern ideas about race developed in the eighteenth century, before biological evolution and natural selection were understood. Then science, perceived as reflecting rationality and objectivity, was used to provide a legitimate and convenient basis for justifying the establishment of a hierarchy based on biological characteristics. The body offered a "natural" trope for the discussion of difference (Goldberg 1990, 305); in fact, it was "the ultimate trope of difference," even though these discrepancies are imagined and constructed along social and political lines in conjunction with the political economy (Gilroy 1990, 264).

Definitions: Ethnicity

"Ethnicity is like family or marriage: everybody knows what it means but nobody can define it" (Smith, cited in Alonso 1994, 379). Ethnicity, nationality, and race are often used in similar ways, although it is important to disarticulate them. Ethnicity involves a "subjective belief in . . . common descent because of [subjectively perceived] similarities of physical types or customs or both, or because of memories of colonization and migration" (Weber, cited in Alonso 1994, 391). Often shared geographic origins (real or imagined) are at the base of ethnic categories. As with racial categories, these groups are first seen as different from one another and then assigned attributes of difference (Jones 1997, xiii). However, as Dawdy notes, the most acceptable definition for *elective* (as opposed to ascribed) ethnic identity relies on self-identification (Dawdy 2006, 155; Jones 1997, 84), making it different from race (although "whiteness" and other racial affiliations may at times be elective). Ethnicity is especially relevant in state societies where it is an important dimension of identity and is employed in negotiating status, often through the use of specific markers that reference language, dress, foodways, and other customs (Alonso 1994, 391). One contrast between ethnicity and race is that the latter mostly uses physical differences as markers, whereas for ethnicity, the identifiers tend to be cultural and therefore are more subtle; a crucial difference is that some forms of ethnicity are easily adopted. In seventeenth- and eighteenth-century New York City, for example, various "Dutch" or "English" residents consciously manipulated their ethnic identity. As the English became politically dominant in New Amsterdam after their conquest in 1664, some emigrants originally from the Dutch provinces altered their names and switched their language and religion to become members of the group that was then in power. One man originally of English background changed his name from Bridges to Van Brugge when the colony was Dutch and back to Bridges with the English conquest (Rothschild 1990, 87). The situational flexibility of ethnic identity should not be surprising as individuals may hold more than one such identity, and these are always being renegotiated in new contexts. Unfortunately, what may be more surprising is archaeologists' desire to fix such identities and link them to a series of material traits, making the assumption that the larger cultural systems of which the identities are part are static (Upton 1996, cited in Shackel 2010, 58).

Although race and ethnicity differ in significant ways from one another, they have points of intersection and overlap. Each may involve the ascription of group membership to an individual, and both serve political agendas, although the agendas may belong to the individual members of either the ethnic or racial group or of the dominant culture. They may also be mutable. In American culture, some groups such as the Jews and the Irish were historically seen as races, that is, as nonwhites. Although they used different means to alter this status, by the mid-twentieth century both groups came to be ethnically, rather than racially, defined. Noel Ignatiev (1995) portrays the change among the Irish in the late nineteenth century as they became politically active members of the working class and supported the concept of white supremacy, thereby gaining the jobs from which African Americans had been excluded. Karen Sacks (1994) suggests that the changed attribution for Jews was linked closely to their movement toward the middle class, which was enabled in large part by access to college-level education.

The Archaeological Study of Ethnicity in American Cities

One of the aspects of ethnic identity especially relevant to archaeologists is the use of material objects as cultural symbols of ethnicity. Material culture has multiple functions, but it is produced by social practice and is constitutive of it (Hodder, cited in Jones 1997, 117). The underlying assumption for the use of such markers ("ethnic signifiers") is that they were designed to communicate identity. There is a considerable literature investigating the communicative abilities of objects through aspects of style (see, e.g., Binford 1962; Conkey and Hastorf 1990; Hodder 1982; Sackett 1977, 1985; Wiessner 1983, 1984, 1985; Wobst 1977). This investigation has shown that classes of artifacts cannot consistently be associated with particular social groups or with specific meanings. Do similarities reflect contact? Borrowing? The dominance of one group over another? A wish to emulate another group? There have been some successes in linking a specific kind of artifact, often with symbolic value (such as an emblem on a smoking pipe [Reckner and Brighton 1999]) to a particular group, but the majority of ethnic "signifiers" are found in multiple contexts and are difficult to interpret. A perception of ethnicity as rooted in *habitus* (Bourdieu 1977) seems more useful than focusing on uses of material culture that involved conscious choice, as some aspects of ethnicity, based in practice (eating habits, for example), may be unconscious and used without reflection (Praetzellis and Praetzellis 2004, 317). In any case, as we suggest below, the intersections between material culture and both race and ethnicity are complex. We report on a number of studies that consider the expression of identity in objects, and whether they reflect a wish to assimilate with a dominant group or express a form of agency by the consumers, they also inevitably note the intersection of class and racial or ethnic identity.

The social landscape is particularly relevant in examining questions in the racially and ethnically mixed communities found in almost all American cities. Places are not neutral and passive, but people use them in active and dynamic ways to help shape their perception of where they are in the world socially as well as spatially (Basso 1996); space, like race and ethnicity, is socially constructed (Soja 1996). New settlers in a city often live near others to whom they have connections (such as kin ties or shared place of origin, religion, language, or "race") for mutual aid and comfort and to mitigate discrimination. Life in seventeenth- and eighteenth-century New York was defined according to certain parameters of ethnicity and class. Social and ethnic factors influenced settlers' choices of places to live. New Amsterdam/New York was different from many early cities in the ethnic diversity of its early settlers. Data from

1703 showed that the Dutch and English (the predominant ethnic groups in the city at that time) lived somewhat separately from one another, with Huguenots choosing to live near the British. By the end of the century these clusters had broken down, and the descendants of the early occupants were aggregated more according to class than ethnicity. However, ethnicity was still a dominant factor in choosing a place to live for later immigrant groups (such as the Scots and Germans), and racial assignments were important in somewhat isolating the members of two groups from the dominant European settlers: free Africans and Jews (Rothschild 1990).

New York City continues today to attract diverse immigrants and to demonstrate this kind of social geography: new immigrants settle where there are others like them, and then if they are able and willing to assimilate, they move to other locations consonant with their class position. As social lives reorganize with new immigrants, spatial life is restructured to reify change. Although landscape perspectives are important, material culture studies also allow for examination of the complexities of ethnic and racial identity. Boundary marking, associated with racial and ethnic categories, whether internal or external, makes the invalid assumption that groups thus defined represent "populations with distinct, homogeneous and bounded cultures" (Alonso 1994, 392). However, in reality, ethnicity and race are dynamic and situational; they can be seen as instrumental or strategically manipulated for political or economic ends (Jones 1997, 75), and the studies cited below have found clear evidence of this.

For the remainder of this chapter we discuss a number of groups that archaeologists have examined in American cities. We have grouped the reports by the broad racial or ethnic cultural categories to which the subjects of the reports are assigned or with which they identify. Many different insights into the material expression of the construction of race and/or ethnicity are found within each section.

Archaeological Explorations of the Intersection of Race and Ethnicity

Studies of Spanish and French settlements in the New World demonstrate one of the ways in which race and ethnicity intersect. Because the simple act of baptism and conversion to Catholicism made indigenous and other women eligible as sexual partners, it produced genetic mixing regarded as social destabilization by Europeans. Spanish and French colonizers had rather different reactions to this situation, with Spanish efforts oriented toward maintaining boundaries while those of the French were more relaxed about breaching them. Spanish settlements in Florida, New Mexico, Arizona, and California were structured by Spanish views of race and caste (Deagan 1983; Rothschild 2003). The Spanish believed in "racial purity" and classified people by the amount of Indian, African, and European blood each had. The *casta* system employed racial categories as cognitive labels referring to groups with contrasting positions in the sociopolitical system and the economic organization of production (Seed, cited in Jackson 1999, 10). It was a racist system organized initially on what were thought to be hereditary differences and then adding class and manners to phenotypic markers such as skin color (Linn pers. comm.; Rothschild 2008). Although the population was genetically quite mixed by the end of the eighteenth century (Bustamante 1991, 162), social differences validated by perceived physical differences continued to define behavior or position.

The French, also Catholic, had a rather different attitude toward "racial" mixture than the Spanish, as archaeologists have shown in New Orleans. One hint of this derives from an analysis of the human remains of twenty-nine individuals found during a construction project at the first cemetery in New Orleans, the St. Peter Street Cemetery (Dawdy and Matthews 2010), described in chapter 7, below. Although New Orleans was colonized by the Spanish and Americans after the French, it seems that a unique combination of ethnicities existed along with an attitude that allowed local people to accept continuing changes from the outside without having to prioritize one group over another. "The other side of the story is not how an Indian town became an Afro-French one or how a French town became an American one. Rather it is how everyone in New Orleans eventually becomes Creole" (Dawdy and Matthews 2010, 282).

Creolization, as a form of mixing or blending, discussed by Dawdy in linguistic, biological, and cultural terms (2000), became a consumable and defining product for the culture of New Orleans and provided a basis for the construction of its history (Dawdy and Matthews 2010, 289). Creolization is especially visible in a diet that employed Native American, European, and African ingredients and recombined them for a Creole cooking tradition which was then adopted by Anglo-Americans. Since the colonizers were mostly white men, and cooking was done by women (often of mixed backgrounds or enslaved Afro-Louisianians), this aspect of culture was ignored by the Europeans and did not change when Americans took over as rulers; it was constructed as women's (or Africans') work. An interesting parallel to this situation is described by Deagan in St. Augustine (1983). There, too, white males had food cooked by (in this case) indigenous women, as few European women came to this colony in its early years. The artifacts from colonial households reflected the dual use of local indigenous items from the (female-dominated) kitchen and high-status majolicas from the (male-dominated) dining room. Although the Spanish were concerned about the maintenance of racial or casta boundaries, it seems that the mixing of foodways, as a part of everyday practice, was ignored.

An insight into the relationship between Europeans and Native Americans (especially the Natchez) in New Orleans derives from analyzing the presence of Native American pottery, which was not recovered in early deposits. The 1729 Natchez Rebellion (aided by captive Africans), which destroyed a European settlement near Natchez, was a reaction to Indian perceptions that, although allies, they had been cut out of the economic trade loop. The French subsequently changed their strategy (Dawdy and Matthews 2010, 283), and Native American vessels appear in later strata, suggesting that they had been reincorporated into trade.

African Americans

For several decades the archaeological examination of sites associated with African Americans has been a growth industry within the discipline. It has produced a great deal of information on the lives (and deaths) of enslaved and free blacks in urban America. Perhaps most significantly, it has counteracted many stereotypic views of the ways of life of African Americans. Most archaeologists doing this kind of research in North America analyze material culture found in what are thought to be domestic deposits because most of the sites excavated from African American contexts (in fact, from a majority of all sites) are domestic ones. Researchers interpret documentary evidence along with material data to consider recorded information on occupation, amount of education, whether people owned or rented their homes, taxes paid, and similar descriptors. These data may also be useful in examining the degree of segregation or separation that characterizes settlements within a community, a form of landscape analysis.

There is rather little archaeological (or documentary) evidence of African Americans in urban areas prior to the nineteenth century. Important exceptions include the African Burial Ground in New York City and several sites in Annapolis, Maryland (Leone 2005; see below). One of the most significant eighteenth-century African sites is not a domestic one; it is the African Burial Ground, excavated in 1991–92, in which more than 400 sets of human remains were excavated. This site provided an enormous amount of information on disease, work stress, causes of death, and a demographic population profile; we discuss this further in chapter 7. The consistency of burial practices revealed there shows the strength of community religious practices.

During the colonial period, free blacks were few in number and not always recorded in government tabulations, whereas enslaved people who lived in cities often lived in the homes of those who enslaved them and thus had little separate material culture, unless it was hidden in the form of spirit bundles or caches, made up of seemingly ordinary objects such as quartz stones, buttons, pins, doll parts, beads, and such, described in Annapolis (Leone 2005, 203ff).[1] The analysis of caches found in the portions of houses used by Africans—kitchens, laundries, and their living spaces—along with the examination of markings etched into rocks, onto ceramic and other objects, or onto a floor (Leone 2005,

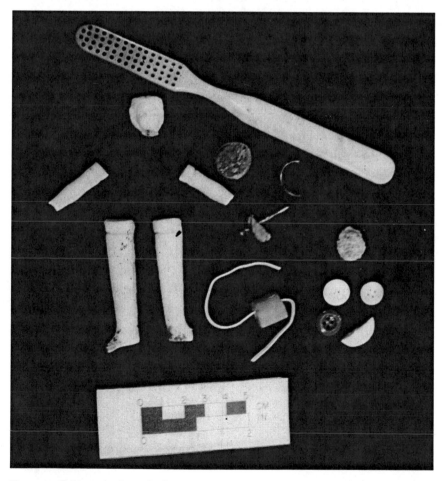

Figure 5.1. Spirit cache from the hearth, Slayton House kitchen. (Courtesy of Archaeology in Annapolis.)

218) is part of an emerging study of creolization within the development of African American culture (Figure 5.1).

Archaeologists have successfully examined the experiences of African Americans in a number of nineteenth-century American cities, including Boston, Mobile, Sacramento and West Oakland, California, and Annapolis. It is interesting to note that communities identified as "black" by outsiders were in fact usually racially mixed (Shackel 2010, 16; Killion et al. 2001). Perhaps this form of description is analogous to the "one drop of black blood" marking an individual as a member of the "black race": the presence of a few black residents marks a community as "black," no matter the number of their "white" neighbors. In many instances the people being examined in these projects were members of the black middle class; they are usually represented in the documentary record because they were often property owners. In general, historical archaeologists have good access to those who owned property or rented it for several years, because they tend to be recorded in census data as well as tax records. However, archaeologists can also provide insights into more transient communities that documents cannot provide if archaeological deposits were left by members of the same ethnic or racial group and class.

Archaeologists have used material aspects to compare black and white lifestyles, focusing primarily on household objects and elements related to foodways. Ceramics and food remains are the materials most frequently recovered from sites and thus are often discussed in the literature. Several studies below compare African American and European American uses of ceramics, especially teawares, and other domestic objects. The authors vary in their interpretations of similarities and differences in the archaeological record, depending on their political and theoretical orientations. However, it seems likely that consumption practices for everyone (not just African Americans) may have been influenced by different circumstances: a midwife living at the edge of a town might purchase a figurine for a different reason than a barber living in the middle of town, thus supporting Mullins's argument (1999, xi) about the lack of common black practice.[2] It is significant that only archaeology has been able to provide these insights and helped to "denaturalize" the concept of race.[3]

African American Consumption Practices

Archaeologists have noted that the intersection of race and class created differences *within* African American consumption patterns as well as *between* black and white cultural practice. It is almost impossible to separate the influences of these two vectors in many of the studies that we cite. Paul Mullins (1999) has written convincingly that there was no "monolithic black experience" and that African Americans as consumers established their own ideas of what was important to have in their homes. African American purchasing practices were meant to define a comfortable existence and to circumvent racism. Thus shopping was a political act as well as an economic one. Mullins suggests that, in Annapolis, black female domestics acquired ideas from their employers' households about what the dominant culture determined homes could or should contain. They wanted full purchasing privileges but did not simply imitate white patterns, making their own selections according to their own values, even though some whites saw the buying habits of blacks as imitative. Mullins also believes that through consumption practice African Americans thought that they could combine the two strands of their identity: blackness and American-ness.

Mullins, Mark Warner, Laurie Wilkie, and Adrian and Mary Praetzellis consider the similarities and differences between the contents of African American and European American homes. In Annapolis, Warner (1998, 202) notes that within the black community stratification was expressed by wealth, rates of residential stability, and leadership positions. First the Maynard family and, subsequently, the Burgesses lived in one house in Annapolis from 1847 until the twentieth century (Leone 2005, 197). Their elite rank among African Americans in the nineteenth century is reflected in the fact that they served tea in wares designated for that purpose, unlike an African American working-class family living nearby in Gott Court (Warner 1998, 205). They differed, however, from a middle-class white family in the study by not using matched tea sets. Mullins believes that the use of diverse ceramics is not because such families were poor but because they kept their ceramics for a long time or may have purchased their ceramics in small amounts (1999, 148). Thus drinking tea in unmatched teawares could perhaps both demonstrate class status within the black community and differentiate black community members from white Annapolitans, having both pragmatic and symbolic aspects.

Diana Wall, observing the lack of matched dishes in both tea and table wares in nineteenth-century African American homes, has suggested another explanation. She posits that it is possible that the group used a different "language of dishes," whereby the desired end was not to have matched sets and thus mark the corporate unit of the household, but instead that each individual household member had his or her own individual dishes, perhaps to underscore the value of each individual. If the goal is for each individual to have his or her own plate, the dishes cannot match, or household members would not be able to tell which plate belonged to whom (1999, 114). This was in fact the custom in late twentieth-century Belize. Alice Baldwin-Jones notes: "In the face of slavery where people of various cultures were brought together as property and [were] treated as less than human, [one might be forced] to create a sense of individuality that would lead to using unmatched dishes and other personal items to create . . . autonomy" (1995, 3–4).

In Mobile, Lucrecia Perryman, an African American midwife, was an important member of her community. Her material culture reflects the purchasing practices of the dominant white culture to some degree (Wilkie 2003, 96). Ceramics were diverse, including porcelains, whitewares, yellow and redwares, as well as coarse earthenwares and stonewares. She used plain wares for setting the table, which Wilkie suggests may have created the appearance of a matched set, whereas her teawares were more colorful (cf. Mullins and Warner above). Some special-purpose forms were found in her assemblages, including two teapots depicting Rebecca at the well, thought to reflect a nineteenth-century view of American women as spiritual and physical protectors of the household, and a powerful symbol for American women regardless of race. The location of the Perryman's home, on the outskirts but incorporated within Mobile, positioned the family in a somewhat ambiguous situation, for us and perhaps for them also, in defining them as urban or rural, but it may have allowed them to distance themselves from racial politics. Wilkie and Shorter comment that the absence of artifacts that reflect skin bleaching or hair straightening can be seen as evidence of racial pride (2001, 38) or at least acceptance of their status.

As a midwife, Perryman served as a generational mediator (Wilkie 2003, 120), combining culturally conservative and innovative practices (using new tools as well as traditional herbal and magical remedies), merging African traditions with New World customs. Another significant aspect of her life associated with middle-class status in the post-Emancipation period was her ability to remain at home with her children rather than having to go out to work (Wilkie and Shorter 2001:23; Mullins 1999:190), although some African American women had to work at home because white women frequently refused to work alongside blacks.

On the West Coast, Adrian and Mary Praetzellis undertook a comparative analysis of the material culture associated with African Americans and Irish Americans in late nineteenth-century Sacramento. The Cook family escaped slavery by following the Underground Railroad to Canada and then settled in California in 1870 (Praetzellis and Praetzellis 1992). Race and racism's influence permeated all aspects of life in Sacramento in the late nineteenth and early twentieth centuries and was as significant in dominating life as was the poor local economy characterized by high unemployment. Racism kept black residents from owning land or voting and from holding positions of authority in most industries. They could not compete on equal terms with whites.

These factors led to the development of specific occupational niches for African Americans. Thomas Cook was an independent businessman, a barber—an elite occupation for a black man at that time. His family's household assemblages date to 1901–1908, when he had a shop in the center of town in which his son also worked (Praetzellis and Praetzellis 1992, 111). Another son was in school at fifteen, when most youths were working.[4] The Cooks' house was full of the kind of mass-marketed consumer goods that were found in many white homes.

The Collinses lived a few blocks away. A white family consisting of a widow and two children, they left archaeological materials dating to 1902–1905. Similar material culture is found in the Cook and Collins homes: popular mass-produced colorful ceramics (those in the Cooks' deposit were more expensive as their set was gilded). As was true at the African Meeting House (below), beef was the favored meat for both families, although the Collins family ate a slightly higher percentage of expensive cuts than the Cooks (23 percent vs. 16 percent); however, the expensive cuts each chose differed, with the Collins family preferring loin steaks and the Cooks enjoying ribs (Praetzellis and Praetzellis 1992).

In a different project, this one in West Oakland, the Praetzellises examined the contents of a number of privies from the households of black porters dating to the late nineteenth century (also see chapter 6). They revealed the use of gracious ceramics and ornaments in the home. The use of "genteel" material culture from the wider society in the 1880s gave owners a sense of dignity, but they used their own aesthetics in selecting what they bought, based on community values. The contents of these privies suggest that dining was formal; tea and alcohol were served, and homes had fresh flowers, bric-a-brac, dolls, and memorabilia. The evidence of formal serving practices suggests that they may have replicated the "Victorian formality and opulence found in the Pullman cars" where the men of these households worked (Praetzellis and Praetzellis, 2004, 281).

African Americans and the Urban Landscape

One element common to the African American experience is the frequency with which they were geographically dislocated by members of the dominant culture. In a macro-scale examination of this same black community in West Oakland, the Praetzellises applied an archaeological perspective and a landscape orientation to documentary records within a broad temporal frame, outlining a hundred-year period in that city. Initially a middle-class black community flourished there, but it was destroyed by the post-WWII decline in skilled industrial jobs and a rise in unemployment, and it became a victim of the unsuccessful 1960s federal policy of urban redevelopment (M. Praetzellis and A. Praetzellis 2004).

Originally West Oakland was a small community formed around a school and a church, but then the western terminus of the Central Pacific Railroad located there in 1869. The Pullman Palace Car Company's policy of hiring only black porters attracted a great many to the city. Although these were service positions, they were ranked high in status in the African American community. The expanding community included barbers, porters, hairdressers, and musicians, who formed a network of institutions, including churches, unions, and a branch of the Universal Negro Improvement Association (associated with Marcus Garvey), which promoted black business ownership. Middle-class "race women" (who worked for the betterment of the African American image) had separate institutions from those of white women or black men. Education was valued, and by all accounts religious faith was an important aspect of the residents' lives, as were personal achievement, which provided uplift, and "race work." In contrast to policy in Oakland itself, blacks in West Oakland were allowed to buy homes in the early 1900s.

This period of economic and cultural optimism continued into the early twentieth century, with more jobs opening during World War I because of a labor shortage and again during World War II in the shipyards, and the African American population increased from 8,400 to more than 50,000 between 1940 and 1950, leading to a shortage of housing. However, after the Depression and the war, the situation changed abruptly, as blacks were the first to be laid off after the war. The loss of employment and the huge population increase resulted in the formation of "slums," which were then thought appropriate for urban "renewal" by local government.

A different form of the dislocation of African Americans is found in Reno, a suburb of Washington, D.C. (now Fort Reno Park). It was originally settled during or just after the Civil War by residents who were able to buy lots inexpensively; thus many were homeowners. For quite a while it was a comfortable, racially mixed community, housing both skilled and unskilled workers (Killion et al. 2001, 29). African Americans built Baptist and Methodist Episcopal churches there between 1872 and 1888. However, as affluent whites increasingly settled the area around Reno, the black neighborhood came to be characterized as a blighted slum. Using the rationale that the viewscape of the affluent should be protected, the city redefined the Reno area as public land and made it into a park. The Fort Reno area probably contains a buried archaeological site that would tell us about this mixed working-class community from the time it was created until it was razed for building the park. Examples such as these bring home the frequency of a pattern in which a stable African American community, with its own institutions, is subject to more powerful people who want their land and evict them using a variety of rationales. Archaeologists have documented this pattern time and again in their studies of changing land use and have brought it into modern consciousness.

The Church

Institutions such as churches and schools were extremely important in African American communities. The church was particularly important in that it fostered morality and cohesiveness and served as a locus for organizing mutual aid. Black churches have centered African American communities throughout the United States from the late eighteenth century through the present and have served as gathering places for abolitionists and civil rights workers as well as venues for education, black pride, and resistance to oppression. Most communities with significant clusters of free African American residents had at least one church. Black communities in the nineteenth century showed their self-sufficiency in creating independent and somewhat separate institutions.

The African Meeting House (AMH) project in Boston involved the study of the "oldest black church edifice still standing in the United States" (Landon n.d., 1; Figure 5.2). Built on Beacon Hill in 1806, it was managed by free people and was a significant symbol of emancipation as well as a sign of the economic power of the community (Landon and Dujnic 2007, 178). (Slavery was officially brought to an end in Massachusetts in 1783, considerably earlier than in other northern states such as New York.)[5]

Archaeology was conducted at the AMH in the 1970s and in 2005 (Bower 1986; Landon and Dujnic 2007). The more recent excavations revealed deposits from two different, though contemporaneous, contexts, in what appears to have been a middle-class community. One set came from a basement apartment within the church (with artifacts dating from 1806 to 1840), and

Figure 5.2. The African Meeting House, Boston (S. N. Dickinson, *The Boston Almanac for the Year 1843*. Thomas Groom, Boston.)

the other, dating from 1811 to 1838, from a privy in an adjacent building where African Americans were tenants. In both settings, the documents and recovered artifacts hint of a middle-class life for black men, suggesting skilled occupations—waiters, tailors, and hairdressers—in this portion of Boston's black community. Women's occupations and class status were less clearly evident. The church basement apartment had vast quantities of high-quality ceramics from a caterer (Landon and Dujnic 2007, 175), Domingo Williams. There is no evidence of matched sets, a situation we have noted above and elsewhere for African American homes, but the patterns used would have complemented each other in color and design; these may have been used for community dinners (Landon n.d., 8). Faunal remains at the AMH came from several legs of lamb (an expensive cut) and may have been associated with either community or catered dinners. The preponderance of plates as opposed to bowls among the dishes reinforces the suggestion that some meat was served in the form of roasts and chops, rather than the stews that have been typically associated with less affluent African Americans (Landon and Dujnic 2007). The archaeologists also recovered literacy-related artifacts (pencils and a slate), which reinforce the belief held strongly by middle-class black Americans that education was an important road to equality even if schools were segregated (Wall et al. 2008).

The analysis of the 2005 excavations at the AMH included a study of health through evidence of parasites, medicine containers, and plant and insect remains. Roundworm parasites were notably present; insect remains suggest that some of the grain consumed was of poor quality (Landon and Dujnic 2007, 176–77); and botanical remains and medicine containers suggest that members of the community were using western medicines as well as traditional plant-based remedies. Project analysts suggest that residents were obtaining medicines from pharmacies but avoiding patent medicines.

Food remains at the AMH are consistent with other urban African American assemblages in that domestic mammals were dominant (not surprising in an urban environment), especially beef, followed by mutton, pork, and fowl. Fish and wild mammals were absent, and meat was purchased already butchered. Remains from a wide variety of fruits were recovered, as well as squash. Little evidence of liquor or tobacco consumption at the AMH reinforces the suggestion that temperance was highly valued in this community (Landon and Dujnic 2007, 170).

This site represents several significant elements. Although the deposits were not from the church itself, the foodways, artifacts, and medical practices they reflect suggest a well-established middle-class community whose members were active in pursuing the way of life they desired (Landon n.d., 12). The analysis of the material is quite informative about the way some middle-class black Bostonians lived in the antebellum period.

Middle-class African American communities reveal a number of similarities, whether they were located in California, Massachusetts, or Maryland. Ceramic wares were similar in style and decoration to those used by whites for the period, and although they were apparently not used in matched sets, they often appeared to be similar to or harmonious with each other. Teawares were distinctive and colorful, and many household assemblages contained symbols of gentility such as household ornaments and vases for flowers. Among the middle class there was a preference for beef. Of course, even when there were similarities to objects found in white homes, we cannot assume that the meanings of these objects were the same.

The Chinese in the United States

A large number of Chinese emigrated to many parts of the world including the United States in the nineteenth century; initially they went to the West Coast and later to the East Coast. Conditions in China (famine, government corruption, concern with European colonialism) and the lack of barriers to immigration were factors, and the gold rush in the United States was a powerful attraction (Orser 2007). By the 1860s there were substantial Chinese communities in North America, the Caribbean, and around the Pacific Rim in Peru, Australia, New Zealand, and Southeast Asia (Voss 2005, 424). European Americans believed that these immigrants were soujourners who only planned to make money, send it home, and return to China themselves when they had achieved success (M. Praetzellis 2004b, 237). Typical occupations for the Chinese were railroad work, mining, laundering, and gardening. Historical archaeologists for the most part are concerned with how these immigrants articulated with the rest of their urban community by looking at how Asian material culture was used, reused, and adapted in the United States. We can gain insights into these questions by examining the lives of particular individuals through documents and artifacts.

The kinds of questions archaeologists explore in looking at Chinese American sites are somewhat different from those considered in the examination of African American ones. When examining Chinese sites, there is an emphasis on "different-ness" and self-segregation, while the focus at African American sites is on the integration with white material culture. It is not totally clear whether this distinction derives from the assumptions of the analysts or the nature of those being analyzed, though it is probably the former. Be that as it may, historical archaeologists have contributed to an increasing appreciation of the variability and complexity of Chinese culture as seen in the United States and have attempted to do away with essentialist notions of who the overseas Chinese were. However, the study of Chinese communities has, in the views of Barbara Voss, been marginalized (2005, 425), and it is fair to say that until recently the perception of these communities has been that they were withdrawn and resistant to adoption of American ways. This may be true in part because the Chinese tended, for reasons of language and culture as well as safety and comfort, to live among or be associated with their own people. African Americans have done that, too, to some degree, but the distinctions between Chinese and non-Chinese have been emphasized by archaeologists.

In any case, archaeology has contributed in a significant way to understanding the complexity of practices within these communities, the uses of Chinese as opposed to American objects in both Chinese and American homes, and the permeability of the boundaries surrounding clusters of Chinese urban residents. There has also been archaeological examination of Chinese immigrants in other parts of the world. In Australia, Jane Lydon (cited in Voss 2005) points out that as in the United States, the Chinese community at The Rocks in Sydney was stereotyped by European Australians as exotic and frightening, poor and immoral, but in fact little united the Chinese community beyond western perceptions and a common origin; the community was subdivided by class and included a range of occupations. In other countries the overseas Chinese represent a national identity and have been racialized, although clearly both the "nation" and the "race" are cultural constructs (Voss and Allen 2008, 5).

During the nineteenth century, Americans and Europeans adopted a stereotypical view of all peoples who lived east of Europe, or "orientals." All were categorized together, glossing hundreds of different peoples, thousands of years of distinctive histories, and vast regions. Edward Said's work (1978) has perceptively recognized that these attitudes were (and are) formed by an imperialist colonial philosophy, demeaning all people, material culture, and worldviews in a hegemonic attempt at control. Thus it would not be a surprise if in many western countries "Chinese" identity was a product of western imagination.

Voss has suggested that historical archaeologists have emphasized the boundaries around Chinese communities because they relied on an acculturation model, with its image of the United States as a "melting pot," which was popular in sociology and sociocultural anthropology in the 1960s.[6] At that time many social scientists looked on acculturation or assimilation as a desired goal and concluded that if the Chinese did not become more Americanized, it was because they preferred not to, which was interpreted as an act of resistance (Voss 2005, 427). Of course there was an alternative explanation, supported today, of Chinese agency, following some of the ideas suggested above for African Americans. The first studies in the early and mid-twentieth century used artifact ratios to measure assimilation, a very simplistic method based on an even more simplistic assumption: the higher the percentage of European American artifacts in an assemblage, the greater the degree of assimilation. Subsequent studies during the 1960s and 1970s continued to focus on the assumed Chinese wish to maintain ethnic separation, regardless of the proportions of European American artifacts found in their assemblages. Voss suggests that the separation of Chinese from other populations in their towns or cities has been overstated, and that there were often clear social, cultural, and geographic boundaries around clusters of Chinese residents, but those performing some forms of services (e.g., laundrymen and restaurant workers) were likely to be geographically dispersed throughout a community and not restricted to Chinatown (Voss 2005). One recent study of a Chinese cemetery in Portland, Oregon, suggests that nineteenth-century Chinese Americans in that city were able to incorporate both their Chinese-ness and their American-ness in a hybrid identity (discussed in chapter 7, below; Smits 2008).

Chinatowns developed in many towns in the West and the East, providing a relatively permanent population of cheap labor, important in construction, agriculture, and local "cottage industries" (M. Praetzellis 2004b, 238). A small number of Chinese merchants controlled the communities and profited from them and encouraged the promotion of Chinatowns as exotic tourist attractions from the early twentieth century onward. Archaeological examination of these urban settlements has mostly occurred in California and in the Southwest, including El Paso (Staski 1993) and Tucson (see below), but the archaeology of the Chinese in rural settings is extensive. The Chinese were the targets of waves of prejudice and legal and illegal attempts at exclusion by the dominant society, and they frequently had to relocate (M. Praetzellis 2004b, 241), as did African Americans. An anti-immigration law was passed in California in 1879, and the Chinese Exclusion Act was signed by the federal government in 1882, which prevented any more Chinese immigration and denied them citizenship. This was the only American immigration act to target a specific racial or ethnic group (see chapter 4). Many Chinese at that point left the United States. The Act was predicated on a European American concern that the Chinese were taking jobs, as well as on the erroneous belief that the Chinese had brought bubonic plague to San Francisco (Kraut 1994 in Linn 2008) and was part of a set of practices defining immigrants as diseased in both moral and physical ways (Stallybrass and White 2007).

The typical Chinese community has been described as rather self-sufficient. The majority consisted of rural folk, laborers working in the mines and on the railroad, as long as that work lasted; urban Chinese were service providers, with a few elite merchants and entrepreneurs (M. Praetzellis 2004b, 238). Archaeologists have focused on a few aspects of Chinese life, rather stereotypical ones, such as their association with laundries, gambling, and opium. They have also been particularly interested in the mixture of Chinese and European American objects (ceramics, medicine containers) and food remains in domestic deposits. Voss's examination of a Chinatown on Market Street in San Jose, California (destroyed by arson in 1887) shows that its residents did not experience their lives through the expected oppositions of East and West or tradition and modernity as they used artifacts crossing these binary categories.

People in these communities seemed to have had close relationships with non-Chinese for business purposes as well as continued involvement with mainland Chinese culture, all expressed in an integrated Chinese, American, and European creolized material culture (Voss 2005, 431). Market Street in San Jose was an ethnic enclave with physical boundaries that served as a refuge and cultural home to a considerable Chinese population, although only about a quarter to a third of the Chinese in San Jose lived in that community. Many others lived near their employers, sometimes in the country, although Chinatown was their cultural and economic center as well as a sanctuary. Chinese children went to integrated schools, so the community was both segregated from and connected to whites.

Voss shows that the material life of the Chinese of San Jose in the late nineteenth century was mixed, especially in foodways, medicines, and drug use, demonstrating again the importance of observing practice rather than rhetoric. Both American patent and Chinese medicines from a local (non-Chinese) pharmacy were used. Residents drank tonic water and American liquor along with rice wine, and they used opium; the Chinese living in Tucson also consumed wine and liquor and used opium. And almost three-quarters of the ceramics recovered were Chinese, while the rest were British American (Voss 2005, 431).

Mary Praetzellis offers another perspective on the connections between Chinese and non-Chinese neighbors in West Oakland in the household deposits of an Irish American family who lived only a few blocks from an established laundry operating from 1880 to 1912 (2004b, 256). The McLaughlin-O'Brien family was the landlord for the nearby laundry, and their own assemblages contained an unusually large quantity of Asian ceramics, showing that the family had an interest in Chinese things. It is interesting to speculate on how these might have been acquired: By purchase? As gifts? Containing food? Or in exchange? In any case, the absence of isolation of the Chinese tenants is clear in the artifacts recovered here.

As discussed in chapter 4, laundries became a common niche for Chinese immigrants in West Oakland and elsewhere in the 1870s and are still today in many cities. Although it was women's work in China, it was often a male enterprise for the Chinese in the New World. Laundrymen (frequently from educated families with other occupations in China) formed a guild to divide work, set prices, and fight harassing ordinances and acts of anti-Chinese terrorism.

The laundries themselves were staffed by family or village members, and there is evidence from archaeological domestic deposits associated with laundries (jewelry, clothing fasteners) suggesting that women were present (M. Praetzellis 2004b, 250), although we cannot be certain that they were Asian.

The Praetzellises describe archaeological traces from several laundries, including clothing, a large number of fasteners, blueing, pins, irons, and starch. Because laundries were often robbed, the owners buried some of their coins under the dirt floor, and many have been recovered during excavation. Ceramics and food remains show a mixture of Chinese and western influences. Beef, sheep, and pork were represented more or less equally, and there were small amounts of chicken as well. They ate local fruits, imported olives, and many kinds of sauces and other condiments. Workers at several laundry sites drank bitters, beer, wine, and Chinese liquor and used opium.

One of the stereotypes about Chinese communities refers to gambling as one of the "immoral" practices found there. Julia Costello, who excavated a privy associated with a gambling hall frequented by Chinese gamblers in San Bernardino, California, from 1910 to 1941, suggests that gambling was a traditional activity that has been sensationalized by outsiders. Seventy percent of the artifacts found in the privy were related to gambling (Costello at al. 2008, 139). They include many types of gaming pieces made of glass, domino-like tiles, bone dice, and coins (mostly nineteenth-century Vietnamese coins, brought because Chinese coins were scarce between 1890 and 1895). Gaming represents one of the few forms of entertainment available to the Chinese, and the gambling hall also served as a social club for traditional activities among the predominantly male residents. An interesting phenomenon seen in documentary evidence is that prosecution by the police varied according to the "moral climate" of the time, and that when the gambling "den" attracted more white clients, the number of raids increased.

Homer Thiel and colleagues investigated a rather different Chinese settlement in Tucson, which existed from around 1880 until the early twentieth century (1997, 141). Tucson did not have a well-developed Chinatown, but there were several aggregations of Chinese settlers, with residents scattered throughout the city, often mixed into Mexican American neighborhoods. Chinese settlers lived in small adobe structures, typically in groups of men. Whereas some men sent for wives from China when the laws permitted, many married Mexican women. Some settlers may have moved into Tucson after working on the railroad; they were described in one newspaper account thus: "Tucson is coming to be known as a Mecca for San Francisco Chinese refugees" (cited in

Figure 5.3. Chinese ceramics excavated from the site of a c. 1910 Chinese laundry in Stockton. (Courtesy of Anthropological Studies Center, Sonoma State University.)

Thiel 1997, 8). The completion of the railroad made it possible for them to get Asian goods imported through San Francisco, presumably making their lives more comfortable and familiar (Figure 5.3).

In Tucson, the Chinese undertook predictable endeavors for their ethnic niche, starting laundries and restaurants, but were successful there at growing fruits and vegetables as well. They rented land, watered weekly or sometimes daily, and were quite productive: "The Chinaman makes it a matter of business and he produces all he possibly can, and as often as he possibly can. [In contrast t]he Mexican garden produces a few chili peppers, onions, garbanzos, beans, watermelons, etc." (Drake 1885, cited in Thiel 1997, 19). After 1900, a conflict over the use of water restricted the number of Chinese gardeners, and they turned to other activities, such as raising carp and poultry, although it is clear that these limitations on their opportunities derived from their economic success as "foreigners."

Tucson's Chinese were also a target of discrimination, presumably because of this success. The community was centered on a Tong meeting house, which combined religious and secular activities, fulfilling a function similar to Masonic halls in European American communities. The ceramics from one gardener's household show a mix of Mexican earthenwares (used for food preparation and storage by both Mexicans and Chinese), European American and English wares, and special items imported from China, such as rice bowls, wide-mouth jars (for condiments), and cups for liquor and tea. Fewer plates and more bowls were recovered than would be found in European American homes. It seems that they used European American wares as replacements for Chinese ones, perhaps if the latter became unavailable. They also ate many liquid-based meals, such as soups or stews, using large Mexican and Papago bowls. Their medical practices as well combined traditional Chinese with American medicine, and there is evidence that they drank beer and liquor (including wine and champagne), similar to the Chinese in Oakland (Thiel 1997, 97).

In Tucson, the Chinese diet was more diverse than Mexican or American ones, and healthier. Their diet was based on balancing foods that were perceived as "hot" or "cold," and a starch portion with meat and vegetables. The archaeologists note the incorporation of dried fruits, fish, seaweed, spices, and eggs in a diverse cuisine with the use of Chinese ingredients to maintain a "Chinese taste" in foods. Animal bone recovered indicates that beef was the prevalent meat, at 50%, along with fish, turtle, chicken, duck, pork, rabbit, sheep, and deer. In this area pork and chicken were more expensive than beef and the hog industry was slow to develop as pigs were hard to ship and did not thrive in the hot climate, whereas cattle could be driven to wherever they were to be slaughtered.

The archaeology of Chinese communities in the United States focuses more on artifacts than landscape, except for some accounts of the influence of geomancy, or feng shui, used to organize structures and communities, as described by the Praetzellises and Marley Brown in Sacramento (1987) and by Ritchie in Chinese communities in New Zealand (1993). The analysis of artifacts offers a multifaceted view of the materiality of those in the households and settlements described. It is unfortunate that there is relatively little examination of Chinese sites in the eastern United States. The Chinese have been a presence, at least in New York City, since the mid-nineteenth century, and their numbers have increased dramatically in the late twentieth century, since the Exclusion Acts were repealed and immigration was opened up. In New York City there are now significant Chinese communities in Queens as well as Manhattan, and the Chinese make up the second largest immigrant group in the city.[7]

A Mexican Household

Mexicans and Mexican Americans have formed an important presence in the American West and Southwest for centuries and are becoming more numerous in northern cities today as well. The examination of a Mexican American family from Tucson during the mid-nineteenth century offers an interesting contrast to the contemporary Chinese settlement there. Thiel and his colleagues from Desert Research excavated this site, which belonged to the León family (2005). Arizona was sold by Mexico to the United States in 1856; it remained an American territory until it achieved statehood in 1912. Initially there was interaction between the relatively small number of Anglos (mostly men) who settled in Tucson and the Mexican population, including intermarriage and the growth of a mestizo community. The arrival of the railroad in 1880 changed that, as it brought Anglo women and ultimately produced increasing discrimination, a common phenomenon in colonial situations (Stoler 1997). The mestizo population continued to be significant in Tucson, even after Anglos arrived; some of them became more American, and some became more Mexican.

The León family was a mestizo family who settled in Tucson in the 1840s. Theirs is the first household from the Mexican period to be excavated in that city (Thiel 2005, 197). They built two houses successively, one occupied from before 1862 to the 1870s, and the other from 1874 to 1910. The Leóns became prominent, and several members of the family were appointed to public positions in the nineteenth century. Once the railroad was finished, linking east and west, much more American material culture appeared in Tucson.

Prior to that time, traders brought goods in by wagon from the United States and Mexico. The specific impact of this difference is seen in the León household. During the mid-nineteenth- to early twentieth-century occupation of the house, Native American ceramics were used for storage, cooking, and serving, but once the railroad was in use in the late nineteenth century, some Tohono O'odham vessels were replaced by European-made pottery (brightly colored whitewares, decorated in a variety of styles—transfer-prints, annular and hand-painted—although apparently not in matched sets). Native American ceramics continued in use in the kitchen for a period. Vessel forms changed to some degree also, with cups and plates appearing in greater frequencies. Mexican ceramics (such as majolicas and lead-glazed wares) were used in the earlier period, but again, the same phenomenon occurred with Mexican ceramics in the 1890s as had earlier with Native American pottery: the use of Mexican ceramics declined while that of European American ceramics and metal vessels increased (Thiel 2005, 112). Some artifacts associated with writing (slates and inkwells) and religion (e.g., a cross identified as belonging to a member of the family who was a nun [Thiel 2005, 104]) were also present, and documentary evidence suggests that education was a significant goal for many family members. Artifacts recovered from the León home were not costly; in fact, the ceramics used after 1880 were less expensive than those used earlier, which Thiel and his colleagues suggest is characteristic of middle-class urban Arizonans and is related to the effect of the railroad as transport costs declined.

In some ways, the greatest insight into cultural change in the region as a whole is seen in foodways. After the Spanish came to the Southwest early in the seventeenth century, food choices became complex, in that traditional indigenous and mestizo foods competed with Spanish preferences. The church used food to proselytize more effectively, trying to show converts the superiority of Christian food over pagan foods and customs, although the desert was not hospitable to many Spanish food preferences, such as wheat. However, the presence of wheat, beef, wine, olive oil, and metal and ceramic utensils increased in the León assemblages, replacing a previous reliance on game, corn, and indigenous plants (portraying a Mexican or mestizo influence), prepared with stone manos, metates, and comales. And there was continuity in some food traditions, as green chilis continued in use. Most food was local, but when Americans brought in new foods and beverages with the railroad, the Leóns began to purchase some packaged foods and drinks. The archaeological evidence indicates that the family ate a great deal of wheat (recovered in features), beef (with some mutton but little pork, see above), and little corn; they ate few cactus fruits (saguaro, prickly pear, and barrel), preferring European ones instead. Thiel suggests that these habits were the result of a combination of the Leóns' status (both actual and desired) and availability. The combination of old and new foods, traditional and innovative, characterizes many of the groups described in this chapter.

Europeans: Irish, Jews, and Others

Ethnicity was an operative concept in nineteenth-century cities such as San Francisco and New York, where whole communities were a mixture of immigrants: Irish, Jewish, German, French, Italian and other Europeans, Mexicans, and Chinese. Each of these groups spoke their own language. The consideration of these groups from an archaeological perspective has taken many forms, but most observers are interested in evaluating the degree to which the group in question assimilated or remained separate from the dominant American culture (as was noted in studies of Chinese immigrants, above).

Most of the archaeological information about non-British European immi-

grant groups is derived from the Irish, who were the largest of the groups coming to North America in the mid to late nineteenth century. Both the British
and Americans treated them as a racial group, at the bottom of the social ladder,
and in the United States they were placed in competition for jobs with African
Americans (Ignatiev 1995). This perception of the Irish as nonwhites was reinforced in the nineteenth century by American bioanthropologists (called physical anthropologists in their day; Orser 2007, 90, 102). As they "became white,"
their status improved and their racial classification altered. This change is seen
to some degree archaeologically, in deposits associated with Irish households in
California (Yentsch 2009) and New York City (Yamin 1999; Orser 2007; Linn
2008; Brighton 2009).

The Praetzellises provide significant data in their San Francisco study (A. and
M. Praetzellis 2009). Anne Yentsch notes that Irish and Jewish immigrants had
a better life in California than on the East Coast in terms of opportunities for
jobs, as western society was more open and tolerant, as a result of its "culturally diversified environment where habit and tradition eroded. The result was
a belief in the future, self-reliance and an abundance of hope" (Yentsch 2009,
186). The Irish were particularly likely to use refined earthenwares as their major ceramic form and had many ornamental objects in their homes (including
vases, mirrors, and clocks). They were less likely than other groups to use serving dishes that matched their plates. They drank considerable amounts of soda
water (see Linn 2008, 2010 for an important deconstruction of this practice),
beer and ale, and hard liquor at home—as opposed to Jews living in the same
area, who drank more wine and champagne.

Stephen Brighton has also focused on this population, and along with Meredith Linn (2008) was one of the first archaeologists to examine the Irish from a
transnational perspective, using Irish as well as Irish American data. His concern
is the transition from Irish to Irish American in New York City and Paterson,
New Jersey (2009). He believes that this transition can be dated on a national
basis to around 1880. Based on ceramic and glass data from the Five Points site
in New York and from Paterson, New Jersey, he suggests that an identity shift
from immigrant to citizen reflects a negotiation conducted among Irish immigrants in reaction to their social, political, and economic circumstances and an
increasing involvement in a capitalist consumer society. In particular, he notes
vessel complexity (referring to the number of different types of ceramic forms
recovered) as a marker of changing identity. He posits that an increase in vessel
complexity (as seen in serving platters and dishes of various sizes as well as a

greater variety in forms of glassware) and shifts in meat consumption all express an improved economic ability to participate in the market economy which in turn correlates with the acceptance of becoming American.

Both Brighton and Linn have looked at medical treatment as a means of exploring ethnic identity. Linn discovered that attitudes of non-Irish New Yorkers toward two diseases found among Irish immigrants—typhus fever, depicted as "the Irish disease," and tuberculosis—demonstrate a number of prevalent ideas of the time: concepts of disease in the nineteenth century, treatments chosen for specific forms of illness, and the ways in which specific populations were isolated and characterized by members of the dominant culture. Archaeological assemblages from the Five Points and Paterson sites—the same sites examined by Brighton—yielded evidence of medical practice, as did hospital records and other forms of documentation. Brighton suggests that the racialization of the Irish inspired discrimination against them that would have limited their access to standard medical care (2009, 137), whereas Linn proposes that Irish immigrants' healthcare choices were also shaped by how they perceived their own ailments and that treatment of the Irish established a model for the treatment of subsequent immigrant groups (2008, 4). The agency of these immigrants in finding medical help and contributing to the way medical care was delivered in New York City is clear; what is particularly interesting is that, because of how certain diseases were understood by Americans at the time, the presence of typhus exacerbated the notion that the Irish were outsiders dangerous to resident Americans, whereas the presence of tuberculosis among the same group facilitated their incorporation into American culture by nurturing an image of them as vulnerable and refined (Linn 2008).

Irish and African Americans often lived in the same poor urban neighborhoods, such as the Five Points (see above and below). Ryan Gray and Jill-Karen Yakubik's study of New Orleans in the late nineteenth and early twentieth centuries compares the assemblages of two privies, representing Irish and African American working-class families, respectively, and reveals a number of similarities. The Irish material was deposited at least thirty years before the African American deposit (Gray and Yakubik 2010). Both show that these residents foraged and fished to supplement the meat they acquired through the market economy. Ceramics were similar among the two groups but different from the wares representing a more elite household. Gray and Yakubik note that late in the nineteenth century there was a biracial labor organization called the Cotton Men's Executive Council. However, as prosperity declined and Jim Crow attitudes increased in the twentieth century, this cooperative spirit was stifled.

These same two groups lived in Seneca Village, a middle-class African American community that existed in what is now New York City's Central Park from 1825 to 1858. These residents, like those of so many black communities, were evicted, in this case so that the park could be built. We do not know that the Irish living in Seneca Village were members of the middle class, although some of them did own their land, but it is interesting that the two groups lived there side-by-side in spite of the conflict reported to have existed between them in seeking to move up the socioeconomic ladder. Seneca Village is similar to Weeksville, a middle-class African American community established in 1838 in Brooklyn (Wall et al. 2010), although the latter survived until the 1930s. Both were anchored by several churches and at least one school. Excavation has only recently (2011) been conducted in Seneca Village by the present authors, and we expect to be able to offer meaningful information about its materiality and the lifeways of members of that community. We know a lot about its landscape, which was obliterated when the park was created. The analysis of a small sample of faunal remains associated with black residents from Seneca Village is consistent with other studies noted above of middle-class black settlements. The data here revealed no remains from wild fauna, with beef and mutton dominating. The beef was butchered professionally, but mutton was home butchered, which may mean that villagers kept sheep (Maeda 2012). These studies, as well as the Mexican and Chinese ones described above, are significant in denaturalizing and complicating racial categories and race history in the United States.

There is limited information from archaeology about other groups, as they were less numerous and the buildings in which they lived in urban areas were multifamily tenements jointly occupied by members of a number of ethnic groups, making it difficult to study a particular group. Some material from San Francisco and West Oakland pertains to Jewish immigrants whose religious identity intersected with that of their national origins in Germany, Poland, and other countries. Anne Yentsch notes in a study of San Francisco that kin networks were particularly crucial among Jewish immigrants, some of whom followed a path to "prosperity, a path that included clerking, peddling from wagons across rural California, purchasing small stores, [and] networking between city and country" (Yentsch 2009, 165). The second and third generations of Jewish families (and other immigrant groups) were upwardly mobile and often achieved higher socioeconomic positions than the first generation. But although the families whose assemblages were examined may have been upwardly mobile and held significant property, there was no evidence of wealth in them; the only artifacts that were not strictly utilitarian were a child's ABC dish, a porcelain vase, marbles, a doll, and parts of a miniature tea set. This frugal behavior is seen at the few sites associated with Jewish families both in San Francisco and New York, in contrast to the remnants of Irish households in which "colorful, decorative wares . . . that are easy to display" are common (Yentsch 2009, 145).

One of the most archaeologically sensitive indicators of ethnic identity is faunal material. The Irish at Five Points in the 1840s through the 1860s had a preference for pork (Crabtree and Milne 2000, 2:180, 187) and those in San Francisco purchased pork and the lower priced cuts of other kinds of meat (A. Praetzellis 2009, 307). Jewish families in San Francisco ate mostly beef and mutton. Germans and African Americans consumed beef over other kinds of meat, even more than U.S.-born whites (A. Praetzellis 2004, 80). The relationship between ethnicity and meat choice appears not to follow stereotypic expectations, as some of the Jewish families in San Francisco and West Oakland ate both pork and shellfish in small amounts, although these foods are forbidden to Orthodox Jews. Adrian Praetzellis suggests that these families may have abandoned kosher practices, perhaps to assimilate more easily and advance socially (2004, 70). If so, the transition for Jews from a racially defined group to an ethnic one, mentioned above, does suggest that these changes may have helped to achieve the desired result.

A kosher diet was apparently maintained by the Harris Goldberg family at the Five Points site in New York City. Goldberg, a tailor, lived on Pearl Street during the 1840s and was the sexton of the local synagogue. The faunal material associated with his household contained beef always from the foreshank—a preferred cut for Orthodox Jews—such as roast or brisket, mutton, a lot of fish, and chicken that was probably kosher (Yamin 2000a, 1:96; Crabtree and Milne 2000, 2:162). A feature located in New Orleans was identified as associated with a Prussian-born Jewish merchant. It contained a distinctive faunal assemblage (mostly bird and fish) suggesting a kosher diet and an intriguing collection of fish and egg remains which the authors (Gray and Yakubik 2010, 301) suggest may represent a traditional Jewish feast of mourning.

Conclusion

In this chapter we have considered the many ways in which historical archaeologists have examined sites in the United States through the lenses of race and ethnicity. We emerge from this study with the overarching result that there seem to be few consistent conclusions about material reflections of groups defined by a shared ancestry, whether genetic or cultural. In part, this is because some of the categories we have examined, both racial and ethnic, are flawed by being essentialist and reductionist; thus any expectations for consistency are invalid. Although there are ways in which groups of people make use of consumption and the material aspects of their lives, from foodways to ceramics to tools, to express a dimension of identity, these are complicated by other aspects of identity such as class and gender and geographic locale. It does seem clear that economic limitations and the multiple perceptions associated with objects and food types make all of these choices complex. There is also a role for idiosyncratic practice and particular historical circumstance.

Archaeology has the ability to disentangle some of these attributes and to suggest the complexity of the situation. We have focused on the archaeology of African American and Chinese sites and have also looked at a Mexican household, a few Jewish families, and some Irish families. Each of these groups arrived in the United States at particular times and under specific circumstances. Some emigrated by choice, while others were involuntary immigrants. Some imagined themselves here for a short time, whereas others came with the promise of a new and better life. Each of the groups described here was subjected to negative stereotypic prejudice at some point. We have not described any affluent Mayflower descendants in this chapter, which in and of itself suggests that the categories of racial and ethnic difference apply only to subdominant "others." The methodologies used in these studies are those basic to historical archaeology: excavate, where possible connect deposits to households for which documentary data exist, and look for correlations between some material aspect of the assemblage and some social dimension. Although we should not expect to find neat solutions to complex problems, archaeology offers a unique means to consider the wonderfully variable ways by which people incorporate objects into their lives.

6

Class and Gender in the City

HISTORICAL ARCHAEOLOGISTS have learned a great deal about the constructions of class and gender in urban places in the United States. And just as was true in talking about race and ethnicity in the last chapter, we emphasize that neither of these constructs can exist on its own. Class does not exist without gender, gender does not exist without class, and of course both of them exist only within the contexts of race and ethnicity (and vice versa), as well as at a specific place and time. So our choice of which studies to include in this chapter as opposed to the preceding one, and whether they are discussed under the subheadings of gender or class, is in some ways an arbitrary one, although some particular studies might speak more to examining class, while others speak more to analyzing gender. This organizational problem is compounded by the fact that particularly for the middle and working classes, the archaeological record for the most part documents domestic life, where women's activities are front and center. So, many of these studies are implicitly about women and therefore touch on gender. This focus on women and the quotidian details of daily life in the archaeological record complements the written record, however, which tends to stress the world of work outside the home and the lives of men.

In deciding how to organize our discussion, we follow the intent of our colleagues: those studies that explicitly focus on class will be discussed under class, no matter their relevance to gender, and those that explicitly focus on gender will be discussed under gender, regardless of their relevance to class. We begin with a brief overview of the concept of class. Then we discuss how historical archaeologists working in American cities have looked at class in the archaeological record to learn about the American experience. Finally, we shift our focus to the study of gender, first discussing gender as a concept and then looking at the ways that historical archaeologists have examined it in urban settings.

Class

While class forms an implicit part of almost every study in archaeology, it only plays an explicit role in some of them. Part of the problem is due to the fact that many Americans support the myth that class does not exist in American society, so they tend to ignore its presence. But even when its existence is acknowledged, the concept is used in very different ways. Some look on it descriptively as a set of fixed categories or as "rungs on a ladder of inequality," usually based on income and/or occupation. Others use class in the more traditional Marxist sense of the social relations of production, particularly in the relationship between those who own the means of production and those who supply the labor for it. This approach includes the premise that classes exist only in relation to each other. Several historical archaeologists have begun to confront class and to acknowledge that though it may well be dead in the descriptive sense (i.e., that it is not a powerful analytic tool), it is not dead in the relational sense. Instead, in this regard it is indeed alive and well (Wurst and Fitts 1999).

Archaeology can play an important role in the analysis of class because the materiality that archaeologists analyze plays an important role in class construction. People manipulate artifacts and their meanings as part of the negotiation of class relations (Wurst and Fitts 1999, 3). Material objects in fact may be seen as part of the symbolic and cultural capital that defines the classes (Bourdieu 1984). Our presentation of class in this chapter is intrinsically linked to the analysis of capitalism, considered extensively in chapter 4. In that chapter we focused on the workplace, whereas here we are more concerned with the construction of class in domestic settings and how it works as a manifestation of various forms of capitalism.

In that earlier chapter, we discussed the history of the United States and of the colonies that preceded it and their coincidence with the development of the modern capitalist system, a history that has been characterized by two kinds of capitalism. By the late seventeenth century most of the European colonies in North America were settler colonies. They served as peripheries, supplying resources to European metropoles, with political economies based on merchant capitalism. In the English colonies, merchants were at the top of this hierarchical system. Beneath them were artisans and farmers, who not only provided the colony's subsistence but also produced many of the commodities the merchants dealt in. They in turn were underlain by laborers, both men and women, enslaved, indentured, and free. Enslaved Africans supplied a large part of the labor force in what would become the eastern United States from the time of the first European arrivals throughout much of its history. After the American Revolution, the new nation that comprised the former thirteen English colonies began its transformation from a peripheral area first to a core and ultimately to a hegemonic power, and the political economy of the country was transformed from merchant to industrial capitalism (see Paynter 1982, Johnson 1996, Leone 2005, and Matthews 2010 [among others] for archaeological approaches to the development of capitalism).

It is within these contexts of merchant and industrial capitalism that class formation and negotiation took place, and archaeologists have examined aspects of both of these forms of political economy in urban contexts. In exploring merchant capitalism, they have looked at the merchant elites and at the artisan middling folk of the colonial and early federalist era, in addition to the laboring classes which were made up in large part by enslaved Africans, as discussed in the last chapter. Furthermore, they have examined the formation and makeup of the modern American class system that arose under industrial capitalism in nineteenth-century urban centers, particularly the construction of the middle and working classes.

Colonial and Federalist Elites

Traditionally, historical archaeologists spent a great deal of effort examining the lifeways of the elites during the colonial and early federalist periods. Many of these earlier studies were done under the auspices of the historic preservation movement and focused on the homes of community leaders that local preservation societies looked on as worth preserving. Three of the more interesting studies use different theoretical approaches to show how members of the elite exercised their power over nature in order to maintain and enhance their status. Two are of families in Annapolis, Maryland, while the third is from Philadelphia.

The earliest of these studies was Mark Leone's now-classic 1984 analysis of William Paca's garden in Annapolis. Here, Leone takes the 1760s symmetrical Georgian garden that William Paca, a lawyer and signer of the Declaration of Independence, had built behind his house and subjects it to Althusserian analysis. He shows how the garden, one of many elite contemporary gardens, is "ideologically informed" and draws on classical references, with their implications of historical precedent, to serve to "naturalize" the inequality inherent in the social order (1984, 25) and thus to make hierarchy seem inevitable. These references rationalize and even hide questions about the gross inequities embedded in a society based on slave labor in the context of freedom, in the build-

up to the Revolutionary War. This study has been enormously influential, pro-
voking extensive commentary, both supportive and critical (see, e.g., Beaudry
et al. 1991; Hall 1992, 2000; Johnson 1996; and Hicks 2005).

The other Annapolitan study, incorporated into Anne Yentsch's *A Chesapeake
Family and Their Slaves* (1994), examines the home of Captain Charles Calvert,
who was the governor of Maryland from 1719 to 1727. In this study, which began
as a rescue project in the early 1980s, Yentsch draws on archaeological, written,
and visual evidence to create an extremely rich historical ethnography of the
Calverts and their world, including the enslaved Africans who lived with them
involuntarily. Her study underlines the ways that the members of a premier
colonial family, relatives of Lord Baltimore, signaled their position as being at
the center of British colonial society by emphasizing like Paca, although on a
grander scale, their control over nature. This control was evidenced particularly
by their orangery, a horticultural structure that passed out of American popular
memory long ago. Invented in Roman times, orangeries supplied a protected,
warm environment that people used for raising plants (such as orange trees)
that were adapted to warmer climates. Sophisticated orangeries like the Calverts' consisted of shed-like structures with hypocausts, or fire-boxes, at one
end with (in this case) vaulted brick ducts for conveying the heat. There was
a similar orangery at Lord Baltimore's estate in Britain (1994, 116–18). Yentsch
stresses that the importance of the orangery lies not in what it provided in terms
of comestibles but rather in "its role in maintaining and enhancing [the family's]
prestige" by emphasizing the resources that they had at their disposal to be able
to grow these trees. The orangery was unique to this family in Annapolis, and its
classical roots conferred the prestige of its association with antiquity onto the
family by connecting it to Roman rulers (1994, 116–24; quote on 121).

A third study centers around another iconic feature that conferred status on
the elite by demonstrating their control of nature and was discovered by archaeologists working in Philadelphia at the site of the President's House, the home
of Presidents George Washington and John Adams in the 1790s, when the new
nation's capital was in that city (Yamin 2008, 41; this site is also discussed in
chapter 7). The house belonged to Robert Morris, a friend of Washington,
who rented it to the federal government to house the presidents. Behind the
house, archaeologists working under Rebecca Yamin discovered an octagonally
shaped pit lined with dry-laid stone blocks. Upon excavation, the pit turned out
to be thirteen feet in diameter and nine feet deep, with a gravel floor. At first, the
archaeologists had no idea what the pit was for. Then, after extensive research
in the archives, they discovered that it was the underground remains of an ice

house that Robert Morris had built in the early 1780s, a few years before the government leased the house (Figure 6.1). Morris was fascinated by technological innovations like ice houses, and in 1784 he had advised Washington about how to build one (Yamin 2008, 42–43).

Ice was an important component for elite entertainments in the eighteenth century. It was used in the production of fancy desserts such as ice cream and

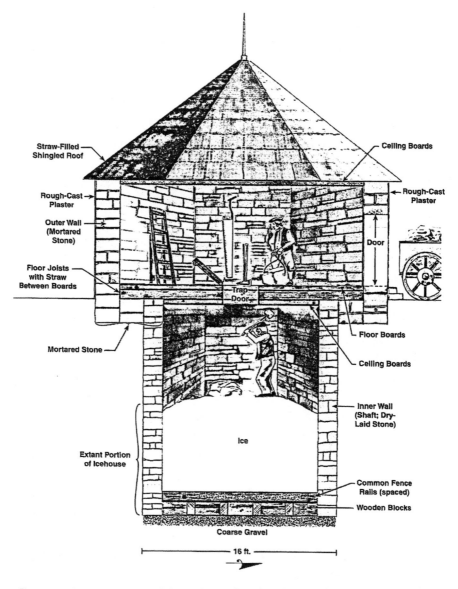

Figure 6.1. A reconstruction of the ice house found on the President's House lot, Philadelphia. (Rendering by Todd Benedict and Rob Schultz; John Milner Associates.)

ices as well as for cooling punch and other confections. With the development of the commercial ice industry in the nineteenth century, ice became a commodity that was harvested and stored in the winter and then sold during the warm summer months (Harris and Pickman 2011); it was widely available to the middle class as well as to the rich. But before that time, ice tended to be available only to the rich, who procured blocks of ice in the winter and stored them in their own ice houses for use in summer to make these high-status comestibles. The presidents' households presumably used the ice house in order to serve the desserts and other treats that one would expect a president of the United States to serve during the long, hot Philadelphia summers. Martha Washington, in fact, is said to have served ice cream and lemonade at the "drawing room" receptions she held weekly on Fridays while the capital was in Philadelphia (Detweiler 1982, 107, 140). A guest described one of these receptions as "brilliant beyond anything you can imagine" (Detweiler 1982, 140).

The president's household in Philadelphia probably harvested the ice from the Schuylkill River during the winter and preserved it for summer use in the specially designed ice house in the backyard (Yamin 2008, 44–46). Like the Pacas' garden and the Calverts' orangerie, the ice house itself along with the extravagant desserts it helped to produce provided an important component of the materiality of elite status in the eighteenth century.

Colonial and Federalist Middling Folk

The end of the Revolutionary War brought an end to Britain's trade and manufacturing restrictions, and the new nation began its development into a core economic area in the capitalist world system. This shift accompanied the beginnings of the transformation of the country's political economy from merchant to industrial capitalism. There have been several archaeological studies on the micro-scale of artisans and other middling folk living in urban areas in the United States during this late colonial and early federalist period. Some of the more interesting of these studies examine the material culture of individual households to see how these changes in the political economy worked themselves out on the ground.

As we discussed in chapter 4, the transformation from the artisanal system of production to the factory system was an uneven, long, and complex process. By the mid-nineteenth century, some trades had converted to the factory system, while others continued to be run as traditional crafts. Most master craftsmen who had been in control of the labor process in the eighteenth century found themselves in new positions, for example, as entrepreneurs or as retailers divorced from the production process, or as supervisors of the work performed in workers' homes or in factories. And most workmen who, in the eighteenth century, had been journeymen with a somewhat realistic hope of becoming masters in their own right became members of a new working class. Furthermore, Americans of African descent who in the eighteenth century had been almost uniformly enslaved had become free in most of the northern states by the mid-nineteenth century. Most of them also had become members of the working class.

The transformation from the moral to the market economy also encompassed changes in home life and in the landscapes of cities. Among the middle class, for example, families moved their homes away from their workplaces and began to enhance the quality of domestic life. Middle-class women tended to have live-in domestics to help with housework, to prepare and serve more complex meals, and to spend more on the accouterments of home life, including more expensive dishes that they purchased in large sets (Wall 1994).

Paul Shackel's study of the workers at the Harpers Ferry Armory (1996) examines some of the changes in the home lives of managers and workers that were integral to the transformation of arms-making from a craft to industrial production in Harpers Ferry, West Virginia. After a great deal of resistance on the part of the workers, changes began to be incorporated into the manufacturing process of the armory in the second quarter of the nineteenth century. Management imposed a new work discipline alongside a new form of production whereby workmen performed piecework by, for example, specializing in manufacturing only one part of a gun as opposed to the whole weapon. Shackel shows how the families of the master armorers who worked in the factory made the switch from the form of domestic life prevalent in the old craft shops to one that characterized the emergence of the new middle class. The changes included the adoption of dishes that were more highly decorated and that were used in more complex sets made up of different kinds of vessels (1996, 122).

But the domestic assemblages of the workers at the armory told a different story. Throughout the early nineteenth century, the position of the workers deteriorated as those who had been craft workers became first pieceworkers and then wage earners. At least some of the workers' families at Harpers Ferry did not participate in the new market system and declined to purchase fashionable consumer goods like their supervisors' families. Instead, they continued to use old-fashioned dishes, such as creamware plates and hand-painted tearwares (1996, 138). This could have been in part a reaction to the decline of real wages that these workers suffered during this period—after all, these dishes were less expensive—but it also suggests that they may have been looking back to an idealized vision of the traditional craft system and rejecting the new factory system.

Rebecca Yamin has also looked at this transformation, this time among artisans in Philadelphia (2008). Adam Everly, a comb maker, provides an example. He began making combs in the 1820s, when new technological improvements made comb production extremely profitable. Like his contemporaries, he not only made combs but also sold them and other accessories to the ladies of Philadelphia. His business flourished, and he became a very rich man. He and his family used part of their fortune to make the transition from living the life of a traditional craftsman to becoming members of the new middle class by moving their home away from their workplace. His wife established a bourgeois home and bought several sets of dishes for setting her table—fancy kinds for special occasions (Figure 6.2) and simpler ones for everyday meals. She also had a

Figure 6.2. Fancy Chinese export porcelain tableware discovered at the middle-class home of Adam and Mary Everly, Philadelphia, 1830s. (Photograph by Juliette Gerhardt; John Milner Associates.)

Chinese export porcelain tea set embellished with the couple's initials, which was specially ordered from abroad. But Adam Everly continued to identify himself as a craftsperson—a comb maker—as long as he continued in the business. When his son William Everly took it over, he changed his identity to a retailer and listed himself not as a comb maker but as a "merchant" dealing in "fancy goods" instead. William Everly may even have abandoned the manufacturing part of the business completely to become a full-time retailer (2008, 31–32).

Yamin also discovered that this transformation was probably not without intrafamily conflict (2008). Alexander Turnbull was a master cabinet maker. Cabinetmaking was one of the "conflict trades" that rapidly expanded in the early nineteenth century to supply the products for the new middle class, and that expansion brought enormous conflict in its wake (Rock 1979). It was in those trades that the position of journeymen deteriorated as their work became deskilled and they were forced to become wage workers. The journeymen cabinet workers in Philadelphia organized and formed the Pennsylvania Society of Journeymen Cabinetmakers in the 1820s. The Turnbull shop thrived in this very competitive environment, suggesting that Turnbull was making economies of scale and could have been exploiting his workers. If so, this position was not supported by his son, Alexander Jr., who, in 1827, after his father's death, founded the *Journeymen Mechanics' Advocate,* a newspaper aimed at organizing journeymen (Yamin 2008, 68–69).

The Middle Class in the Mid-nineteenth Century

Archaeologists have also studied the urban middle class in the mid-nineteenth century. These studies began in the early 1980s, after historical archaeologists Mary and Adrian Praetzellis issued a clarion call for their colleagues to study the dominant culture in the nineteenth century—that of the white, American-born middle class—so that they could use it as *comparandi* (their term) for the studies of ethnicity that so engrossed the discipline at the time: "Archaeologists have devoted altogether too much attention to the problem of archaeological evidence of ethnic differences at the expense of identifying the dominant cultural tradition of nineteenth-century America, as it may or may not be expressed in the archaeological record and the material environment in general" (quoted in M. Praetzellis et al. 1988, 193). The Praetzellises again wrote about the white middle class in a study of what they referred to as Victorianisms in a project in Sacramento, California, where they looked at the consumption patterns of German bootmakers and bakers (1992; A. Praetzellis 1991). They saw these families as inculcating the Victorian values of independence, frugality, industry, and hard work into their children through messages inscribed on their children's dishes: one family had two mugs inscribed with the inscription "For a good Boy." Little girls learned a different lesson about their domestic responsibilities to their families through a material culture that included dolls and dolls' tea sets (Praetzellis and Praetzellis 1992, 90–93).

In a more recent study of the middle class, the Praetzellises reframed their argument within a world of "gentility" and its accouterments, which are invested with meaning (Praetzellis and Praetzellis 2001). In this study they offered a more nuanced interpretation of the cultural hegemonic model by "question[ing] the notion that everyone who used genteel material culture employed these items to convey the same ideas and for the same purposes." Instead, they proposed that even as these signs possessed powerful, conventional meanings that were widely understood, people used their knowledge of these meanings as cultural capital to execute their own strategies, not simply to imitate the upper crust (2001, 647). They used examples of assemblages from the homes of several people of different ethnic and racial groups to make their point. One was Don Mariano Guadalupe Vallejo, the Mexican comandante of Alta California, who used his gothic-style home and the accouterments of Victorian genteel dining to make a place for himself in a new era when Alta California was being transferred to American rule. Another was Tong Ahchick, the agent for the Chinese Young Wo Association, who represented the interests of the association's members in the context of prejudice and discrimination on the part of the dominant culture. The assemblage associated with his home showed a mixture of Chinese- and English-made dishes. The traditional Chinese vessels consisted exclusively of bowls and may have been used in family meals or in entertaining Chinese guests. But the rest were English-made dishes and included bowls, a basin, soup plates, and dinner plates. At least one of the last mentioned was, ironically, in the willow pattern—an English-made, Chinese-derived pattern that was an icon of genteel American culture. These dishes were presumably used to entertain—and impress—his European American guests.

Finally, as mentioned in chapter 5, the Praetzellises also looked at assemblages from African American homes in West Oakland that dated to the late nineteenth century, during the Jim Crow period. Many of the men who lived in these houses at this period were porters who worked in the Pullman cars of the Southern Pacific Railway (2001; 2004). Their households too exhibited a penchant for the table- and teawares that formed part of the genteel tradition. The Praetzellises suggest that the Pullman porters and their wives were not simply emulating the European American middle class but also looked on these goods "as symbols of civility and personal dignity, qualities for which the men strived against the odds" (2001, 651). Following Matthew Johnson, they point out that their case studies contribute to our understanding of "the space between often very powerful master narratives of cultural and social identity and much smaller, stranger and potentially subversive narratives of archaeological material" (2001, 652, quoting Johnson). In this case we can see how those on the margins of society take up the "very icons" of gentility, which in nineteenth-century American culture represented the hegemony and orthodoxy of the middle class (2001, 651), to pursue their own agendas.

Diana Wall and Robert Fitts (working separately) looked at the materiality of the home life of members of the middle class in mid-nineteenth-century New York City and Brooklyn, respectively. Wall showed how middle-class women used different styles of dishes to underline their complementary roles at home. They used dinner dishes in the gothic pattern (the same style used for building churches) to underline their role as the moral guardians of society, and at tea parties they used fancy porcelain dishes in the Italianate pattern (the same style used for building their fashionable homes) as part of the materiality that expressed their role as negotiators for their family's position in the social structure. These parties were the venues for the competitive displays aimed at finding husbands for daughters and employment for sons. But Wall noticed that less affluent women of the middle class apparently exercised only one of these domestic roles: the assemblage from a poorer middle-class family did not include fancy porcelain teacups. She postulated that competitive displays may not have been productive for poorer members of the middle class, who may have had to count on each other for help in times of need (1991). This finding underlines the fact that there is a great deal of diversity among the group that we refer to as the "middle class."

Fitts (1999) also examined the trappings of gentility among middle-class families living in Brooklyn in the mid-nineteenth century, at the time when Brooklyn was a separate city as well as a middle-class suburb to New York, to which it was connected by ferry. He was interested in examining how nineteenth-century middle-class women used material culture to create domestic havens for their families and to see the extent to which they practiced genteel dining, as defined in the prescriptive literature or "how-to" books of the time. These books advised women about how they could become established members of the middle class, but they did not divulge the extent to which women actually complied with this advice. He asked several questions of his material: Were these people (as prescribed) following the one dish per person rule, or were they using communal dishes? Were they (as prescribed) using matched sets of dishes, so that all the plates used to set the table for a meal were in the same pattern, or were the dishes in a hodge-podge of patterns? And, finally, were they (as prescribed) using dishes that were functionally specialized by size and shape, or were they using dishes that could serve several functions? His study allowed him to see that the families in Brooklyn were following the rules established for middle-class life. But what was amazing was that not only were the dishes from each household in just a few patterns but the dishes from neighboring households were in those exact same patterns, too. He saw this conformity as an expression of people marking themselves as members of the middle class during the period of class formation and of the subsequent growth in the number of its members with a worldview stressing uniformity over individuality and formality over informality (1999, 58–59). Furthermore, with one exception, the dishes that Fitts examined in Brooklyn were in the same patterns and forms as those that Wall found in New York, showing that this uniformity among the middle class was not confined to just one city. The exception was that the Brooklyn assemblages contained tablewares in fancy porcelain, whereas the New York ones did not. Instead, the latter contained only the smaller porcelain plates associated with serving tea and desserts. This difference suggests that Brooklynites entertained their friends for dinner and not just for after-dinner tea parties, as their New York counterparts did.

The Working Class

America's working class had invented itself twice by the middle of the nineteenth century (Gutman and Berlin 1987). The first working class, which predated the 1840s, consisted of a heterogeneous group of predominantly native-born people—both white and black and, for the blacks, both enslaved and free—who worked with their hands and who, among the whites, had inherited the republican artisan ideology of the Revolutionary War. But this working class did not reproduce itself to become the working class of midcentury. Instead, it was swamped by the waves of immigrants who began arriving in the 1830s. During the 1830s and 1840s, the Irish and Germans predominated among the immigrant groups, only to be joined by people from southern and eastern Europe and, after the discovery of gold in California, China as well. Furthermore, there were the Mexicans who lived in the new states that had formerly belonged to Mexico. It is these immigrants, for the most part from rural areas in Europe, China, or the West, that took over the working class, outnumbering American-born workers of both African and European descent in America's cities. In the last chapter we examined how archaeologists have approached the study of the ethnicity of these working-class immigrant groups. Here, we look at studies that focus on these groups and their roles in the construction of the American working class.

There have been many archaeological studies of the immigrant working class. One of the most important was the Five Points project in lower Manhattan, where Edward Rutsch and Leonard Bianchi directed the excavations and Rebecca Yamin supervised the analysis. This project was important for several reasons. First, of course, was the visibility of the site itself: The Five Points is one of the most notorious slums in the world. It was visited and written about by Charles Dickens when he was in New York in the 1840s, and it has been sensationalized by countless authors ever since. It was memorialized by Martin Scorsese in the film *Gangs of New York* (2002) and most recently in the television drama *Copper,* aired in 2012 and 2013. Because of the site's notoriety, the project received a lot of publicity and was well-funded both in the field and in the laboratory. Furthermore, its final report was enormous, totaling six separate volumes, and its data have formed the basis of numerous articles and several books (e.g., Brighton 2009; Griggs 1999; Orser 2007; Yamin 2001, 2005). Tragically, the artifacts from the site were destroyed in the attacks on the World Trade Center in 2001, but copies of both the field and artifact records survive.

Yamin drew on "acts of imagination" (Yamin 2001, 163, citing Schrire) along with information about the site gleaned from historical and archeological records to develop narrative vignettes that would "provide alternative images" of the Five Points (Yamin 2001). One of these alternative images concerns the "respectability" of many of the people who lived there. Although the denizens of the Five Points were stereotyped by some members of the middle class as barely human, in fact some of them had a vision of domestic life that would have been familiar in middle-class homes. Yamin has noted that one assemblage, for example, "included matching dishes and serving pieces, as many as six tea sets, including three imported from Staffordshire, one of bone China, and one of Chinese porcelain, and extensive glassware including an unusual lacy pressed square bowl . . . and numerous cut decanters" (Yamin, quoted in Cantwell and Wall 2001, 218).

There have been a substantial number of studies of the nineteenth-century working class in many American cities over the years, and archaeologists have accumulated a lot of data about them. What is exciting about the data is that it allows us to look at members of the working class who came from many different backgrounds, worked in many different industries, and lived in different parts of the country and to compare their ways of life. As archaeologist Jean Howson notes (2009, 227), what we can now explore is how during the mid- to late nineteenth century, peoples of diverse ethnic backgrounds formed themselves into an American working class. We can see this most clearly when we look at ceramics. Whether we look at the working class in San Francisco (Praetzellis and Praetzellis 2009), West Oakland, California (Walker 2004; Praetzellis 2004), Detroit (Branstner and Martin 1987), Paterson, New Jersey (De Cunzo 1983; Yamin 1999), Washington, D.C. (Seifert 1991), Newark, New Jersey (Howson and Bianchi 2009), or the Five Points site in New York City (e.g., Yamin 2000), the ceramics tend to be similar. This similarity in style is what we might expect— more than two decades ago the historian Lizabeth Cohen noted that ethnic variation came to be subsumed within a "consistent American working-class material ethos" (1986, 273–75)—but the styles themselves were not what we anticipated. The conventional wisdom had been that the styles preferred by the working class expressed ornate Victorian tastes as opposed to the simpler Colonial Revival and Arts and Crafts styles preferred by the middle class during the terminal nineteenth and early twentieth centuries (Cohen 1986, 275). But our archaeological assemblages show us that this is not in fact the case. Instead, although members of the working class of many ethnic backgrounds are using dishes in similar patterns, those patterns are not busy Victorian ones, but simple white ironstones, some with molded designs. Howson notes that these patterns "speak to a new American traditionalism (one that fits within a rather leveling aesthetic) rather than to what the 'Victorianism' tea sets might evoke" (Howson and Bianchi 2009, 227).

One of the big questions that scholars have posed in looking at the working class in the United States has to do with class identity. Some have pointed out that, unlike in Britain (Thompson 1964), the extent to which the working class in the United States exhibited class consciousness is not clear. Did the working class develop its own class consciousness that was embedded in its own aesthetic? Or did they look to the middle class (Mrozowski 2006, 151–52)? We should be able to begin to address this question when we compare domestic artifacts between contemporary working- and middle-class households—a research question that has yet to be explored. And if they did look to the middle class, did racial consciousness play a role—in other words, did members of the white working class identify with the white middle class and thus set themselves apart from black working-class Americans? Ultimately this is a question that archaeologists studying material culture will be able to help elucidate.

The Great Transformation

Most archaeologists focus on a few assemblages that date to a single group of people from a similar period ("the late nineteenth-century working class," for example) because they are studying the archaeological remains from individual sites, and the assemblages from the nation's younger cities particularly tend to date to roughly the same period. As the archaeology of urban places has matured, however, some archaeologists have been able to use data from many sites to look at life in the past over a long period of time (e.g., Brighton 2009; Wall 1994). The study that is most relevant in this discussion is Stephen Mrozowski's 2006 book, *The Archaeology of Class in Urban America*. In it, he examines the changing face of "class" in the United States during the transformation from merchant to industrial capitalism by looking at the results of his earlier studies of sites in Newport, Rhode Island, and Lowell, Massachusetts. Newport provides a case study of a society whose economy was based on merchant capitalism, while Lowell (discussed also in chapter 4) allows us to look at industrial capitalism. Lowell is unusual in that it began as a planned factory community with a workforce of native-born young women governed by corporate paternalism, designed to avoid the horrors produced among the working class in England's northern industrial cities. But as the century wore on, that workforce was replaced by immigrant workers.

Mrozowski's work is unusual in that he uses biological and environmental data along with the more traditional data sets popular in historical archeology to give a nuanced view of lived experience during the development of the modern class system in New England. What he is able to document is the fact that working people faced greater health risks than their superiors in the class structure, and these inequalities became more intense as time went on. For example, in Lowell, the workers' boardinghouses showed evidence of greater rat infestations and higher concentrations of lead in the soil than the homes of those higher up in the class structure, and workers lacked indoor plumbing long after it was introduced into wealthier homes. He also shows how the class relationships that developed along with capitalism became written into urban spaces, particularly in Lowell. One of the big changes was the growing importance of the role of ornamental space (as opposed to the premodern pattern of functional space) in negotiating higher positions in the class structure, as evidenced in the artifacts and ecofacts from the backyards of Lowell.

Finally, the examination of class has allowed archaeologists to see on the ground that classes are not monolithic. They are culturally specific and vary through time and space as their members are constantly negotiating and renegotiating their position. Mrozowski underlined that in looking at the working class and how it changed in Lowell (2006), Wall discovered it in looking across the middle class in the mid-nineteenth century in New York City (1991), and Mark Walker found it in looking at mid-nineteenth-century working-class railroad workers in West Oakland (2004).

As mentioned above, although many archaeological studies of class (as well as of ethnicity and race) look particularly closely at domestic life and therefore usually at the lives of women, there are some studies that focus on women explicitly. Now we turn to them and to corresponding studies of men.

Looking at Gender

As the women's movement swept through western society in the 1960s and 1970s as part of the civil rights revolution, many scholars, including some anthropologists, began to ask questions and to design studies that were influenced by, and that contributed to, feminist theory.[1] The publication of Margaret Conkey and Janet Spector's seminal article, "Archaeology and the Study of Gender," in 1984 served as a watershed for archaeologists. But it was only in the early 1990s that historical archaeologists began to explore questions explicitly related to women. Since that time, they have published articles, books, and edited volumes that use feminist or engendered approaches in decoding stereotypes and problematizing issues of gender in looking at the past.[2] Some of these studies have focused on cities and/or issues related to urban studies.

Before we turn to these studies, we need to briefly consider some definitions. The first set considers the differences among sex, gender, and sexuality. The conventional wisdom has been that sex is biologically determined, while gender is socially and culturally constructed. In other words, the presence of specific biological characteristics determines the sex of a person, while that person's gender—what it means to be a member of that sex—is determined by that person's culture.[3] Needless to say, there are many possibilities for overlap between these two categories: for example, to what extent is male aggression determined biologically or culturally? Sexuality (following Voss and Schmidt 2000, 2) refers to "all kinds of sexual relations, including sexual activities, eroticism, sexual identities, sexual meanings, and sexual politics."

Ideally, the term *gender studies* includes the study of the cultural construction of what it means to be a man in relation to what it means to be a woman (and vice versa), but in fact with very few exceptions archaeologists (along with other social scientists) have not focused either on the relationship between the sexes or on men or masculinity alone; instead, they have focused predominantly on issues related to women (but see Brashler 1991; Deagan 1983; Wilkie 2010; and Williams 2008). Finally, the kinds of approaches that archaeologists tend to use in looking at issues of gender for the most part fall into two categories: "engendered" approaches and feminist approaches. Engendered approaches are simply studies of women while feminist approaches are engendered studies that also have the political agenda of changing the power relations between men and women (Little 1994). Here we look at some of the studies of gender and sexuality that archaeologists have worked on in urban areas

Gender and Colonialism

The first engendered analysis in historical archaeology was Kathleen Deagan's study of St. Augustine, Florida, which formed the basis of her dissertation as well as of many subsequent publications (e.g., 1974, 1983). In this extremely important and influential work, she examined how gender relations structured the colonial process in the creole community of eighteenth-century Spanish Saint Augustine in La Florida. St. Augustine, the oldest continuously occupied city in the United States, was founded in 1565 as a presidio, or military town, situated to protect Spanish ships loaded with plundered Aztec and Inka treasure from attacks by privateers while traveling from Mexico back to the home country. Noting that households in St. Augustine were often made up of men of Spanish descent who lived with or were married to women of Native American ancestry, Deagan, using the processual paradigm in vogue at the time, hypothesized that the artifacts used in women's activities, such as food preparation, which are hidden, would be similar to those used in Native American culture, while those used in activities that were "public" and could be seen by outsiders would be Spanish in style. She interpreted this pattern, which she and her students encountered again and again at Spanish sites in the Southeast and in the Caribbean, as meaning that in "the Spanish New World, an extremely potent force in acculturation and adaptive processes was Spanish-Indian intermarriage" (1983, 271) and that Indian women were the primary agents in this process. Today it is hard to appreciate the enormous contribution that Deagan made to historical archaeology because her influence is so ubiquitous that her contributions are simply assumed to have always been part of the discipline. But as Ross Jamieson recently put it, "She was one of the first researchers to turn historical archaeology into a serious anthropological enterprise, taking potsherds and rusty nails and turning them into debates about colonialism, identity, and the birth of the modern world" (2008, 880). And she was groundbreaking in her consideration of gender in this process and in giving indigenous women credit for their contributions in the creation of colonial culture (Voss 2006, 112). Nowadays, of course, some of her interpretations are being questioned. For example, several archaeologists have pointed out that indigenous women in St. Augustine (as elsewhere) were not just confined to domestic roles; instead, they were also active in politics, and some had important economic roles as entrepreneurs, merchants, and artisans as well (see Voss 2008 for a critique of Deagan's hypothesis).

Women and the Middle Class

There have been several studies of middle-class women living in cities in the United States. In looking at these women in early nineteenth-century New York City, Diana Wall examined the role of their agency in the creation of the "cult of domesticity" (1987, 1994). She noted that in colonial times, homes and workplaces were situated in the same buildings, and women played prominent roles in business. But by the mid-nineteenth century, homes and workplaces were located in separate spaces in separate neighborhoods, and middle-class women were virtually confined to their homes or to nurturing roles in society at large. Wall wanted to find out who actually instigated this change—some scholars saw women as victims whose roles were redefined by men and the larger society, while others looked on women as actors in their own right who, along with men, contributed to the restructuring of gender relations. Wall thought that if she could see that women were enhancing domestic life in the old, combined homes and workplaces *before* the spatial separation of the home and workplace occurred, it would suggest that women were actors alongside men in the development of a separate domestic sphere. To explore this issue, she looked at a number of variables for middle-class homes: the increase in the number of domestic servants to help with the growing load of housework; the decrease in the number of children as they became redefined as responsibilities who had to be educated as opposed to being the helpful "little hands" they had been before; and the enhancement of those aspects of domestic life that focused on meals, particularly the dishes used in family dinner. Men and children who had worked together at home in colonial times now went out to work and school, respectively, and returned home late in the day to family dinner, a meal that became more and more important as a family reunion.

Wall discovered that she could see these changes in domestic life beginning in the old, combined homes and workplaces. As time went by in the early nineteenth century, there were more and more servants and fewer and fewer children in these households. She could also see family dinners becoming more important inside the combined homes and workplaces of the city's middle class, as evidenced by the fact that the dishes that women used to serve this meal became fancier and more expensive (Wall 1994). Taken together, the data showed that women began to take the initial steps toward an elaboration of domestic life—steps that led to the creation of the cult of domesticity—inside the combined homes and workplaces in New York, and Wall suggested that women were not simply victims but that they (as well as men) were active in instigating this change. Wall's study was important in that it was one of the first to show how material culture could be used to talk about questions of social change among European Americans in the relatively recent past.

Changing Notions of Masculinity among the Late Nineteenth- and Early Twentieth-Century Middle Class

Gender, of course, is a relational category, and in any specific era and community, the culture of women exists only in relation to the culture of men (and vice versa). But as noted above, gender studies in historical archaeology (and elsewhere) have been biased in that they have focused for the most part on women. There are a couple of exceptions to this, however, and some focus on the construction of masculinity in urban areas. One is Laurie Wilkie's study of Zeta Psi, a University of California fraternity (2010). New construction on the Berkeley campus offered Wilkie the opportunity to conduct an archaeological study of the fraternity and to open two windows on fraternity life, one from an early period (1876–1909) and the other from more recent times (1909–56). Using material culture (including not only archaeological artifacts but also the architectural details of one of the fraternity houses itself), as well as historical records and oral histories, she was able to examine how changes in fraternity life over time facilitated the redefinition of masculinity among elite men. During the early period, the Victorian ideal of the "civilized man" was based on ties of brotherhood created through the vocabulary of nurturing in female domestic space. This was supported by the use in the fraternity of the same plain white china used in middle-class homes, evoking "the sanctity of home life" (Wilkie 2010, 257). Later, in the second period, the masculine ideal had changed to one evoking strength, rigor, and even brutality. Then, members no longer used plain white dishes but ones decorated with the fraternity's crest. While sympathetic to fraternity life, Wilkie is by no means an apologist for the misogynist aspects of fraternity culture that have come to be more and more evident in the most recent phase of the fraternity's history. But she underlines the important roles that fraternities played in providing a safe haven for the social reproduction of privileged white masculinity and the reification of white male power and the role that material culture plays in this process.

Another interesting study looks at the intersection of gender, race, and ethnicity. This is Bryn Williams's study of masculinity among Chinese immigrants in San Jose (2008). Chinese began to immigrate to the United States in numbers with the gold rush, and they stayed on to work on the railroads (see chapters 4 and 5). During the first phase of Chinese immigration, as among many other immigrant groups, the newcomers consisted predominantly of men, who might, after they had established themselves, send for their families. The Chinese exclusion acts of the late nineteenth century were passed in response to protests by many European Americans against the Chinese presence, particularly in the West, and constitute the only American immigration laws that targeted a specific racial group. The passage of the exclusion acts denied the reunification of families by forbidding the immigration of the wives and children of all but the richest merchants. This exclusion led to the creation of so-called bachelor societies.

Williams has looked at definitions of masculinity among the Chinese as constructed by westerners and the Chinese themselves and has explored how these concepts used material culture in their articulation. As we mentioned in chapter 5, westerners tend to view "the East" through the prism of orientalism (Said 1978), whereby all things and individuals from "the East" are interpreted not on their own terms but in contrast to "the West." From the western perspective, one of the tenets embedded in orientalism is the feminization of Chinese culture and of Chinese people, including men. In terms of material culture, this feminization was reified in the West in *chinoiserie,* objects made in a decorative style that originated in China but that were made specifically for the western trade. *Chinoiserie* objects were extremely popular from the sixteenth through much of the nineteenth century in the West, where they were considered part of the decorative arts and therefore were associated with western women. The westerners' image of Chinese men as feminine was reinforced, particularly after the end of the gold rush and the completion of the transcontinental railroad, when they began to settle in western cities. There, many aspects of traditionally masculine Chinese culture as expressed in materiality—their traditional clothing; their long braids or queues; their use of tiny, delicate "teacups" for drinking alcohol—contributed to their feminization in western eyes. Some of their occupations—many operated restaurants and laundries, services traditionally associated with women in western (as well as eastern) culture—added to their feminized image among westerners (Williams 2008).

This "oriental" stereotype of Chinese masculinity among westerners was counterbalanced by two other definitions of masculinity as set forth by the Chinese themselves as expressed in the masculine concepts of *wen* and *wu*. *Wen*, associated with elites, encompassed genteel male qualities as expressed in artistic pursuits, while *wu* embodied the idea of military strength, particularly among the working class. The *wu* expression of masculinity includes such feats as being able to consume large quantities of alcohol in a controlled manner, one aspect of which involved the use of the tiny "teacups." These same "teacups," then, that through western eyes were associated with femininity and gentility, through Chinese eyes were associated with masculinity and working-class life. They provide wonderful examples of multivalence and of how the same objects (such as these cups) can become material manifestations of different meanings in cultural discourses among different groups of people (Williams 2008).

Gender and the Nineteenth-Century Working Class

Archaeologists working in America's cities have done several studies of working-class women, particularly those of Irish descent. These scholars include Steven Brighton (2001, 2005, 2009), Heather Griggs (2001), and Rebecca Yamin (2001), all of whom used data from the Five Points site in New York, and Anne Yentsch (2011), who used data from the San Francisco Bay area. Yentsch's study particularly provides a fascinating picture of Irish women in an American urban environment.

In the mid-nineteenth century, the ideologies of native-born middle-class women and of Irish-born working-class women were almost diametrically opposed. Following the Irish ideology surrounding femininity during that period and which the Irish carried overseas with them in the diaspora, women were expected to be strong and assertive. In Ireland, women were wage earners and entrepreneurs and had financial power almost equal to their husbands. They could own property and often served as the financial managers for their families. And they were also culturally different from their counterparts in the United States (Yentsch 2011). Theirs was not a life of plenty, and they had relatively few objects around the house. Furthermore, their meals were very different—they did not sit down at a table to a meal the family consumed together. Instead, family members sat at the hearth on three-legged stools and ate their dinner, with a wife serving her husband first; she and the children ate later, only after he had finished. The cult of domesticity prevalent among the European American middle class in that period, on the other hand, incorporated the ideals of "purity, piety, domesticity, and submissiveness" to make women "timid, passive, and dependent" (Yentsch 2011, 176). In the middle-class homes in the United States where many young Irish women found work as domestics, their employers considered assertion and strong-mindedness to be "impertinence" (Yentsch 2011).

Looking at Irish immigrant women in Oakland in the nineteenth century, Yentsch discovered that they were both active on their own behalf and assertive, like their sisters at home. They owned property and invested in commercial ventures; their families owned homes at higher rates than the members of other working-class immigrant groups or the middle class. And the material record of these Irish families showed that they had much less concern for middle-class definitions of gentility than their native-born neighbors. They eschewed the white ironstone dishes that were so ubiquitous in middle-class homes, preferring the blue-on-white dishes in the willow pattern that they had cherished in Ireland (Yentsch 2011; Brighton 2005; Wall 2002). And they also preferred pork for their dinners, even though fish was less expensive (Walker 2009).

Later in the century, much of this had changed. Irish women—both first and second generation—were more like their native-born middle-class sisters: they began serving their dinners on white ironstone plates. Several archaeologists have suggested that this might mean that the Irish were adopting the trappings of an American identity and were interested in being perceived as "genteel" members of the middle class (Brighton 2005; Yamin 2001).

Prostitution in the Nineteenth-Century City

During the last two decades, archaeologists led by Donna Seifert have begun to look at prostitution in several cities. These studies were undertaken because a number of development projects required archaeological study in areas that in the nineteenth century had been red-light districts. Archaeologists have unearthed assemblages associated with several brothels in Washington, D.C. (Seifert 1991, 1994; Seifert et al. 2000; Seifert and Balicki 2005), and they have discovered others in New York (Yamin 2005), St. Paul (Ketz et al. 2005), and Los Angeles (Meyer et al. 2005). Their work has underlined the great diversity of brothels that catered to different clienteles. There were high-end parlor houses located in townhouses in the East (e.g., Seifert and Balicki 2005), where prostitutes often knew their clients personally. There were also low-end bawdy houses that catered to everyone. Some, like one in New York (Yamin 2005), were located in basements, while in the West they were often located in "cribs," which were made up of a string of extremely small rooms, each with its own door, laid out in a row, like old-fashioned motels. These architectural differences were also expressed in the artifacts associated with the brothels. In the fancier ones, where girls both lived and worked, archaeologists found exotic foods and fancy dishes for serving clients (Yamin 2005), while the artifacts from the cribs, where no one lived but which a prostitute could hire for the period of a few hours, were extremely sparse (Meyer et al. 2005).

The material culture discovered has provided some insights into the lives of prostitutes and the business of prostitution in the late nineteenth century. Following Donna Seifert, several of these studies have compared the artifacts from brothels with those from contemporary working-class and middle-class homes that were nearby. Not unexpectedly, these comparisons have shown that the brothels exhibit a higher proportion of artifacts associated with grooming and hygiene (including medicine bottles) than working-class homes, reflecting the occupational plusses and hazards of the trade. But more interestingly, the fancier brothels also served diverse and exotic kinds of foods, whether meats or fruits, on fancy dishes. Several authors interpreted this to mean that the prostitutes were able to enjoy a higher standard of living than their working-class sisters who lived at home with their families, but one analysis suggests that this in fact was not the case. A study in St. Paul (Ketz et al. 2005) included excavations in both the front- and backyards of a brothel. The archaeologists discovered that the artifacts and food remains from the front yard—adjacent to where clients were being entertained—reflected a high standard of living, while those from the backyard—near where the prostitutes were living—reflected a standard of living similar to that of the working-class homes. In other words, although the women might have provided exotic foods served from fancy plates when they were entertaining their clients, when they were not working they ate foods similar to those that their working-class sisters ate. Furthermore, there were many more drug bottles from the backyard deposits—underlining the harsh reality of venereal and other kinds of diseases that could be a lethal occupational hazard. In fact, nine empty quart-sized bottles that had held Darby's Prophylactic Fluid, used to ward off both conception and disease, were found associated with the brothel in Los Angeles (Meyer et al. 2005).

Birth control was a concern for most women in the nineteenth century, both among the middle class, where women were interested in keeping birthrates down, and the working class, particularly for prostitutes. Vaseline and boric acid blended into a salve was a popular form of birth control that was also thought to ward off venereal disease (Meyer et al. 2005, 120). Many empty Vaseline jars were found in the brothel features—a dozen came from the Los Angeles privy alone (Meyer et al. 2005, 120). Archaeologists have found containers for vinegar, which may have been used as a spermicide in douches; they have also found fragments of douche syringes (Yamin 2005; Meyer et al. 2005).

Perhaps also related to birth control were the poignant remains of three infants that archaeologists found in the privy associated with a New York brothel (Crist 2005). Two of them had come to term; it is not known if they died of natural causes or were the victims of infanticide. The third, who had not reached term, had aborted, either deliberately or spontaneously. But none of these infants had been buried; instead, their bodies were disposed of secretly, hidden in the backyard privy.

Women and Institutions

Archaeologists have studied several urban institutions associated primarily or exclusively with women, including almshouses and reform societies. In the late 1980s Sherene Baugher directed the excavation of an eighteenth-century almshouse in New York City. Most of its inmates were women and children, because in the eighteenth century, it was they who were looked on as the "deserving poor" and thus entitled to charity. The excavations uncovered the remains of a building thought to have served as the almshouse kitchen. The artifacts suggest that the inmates were making clothing, either for themselves or to sell. Among them were a number of bone buttons and straight pins. In addition, there were bone button blanks, showing that the inmates were manufacturing buttons as well. Although it was thought that the children had a dreary life of work in the almshouse, they also had at least some time for play—the archaeologists discovered a number of marbles at the site (Baugher 2001).

There are also several examples of projects that focused on women and reform among both the working class and the middle class. Using a feminist approach and drawing in part on the work of Dolores Hayden, Suzanne Spencer-Wood has written a great deal about the domestic reform movements that middle-class women organized in Boston during the nineteenth century (e.g., 1991). These movements encouraged the use of the built environment to promote gender equality, with the professionalization of housework and the development of cooperative housekeeping. The movement succeeded in challenging the dominant Victorian ideology. Spencer-Wood urges additional archaeological study of these sites.

During the nineteenth and twentieth centuries, there were also a number of institutions that members of the middle class formed to protect working-class women from the exploitation—sexual and/or economic—that was inherent in the city, according to popular views of the time. Lu Ann De Cunzo made a study of the Magdalen Society and its Asylum, an institution designed to reform "fallen" women in nineteenth-century Philadelphia (1995; 2001). Looking on "reform" as a purification ritual, she was able to demonstrate the importance of the Asylum's architecture, foodways, and dress in that ritual's enactment. Anna Agbe-Davies has been working with community activists on the South Side of Chicago in excavating the site of the early twentieth-century Phyllis Wheatley Home for Girls, which had been run by members of the Phyllis Wheatley Club, a voluntary association for middle-class African American women. Its inmates were young women who had recently arrived in the city from the rural South, often as part of the Great Migration. In addition to safe housing, the home's goal was to provide guidance and "domestic education" for the girls. This project has two parts. Its research component is geared toward examining how "material culture was used to create and reinforce notions of femininity" among the African American girls in the segregated city, while its activist part is focused on highlighting the use of the past "as a tool for social change through education and economic opportunity through heritage tourism" (Agbe-Davies 2008).

Projects like Agbe-Davies's, where an archaeological program is used as a meaningful component of community action, have begun to play an important role in archaeological study during the past few years. In the next chapter we discuss some of these movements that have taken place in urban areas, as well as the cemeteries where many of these movements began.

7

Cemeteries and Commemoration in the City

ARCHAEOLOGISTS DO NOT WORK just in the past; they have also been active in bringing the past into the present, reminding those alive today about people whose lives have often been forgotten. Sometimes this process includes the recovery of lost sites. Cemeteries represent a special class of such sites; and the stories associated with them are intriguing, and the information they contain is often unparalleled in importance. The excavation of these sites has opened the way for the civic engagement of archaeologists with descendant and local communities. This is referred to as community or public archaeology, and many archaeologists today are adopting it as their niche within the profession.

Working with modern-day groups, they use the materiality of the archaeological record to tell stories about peoples, places, and events of the past that have been forgotten and bring them into living memory. Many of these projects have been in urban areas. In this chapter we discuss both the excavation of urban cemeteries and some urban archaeological projects that have involved public participation in understanding the relationship between past and present.

The Study of Urban Cemeteries

The dead are always important to society, valued and/or feared, and are treated variably depending on the time and place and who they are. The transition from being a member of a living society to joining the majority is a difficult one for everyone and is ritualized at multiple points along the way. These points include the treatment of the body, where it is placed on the landscape, and how the living should behave. Attitudes toward the dead were not and are not uniform from one group to another, and among European Americans they were inherited initially from the various colonizers who settled in different parts of what is now the United States. Cities, with their valuable real estate, face particular problems in preserving spaces for the dead, and those designated for the poor and members of marginal groups are often forgotten entirely.

Here, we consider urban cemeteries as valuable in several ways. First is the information they contain about urban growth patterns and changing attitudes toward the dead, which we can infer by noting the placement of cemeteries and their arrangement and rearrangement on the urban landscape. Second, we may observe the manifestation of specific historicized ideas concerning the disposition of the dead because cities, with their relatively large and varied populations, often bring together a range of ideas and practices and reveal new as well as old customs in the same space. We discuss two important sets of ideas below, the concept of a "Good Death" and a nineteenth-century movement called the "Beautification of Death." Third, many studies have focused on the ways in which the dead and their treatment express the social, economic, racial, and ethnic structure of the city, examining, for example, the arrangement of cemetery space and variation in grave markers. Some differences among the living are inscribed in the bodies themselves, because some of the difficult conditions of their lives and deaths leave physical traces. Urban cemeteries are particularly revealing because they yield such large samples of the dead. In cases where bioarchaeologists are able to study the human remains and forms of burial before reinterment, we can learn a great deal of primary information that cannot be recovered by any other means. Age at death, sex, diet and health, types of disease, skeletal modifications through repeated muscular actions: all of these offer glimpses of how people lived in the past. DNA analysis can provide information of peoples' origins, life histories, and connections; bones and teeth reveal childhood diet.

Cemeteries, Their Composition, and the Urban Landscape

Early colonial American cemeteries were located within the community. In colonial cities, people often tried to contain the dead in religious institutions, burying them under church floors (such as in New Mexico) or in adjacent graveyards (as at Trinity Church, New York City). However, not everyone was welcome in a graveyard associated with a religious institution, and the institutions got more particular as to whom they would bury, privileging the devout or the elite, as time went by. In some urban communities, a common burying place continued in use until its spaces got filled. As urban centers expanded, they needed to find additional places to dispose of their dead. Later landscapes show that people began to separate the dead from the living (Will de Chaparro 2007, xvi), placing cemeteries at the edges of the settlement.

One aspect of attitudes toward death is reflected in the composition of cemeteries and who was buried in them. In some cases, even within a common ground, the cemetery landscape replicated the community's social structure, so that the cemetery was racially and socially segregated (Davidson 2004, 46). This practice accelerated as cities expanded; urbanization is often associated with increasing socioeconomic stratification. The imposition of class and racial structures on the burial of the dead correlates with urban growth, and cemeteries themselves acquire particular statuses. An extreme form of separation is seen in potter's fields, burial sites for those without members of the living community to pay for their interment, usually the poor and unknown but also other marginal community members. The existence of such places is ancient in cities of the world, but they first appeared in American cities late in the eighteenth century, and they are still in use today.

Cemeteries that are not part of other institutions or that are used by those excluded from other graveyards (such as New York's African Burial Ground) are usually located away from town centers, mirroring another element of landscape practice (or urban planning) which places devalued, dangerous, and/or land-extensive activities on urban peripheries. Miasmatic theories of disease sometimes played a part in the placement of cemeteries. This belief that the circulation of bad air (miasmas) led to disease and equating bad smells with epidemics persisted until the mid-nineteenth century (Heilen and Gray 2011, 169; Will de Chaparro 2007, 142). Of course, as cities grew, their edges, including their cemeteries, were incorporated within settled space, and the latter were paved over, turned into parks, or developed as part of the city.

When cemeteries were redeveloped, sometimes an effort was made to remove the human remains, but not always, and even when such an effort was made, many of the bodies, particularly those in unmarked graves, were left behind. So the archaeological studies associated with today's new urban development projects often lead to rediscovering these forgotten places. These studies have contributed to community life by recovering these extinct places for the dead and bringing them into living memory. Not only are the dead remembered anew but their lives are revived and made meaningful to the living today, along with the period in which they lived. Occasionally the bodies are left in the ground and the cemetery is preserved, but usually the bodies are moved and then reinterred somewhere else as the development moves ahead.

Sites of Common Burial

There are at least four archaeologically examined examples of cemeteries where all the dead were buried in the same location, regardless of religion. We look at Shannon Dawdy's work in New Orleans, James Davidson's research in Dallas, David Pollack et al.'s work in Frankfort, Kentucky, and a project directed by Michael Heilen in Tucson. Burials were exposed in an early New Orleans cemetery (St. Peter's), in use between 1725 and 1788 (Dawdy 2008, 139), during construction of a condominium building in 1994. The recovered sample was small and racially mixed (although see below on the difficulties of assigning meaningful racial categories to human remains). "People of African, European, and Indian ancestry, as well as those of mixed ancestries, lay side by side in simple wooden coffins" (Dawdy and Matthews 2010, 9). Most of the burials were African men, but there were also European and African European adults, and European or racially mixed children, including at least one of mixed Native American and European heritage (Dawdy 2008, 140). But despite the differences in ancestry, there were few differences among them in terms of burial treatment. All the coffins were simple, and no objects were found with the bodies, except for one individual who was buried with a jeweled rosary, saints' medals, and an elaborate medallion. Dawdy notes that in the eighteenth century, cemetery areas were held by families or households, regardless of wealth, and she suspects that those in adjacent plots were related, with spaces between coffins kept for later burials (an interpretation that perhaps now could be evaluated with DNA analysis). This spatially orderly, but racially diverse, collection suggests to Dawdy that racial mixing (métissage) was a consistent and consensual practice.

The Old Frankfort Cemetery in Frankfort, the capital of nineteenth-century Kentucky, was discovered by workmen in 2002 as backhoes were preparing the land for a new state building. No headstones or other evidence marked this cemetery, and no one knew that it was there. First (1810) it was located at the edge of town, but then in the 1830s it was incorporated with town growth and became a neighborhood graveyard. It was used by all, the elite, the poor, and members of the working class, whether of European, African, or mixed heritage. More than 240 people were buried there, 38 percent of whom were under thirteen (Pollack et al. 2009, 29).

In the mid-1840s a new cemetery was begun on a bluff overlooking the old one; some contemporary accounts refer to the dilapidated condition of the Old Frankfort Cemetery, and some of those buried in the old cemetery were moved to the new one. The old cemetery was in use before the undertaking industry was developed after the Civil War, so the burials were prepared by family and friends and were not embalmed. Most of the dead were buried in simple clothing or shrouds; a few had jewelry or coins placed on their eyelids; one European man had eyeglasses in his shirt pocket. Although most were in wooden hexagonal or rectangular coffins, some were in stone-lined graves. A few had limestone slabs placed over the coffin so that the earth would not crush it.

Studies of the bones revealed variations in diet; for some individuals (presumably poorer ones) as much as 75 percent of their diet came from corn and corn-based foods, resulting in deficiencies in some essential vitamins and protein. Almost all burials showed incidents of nutritional stress when the individuals were young (with enamel hypoplasias on their teeth and Harris lines on their long bones), suggesting that most children were weaned early. There is considerable evidence of arthritis, even among children, presumably related to physical labor performed during life. Other illnesses, such as staphylococcus infection, tuberculosis, cerebral palsy, rickets, and brucellosis (from pigs or unpasteurized milk; Pollack et al. 2009, 35), indicate the difficulties of these lives. After excavation and analysis, the human remains from the Old Frankfort Cemetery were reburied in the later cemetery at the top of the bluff.

A similar process of cemetery replacement was seen at another Kentucky cemetery, this one in Louisville (Stottman 2010), but although this cemetery was used by all, the space was organized to match social divisions among the living. The Western Cemetery was Louisville's second, created at the edge of the city when the first was filled in the 1830s. It was divided into segments: one for community members and one for strangers. Private plots lay in the center, and Catholics and Africans were buried at either end of the space. The first landscaped, garden-type cemetery (Cave Hill) was developed in Louisville in the 1840s, and it became the preferred burial place for the town. The Western Cemetery continued in use, but it was not maintained. The headstones were removed or broken, and a playground and park were established there. A 1992 traffic improvement project brought the cemetery back into public awareness. The archaeologists identified more than 600 grave shafts and estimated that thousands might still remain, so the proposed project was curtailed.

The Alameda-Stone Cemetery

A recent project involving the construction of new law courts in the city of Tucson resulted in a major urban cemetery excavation completed in 2008. It was conducted by SRI with contributions by many archaeologists; ultimate oversight was by Roger Anyon of Pima County. The Joint Courts Complex was planned in an area containing the Alameda-Stone (or National) Cemetery, which was in use from 1862 until 1881, from the Territorial Period until after Tucson became a city in 1877. The project was important because the cemetery was so large. It included at least 1,800 burials (Heilen and Gray 2011, 12), and all of Tucson's dead (Native Americans, Hispanics, and Anglo-Americans) were buried there. There was also a small military component. The civilian cemetery was closed in 1875 and the military one in 1881, as Tucson's expansion required the land upon which the old cemetery was located. Beginning in 1890, the area was developed and redeveloped, and all surface traces of the cemetery including fences, walls, headstones, burial vaults, and other markers were destroyed. Archaeological excavation, however, uncovered the remains of close to 1,400 burials, of which almost half were undisturbed. Members of several descendant communities (including Hispanics, Native Americans, veterans of the armed forces, Catholics, and Jews) were consulted as the project moved forward.

Five areas were identified within the cemetery, one for the military and their families and four for civilians. This division was evident based on variations in grave size, depth, spacing, density, burial orientation, and gaps between graves (Heilen and Gray 2011, 5, 238). One of the areas may have been the portion of the site in which the church had been located, as burials there were more densely packed than in the others. Graves in the northern part of the cemetery tended to have their heads facing east (toward the chapel); those in the south had heads facing west. The northern portion of the cemetery included mostly Hispanic individuals (based on a combination of contextual, osteological, and historic evidence), of whom more than 50 percent were juveniles, whereas the southern part contained European American men primarily.

Analysis of Hispanic burial customs showed that burials were generally simple, in wooden coffins, oriented on an east–west alignment, without grave markers or costly mortuary accessories. Some coffins were painted bright colors. Some buttons from clothing and small religious or personal items (such as picture frames, bottles, pipes, toys [associated with children], and tools) were interred with the dead. Some objects were engendered: men were associated with coins and particular forms of buttons while women and children had more items of adornment, and Hispanic children were often buried with floral crowns (some of the artificial flowers were recovered [Heilen 2012, 170]). Rosaries often accompanied adults, but religious medals were found with both adults and children.

Osteological analysis on this burial population produced abundant information on health and disease. For example, enamel hypoplasias (indicative of nutritional stress) and dental caries (suggesting a high sugar content in diet) were higher among European Americans in the southern portion of the cemetery, whereas more osteoporosis and work-related bone changes were found among the Hispanic dead (Heilen and Gray 2011, 238). There was more evidence of systemic infection among the adult males in the southern area (members of the military and travelers), although active disease at death was found more commonly among juveniles than adults.

One of the significant aspects of the report on the Alameda-Stone Cemetery lies in its use of comparative data from a number of other roughly contemporaneous cemeteries. These show differences in (1) work-related body changes seen in joint degeneration (different locations of evidence of stress on the body suggests different work patterns requiring specific muscles), (2) diet and nutritional stress, (3) dental pathologies by gender and ethnicity, and (4) the rate of epidemic disease within the population. Some indicators of nutritional stress (cribra orbitalia, porotic hyperostosis) were found in several of the cemeteries analyzed in the Alameda-Stone report. It appears that the bones of children in all cemeteries examined showed evidence of infection (periosteal new bone, osteomyelitis), nutritional stress (enamel hypoplasias), or trauma and at consistently higher frequencies than the adults buried in the same cemeteries. Close to 45 percent of adult bodies (and 55 percent of males from all cemeteries) showed evidence of trauma, although surprisingly, given Tucson's reputation as a wild frontier town, few traumatic injuries were from weapons (Heilen and Gray 2011, 193–94). The intensive analysis of data from this cemetery reveals how productive archaeological investigations of burials can be.

The "Good Death"

Historical and archaeological study of the treatment of the dead during the eighteenth century in the Catholic and Spanish-influenced areas of Arizona and New Mexico reveal significant differences between them and the British and Protestant-dominated eastern portion of the United States. However, by the mid-nineteenth century, most Americans had accepted the baroque concept of a "Good Death," which required the dying person to be among the living at the moment of death. It also involved the person's recognition of impending death, a willingness to accept death, and an expression of belief in God (Faust 2008).

Similar to keeping the dying person within the living community, the cemetery was an important part of the local landscape in the eighteenth-century American Southwest. It was neither physically nor conceptually separated from the space of the living (Will de Chaparro 2007, 113). The process of death incorporated the living both before and after the moment of death, and bodies were not afforded much in the way of processing (Heilen and Gray 2011, 219). Many were buried under a church floor, preferably close to relics of saints, so that when others walked on the bones of kin and friends it made them aware of their own future deaths. In the Southwest, the population beneath the floor was often mixed, with Spanish, Indian, and Mestizo present, reflecting the living population (Will de Chaparro 2007, 115). The absence of grave markers may suggest piety (Heilen and Gray 2011, 222) and less concern with social hierarchy than was found in Europe (Heilen 2012, 71), but it also meant that graves were reused, new burials intruded into older ones, and bodies were concentrated in specific areas (Heilen and Gray 2011, 221).

In many urban communities, a number of concurrent processes occurred from the mid-eighteenth century onward. In the Southwest a series of public health reforms promoted new ideas about urban life and new institutions to protect citizens, including marginal people such as the sick and those considered undesirable, condemning dirty streets and open sewers, roaming animals, and public drunks (Will de Chaparro 2007, 143). Bodily hygiene was extended to larger ideas about society, and plazas were swept, animals confined, midwives licensed, and dogs leashed. New rules banned throwing garbage in rivers, and information about smallpox, other diseases, and inoculation was made available.

Burial reforms were part of the innovations in scientific and medical issues, changing ideas of where authority lay and what role the individual played in society. Around this time, it began to be thought important to separate the dead from the living, suggesting that it was now thought that cohabitation was dangerous and calling for less crowded cemeteries. As well, elites began to think churches should be places of propriety, piety, and sober thoughts, whereas cemeteries were seen as more mundane spaces, and burials became more secular and less elaborate. Health concerns for the living won out so that the dead were moved away, and finally in the late nineteenth century cemeteries came under civil control. Albuquerque and other cities built secular cemeteries for all, and the state assumed authority over death and burial, while traditional ways survived in rural areas.

The "Beautification of Death"

The set of customs associated with the "Beautification of Death" movement emerged during the Civil War, when hundreds of thousands of soldiers died at a distance from their homes. Death far away, on the battlefield, in a prison or hospital, interfered with the practice of a "Good Death," as loved ones were not present, although friends, chaplains, and others tried to replicate the environment of a loving community for the dying (Faust 2008, 12, 14). These problems generated the wish to preserve the body of a loved one by embalming it and creating refrigerated coffins, so at least some of these men could be shipped home and viewed by their loved ones before burial. A concurrent development was the emergence of death specialists or undertakers (Heilen and Gray 2011, 223), mostly based in cities. The "Beautification of Death" movement expressed Victorian concepts that romanticized and idealized the dead. It generated elaborate burial and mourning practices and led to innovations in the way the body was treated after death, the use of elaborate coffins and hardware, the creation of park-like cemeteries, and mourning customs, including special jewelry, clothing, and behavior.

Here, we discuss two excavations that reveal the impact of this movement on mortuary populations in Dallas (Davidson 2004), and in Alexandria, Virginia (Bromberg and Shephard 2006, 175). This movement was not restricted to the upper economic strata of society; some of the available coffin hardware was relatively inexpensive and was found, for example, in paupers' graves in Uxbridge, Massachusetts, leading one archaeologist, Edward Bell, to suggest that the presence of these elements represents an archaeological horizon (1990, 50).

The Freedman's Cemetery

Dallas was established in 1841 as an agricultural town, with some enslaved blacks working on local farms (Davidson 2004, 18). In spite of the fact that Reconstruction was marked by intense violence against blacks, James Davidson notes that Dallas became a magnet for free African Americans, and a number of Free African American communities were established on its periphery. As Reconstruction ended in 1872 and white supremacy was restored, episodes of racial violence were somewhat reduced. There were also some short-lived interracial cooperative efforts in the labor movement in the 1890s.

The Freedman's cemetery in Dallas opened just after the Old Burial Ground, formerly used by all, was closed in 1869 (McDavid 2011; Davidson 2004, 62). It continued in use until 1907, after African Americans had established a new, orderly, park-like burial place, Woodland Cemetery, in 1901. The old cemetery was partially excavated when a highway expansion project necessitated the removal of more than 1,100 burials from a place which had, like so many other urban cemeteries, been transformed into a city park.

In examining the cemetery data, Davidson focused on the intersection of race and class with mortuary behavior. He interpreted that the choice of elaborate coffins and expensive hardware—evidence of the "Beautification of Death" movement—expressed resistance to the domination of white culture but incorporated some of the symbols of the racist society to do so. Some contemporary observers noted that it was improper for the "lower classes" to have expensive funerals, missing the point that those who did so were actually members of the middle class. Davidson cites Mullins's views on consumption and suggests that in Dallas, as elsewhere, postbellum African Americans used the acquisition of material goods to demonstrate that they were neither inferior nor indigent (Mullins 1999). Davidson found that whereas paupers had no coffin hardware or decoration (2004, 222), the money spent on such elements by other African Americans increased over time.

Davidson also examined vernacular inclusions in a small number of graves that he saw as authentically African or at least incorporating traditional African American elements. Knives, ceramic bowls, medicine bottles, dolls, coins, and other items were found in graves; historical accounts suggest that these and other items such as shells and household objects were placed on top of graves after they were filled in. A single shoe was sometimes placed on the coffin lid here and in other African American cemeteries (e.g., the First African Baptist Church in Philadelphia) to trap the devil. Davidson suggests that some of these customs have metaphorical significance (such as seashells suggesting a connection to the soul or lamps upon a grave to lead the soul to the spirit world),[1] while others were spiritually relevant (including things touched by the dead person just prior to death, dishes, and medicine). His interesting conclusion is that there were two mutually exclusive groups of people using the Freedman's Cemetery: those who chose to adhere to an "African" or traditional mortuary ritual and those who participated in the "Beautification of Death" movement. The latter were members of the middle class, whereas the former were working class. Davidson shows that more money was spent on the funerals of middle-class women (defined as those without osteoarthritis) than on those who were involved in heavy labor. The intersection of race and class appears in many aspects of culture; we should not be surprised that it is part of the set of behaviors surrounding death. Randall McGuire's work, discussed below, provides additional evidence of the phenomenon in which earlier graves mask social differences whereas later ones emphasize them.

Quaker Burying Ground, Alexandria

Bromberg and Shephard's (2006) archaeological assessment of burial practices among the Society of Friends living in late eighteenth- and nineteenth-century Virginia represents another examination of the influence of the "Beautification of Death" movement. It is based on the excavation of sixty-four burials before the construction of a library. Because this new set of beliefs was accompanied by material symbols (inscriptions on headstones, increased decoration of coffins, and special Victorian mourning dress and ritual), the Quakers are an interesting case study to examine (Bromberg and Shephard 2006, 64, 183). They were an educated, relatively affluent population with an avowed commitment to egalitarianism, simple speech and dress, and an avoidance of ostentation in burial. "The corpse is deposed in a plain coffin . . . depriving the dead body of ornaments and outward honors. For stripped in this manner, they conceive it to approach to its nearest worthlessness of dust" (Clarkson, cited in Bromberg 2000, 177).

The archaeologists were interested in whether later Quaker burials at this cemetery showed the influence of the "Beautification of Death" movement in their treatment of the dead, and thus examined such elements as coffin style, decoration, and artifacts included in graves. They also were interested in determining the health of the deceased as seen through the examination of their teeth. The bodies were generally in poor condition, and although the contemporary Society of Friends did not wish to subject them to detailed osteological analysis, they thought it was appropriate to investigate the teeth as well as the coffins and their trimmings.

The archaeologists found that indeed there was evidence of the adoption of some "Beautification of Death" practices, seen in a concern for prolonging the preservation of the body, associated with burials which appeared to be from the later nineteenth century. Coffin decoration was also found among some of the late-period burials. The archaeologists noted that the rate of coffin decoration was lower than at the potter's field in Uxbridge, Massachusetts, and much lower than in the cemetery of a wealthy family in Manassas, Virginia (Bromberg 2000). Gravestones continued to be simple in all periods, perhaps because these were visible to all.

Serious childhood disease was prevalent even among this relatively affluent and well-educated population; enamel hypoplasias were found, suggesting malnutrition and disease at early ages. Archaeologists anticipated evidence of dental work, but it was only found in two of the sixteen individuals with dental disease (Bromberg 2000, 371).

Cemeteries Reflecting Socioeconomic, Racial, and Ethnic Status

Several studies have used cemeteries to look at the construction of class, ethnicity, and race in various times and places. There seems to be a trend toward increasing stratification within and between cemeteries over time, as noted particularly in McGuire's (below) and Davidson's (above) reports, but hinted at in others. Archaeological information on racial or ethnic groups is most commonly found in the examination of African American cemeteries, although we note Michael Blakey's discussion of the problems associated with assigning racial categories to bodies, as these races are modern cultural constructs (Blakey and Rankin-Hill 2009).

However, an interesting excavation of the Chinese portion of the Lone Fir Cemetery in Portland, Oregon, by Nicholas Smits revealed a small cemetery with fewer than 300 bodies. There were so few bodies because most Chinese wanted to have their bones shipped back to China so that they could join their ancestors (Smits 2008, 111). An analysis of the artifacts recovered with the burials in the cemetery, in use between 1854 and 1928, was quite revealing. The majority of the artifacts were those that would have been used in feasts left at the grave for consumption by both the living and the dead, including meat, fruit, rice, wine, and liquor. Plants and flowers also served as offerings. The analysis of these materials suggests that the Chinese were maintaining aspects of their traditional mortuary customs but also participating in American consumer society by purchasing mass-produced goods such as undecorated white dishes or decorated vessels that were similar in design to Chinese wares. Smits believes that these artifacts reveal a transnational orientation for Portland's Chinese Americans, a hybrid identity that allowed the incorporation of selected elements from both traditions.

Broome County, New York

In Binghamton, New York, Randall McGuire examined gravestones and city records from the mid-nineteenth century to 1980 among a mostly European American burial population to see what gravestones could reveal about social stratification. He looked on the material culture found in cemeteries as expressing broad cultural attitudes toward death, mirroring the dominant ideology in a way that is nuanced and tempered by the issues urban elites faced as they were impacted by nineteenth-century industrial capitalism. Basically he found that sometimes gravestones mirror stratification and in other periods they do not but seem to follow broader social changes (McGuire 1988, 436–37). McGuire notes that as elites change their behavior, others do not always imitate them, with members of the working class especially resistant.

Broome County, in which Binghamton is situated, was a manufacturing center in the nineteenth century; factories there were known for their shoes and cigars. However, in the 1830s the people of Broome County began to perceive their old community cemeteries (which buried all community members) as filthy, unhealthy, and ugly. The new cemetery type, involving a lawn and a park-like landscape, was developed in the 1860s. The Victorians established a dialogue with the dead and saw the cemetery as linking the dead and living. However, by the early twentieth century, new ways of burying people developed and new types of stones and markers appeared in Binghamton. Family plots were organized around a large central monument associated with the eldest male, and other individuals were buried in relation to the central person. McGuire interprets phenomena dating to the early nineteenth-century cemetery as denying inequality and affirming an ideology that masks power relations. In the later nineteenth and early twentieth centuries, inequality was naturalized and emphasized in cemetery monuments by glorifying individual success. Then people competed to build the largest mausoleum or one that commanded the landscape from the highest ground. A concurrent development was the design of smaller, lower stones for working-class individuals, located on the edges of high prestige cemeteries or placed in separate burial grounds with lower prestige (see Davidson, above). However, in the early decades of the twentieth century, investments in monuments declined, and families developed new customs according to their ethnicity or religion, with some families continuing to erect mausoleums while others used smaller, more uniform markers. The overall appearance of cemeteries became more consistent and differences between individuals less relevant because the mass production that increased access to consumer goods across society made uniform gravestones available to all. After World War II, plots for a married couple replaced family ones, suggesting a decline in the significance of the extended family. McGuire believes one cannot interpret changes in the cemetery alone without examining broader changes in culture, family organization, and attitudes toward death.

Some ethnic groups reacted to changes in the dominant group with their own innovations, so that the material culture of cemeteries may objectify distinctions between groups. Separate Catholic cemeteries were established in Binghamton in the mid-nineteenth century, and Irish gravestones emulated Protestant trends, with a slight time lag. And Jewish cemeteries were developed there around that time; their gravestones were similar to other markers but centered on a Star of David rather than a cross, as these families aspired to middle-class, mainstream American positions.

Spring Street Presbyterian Church Cemetery

A very different type of cemetery, associated with a specific church, was found in conjunction with the proposed construction of a Trump hotel in New York City in 2006 and excavated by Douglas Mooney of URS Corporation, under the oversight of Diane Dallal of AKRF. This primarily working-class cemetery dated to the nineteenth century and was associated with a church that had been in existence from 1810 onward. It had a racially integrated congregation with abolitionist views and was destroyed in 1834 by an anti-abolitionist mob that was only finally dispersed by the National Guard. Some of the rioters then went on to destroy the home of its minister, an outspoken abolitionist. The church was rebuilt in 1836 and survived for more than a century until, with its congregation dwindling, it was dissolved in 1963. The archaeologists discovered three burial vaults containing mostly disarticulated bones from ninety-three individuals, although originally the cemetery included many more people. The normal nineteenth-century "regulation" of the vaults and then the final destruction of the property, which exposed and filled in the vaults in the 1960s, are responsible for a great deal of the disturbance to the human remains (Mooney et al. 2008, ii, 4.29). Analysis combining church documents and archaeological evidence suggests that the cemetery was in use from about 1820 to the early 1840s—during the period when the church was most active in the abolitionist cause.

Burials were placed in typical (for the time) hexagonal wooden coffins with flat tops so they could be stacked. Some coffins appear to have been stained or painted, but no other decorations were identified. Coffin plates giving the name, date of death, and exact age of the deceased were found, but they could not be associated with specific individuals. Research identified specific parishioners whose plates were recovered, giving a snapshot of some of the church's congregation. The extant burial population seems to represent a good cross-section of those who were in the congregation: adult men and women of varied ages, and a number of children; in one vault more than half of the bodies were of subadults. Shroud pins were by far the most frequent item found in graves; buttons and saucers were also quite common. Apparently both West African and European mortuary practices include placing a ceramic plate with the deceased (also noted in the Quaker Burying Ground report, Bromberg and Shephard 2006). In Scottish, Irish, and Welsh traditions, the plate was used for salt, and the report suggests there may have been an attempt to reduce odor by placing a mixture of salt and sulphuric acid in a dish, yielding a chlorine gas (Mooney et al. 2008, 5.34). The mostly working-class population did not demonstrate the kind of arthritic joint problems associated with heavy manual labor, as found at the African Burial Ground, discussed below, and there was little suggestion that tuberculosis was prevalent. Age at death varied by gender, with more than half of women dying under thirty years of age (presumably from childbirth-related factors), and few adults living past forty-five years. Over 40 percent of the children died before they were eighteen months old, but if they lived to that age, their chances of survival increased markedly.

Seeing Changing Attitudes toward African Americans in Burial Customs

An interesting insight into race relations is described by Leland Ferguson (2011) in discussing Moravian burial practices among the Wachovian community in North Carolina, mentioned in chapter 3. Initially the Moravians regarded slavery as "an act of providence that supplied the additional labor necessary for their project" (Ferguson 2011, 56), but they accepted Africans as members of their church community. Gradually, various forms of segregation developed, and in the mid-nineteenth century the Moravians built two racially separate cemeteries (Ferguson 2011, 63). By then, grave location was based on a number of parameters, including piety, race, gender, age, and rank, with strangers buried in the "non-white" cemetery. Initially all the dead had gravestones, but as segregation increased, many in the "lower" graveyard, which included African Americans, were in unmarked graves, and the earlier gravestones of African Americans were covered up or removed.

In another study, James Garman examined gravestones in Newport, Rhode Island, which also demonstrated how changes in race relations were expressed in burial practices. During the period of enslavement in that state, the stones of the African Americans listed their masters' names and the slave-master relationship, presumably because the master paid for the engraving (Garman 1994). Gravestones for blacks were similar in size to those for whites, suggesting size was standard, but had less carving, suggesting that the plainer ones cost less. After the revolution, as slavery formally ended in Rhode Island (but racism did not), grave markers changed, and all stones became more similar in style. However, those of the African Americans rarely mentioned race, which Garman interprets as a sign that the messages were directed to other members of the black community who would have known who the dead were (1994, 87).

Cemeteries, Communities, and Archaeology

Some of the most interesting cemetery projects have involved the study of human remains from black cemeteries, important in part because we know so little about the African American experience from documentary records. But some of the excavations associated with these cemeteries are also significant because they were done with the participation of members of their descendant communities. In 1990, Congress passed the Native American Grave Protection and Repatriation Act (NAGPRA), which called for the repatriation of Native American human remains and religious and funerary objects under federal jurisdiction, whether in museums or in the ground. This process requires consultation between Native American descendant communities and archaeologists, but it does not cover African Americans or the members of other groups. Archaeologists Daniel Roberts and John McCarthy have suggested that community participation, which can satisfy both scientific and nonscientific interests within the group (1995, 26), is an important way of dealing equitably in contested situations. The Freedman's Cemetery and the African Burial Ground have both benefited from community participation, and the President's House in Philadelphia, although not a cemetery, is an excellent example of the negotiation of a partnership between community activists and government representatives in commemorating a site, a negotiation in which archaeological excavation played an important role.

The African Burial Ground

The African Burial Ground (ABG) is in some ways the most significant urban site ever excavated in the United States. We say that for many reasons: because of the archaeological material recovered and the information that has been learned from it; because of the attention the site has received on both the national and international levels; and because in some ways, the information recovered from the analysis of this site rewrote the national discourse on race in the United States, which had originally minimized the existence of slavery in the North. The data that this project provided about a virtually undocumented group—the enslaved Africans who made up almost a fifth of New York City's population in the eighteenth century—was unprecedented. The disinterred human remains represent the earliest and largest burial population of people of African descent in the Americas (LaRoche 2011, 629).

This project began in the late 1980s, when the federal government began plans to build an office tower in lower Manhattan and arranged for an environmental impact study of the area. Those doing the archaeological part of the study discovered that there had been a burial ground there for the city's enslaved Africans throughout most of the eighteenth century. But when they looked at the records of the buildings that had subsequently been built on top of the cemetery, they saw that they all had deep basements, which, they thought, would have destroyed the cemetery (Ingle et al. 1990). So although their report mentioned that the cemetery had been located there, no one imagined that it had been preserved. Once excavations began, however, the archaeologists discovered that after the burial ground had been abandoned, but before it was developed in the 1790s, twenty to twenty-five feet of landfill had been added to the area, burying the cemetery. Therefore, most of the burials were still intact beneath the deep basements and the fill. By the time the project was halted a year later, more than 400 sets of human remains had been removed from part of the site (Figure 7.1).

Figure 7.1. Excavating at the African Burial Ground; note the number of archaeologists working in close quarters. (General Services Administration.)

Bioarchaeologist Michael Blakey, then of Howard University, led the project team in its study, which included data on the demography, trauma, nutritional stress, and the effects of malnutrition in the lives of the city's enslaved Africans. Seventy percent of the people whose bones were analyzed had enamel hypoplasias—lines on their teeth indicating that growth had been arrested—suggesting generalized stress in childhood. Children born in colonial New York "within the condition of slavery were more vulnerable to health risks and early death due to nutritional deficiencies and illness than is evident for the childhoods of those who were likely to have been born in Africa" (Blakey and Rankin-Hill 2009, 331); these indicators were high in the ABG population "regardless of age or sex" (Blakey and Rankin-Hill 2009, 398), and stress levels in ABG children were higher than those among contemporary populations of enslaved people in Maryland or in Barbados (the only places from which there were comparable data). Furthermore, the brutalities of slavery altered the body's skeletal structure. This was seen in bone hypertrophy and remodeling as a result of intensive labor as well as the development of rugged muscle attachments related to heavy tasks and the presence of osteoarthritis and bone lesions at places where tendons and ligaments attach to bone. These skeletal indicators of intense workloads were found in both men and women. Women had particularly high rates of lumbar osteoarthritis (around 58 percent of the sixty-nine individuals studied), suggesting the effects of strenuous labor on the vertebral column (Blakey and Rankin-Hill 2009, 412); there were also many examples of cervical osteophytosis, or deformation of vertebral elements, which comes from carrying heavy loads on the head or similar activities. Furthermore, there were a large number of fractures in the population; most were inflicted on the cranium (seen in 11 percent of the males) or femur (seen in 12 percent of the females). Cranial fractures usually indicate violence or a serious accident.

One young adult female had thirty-two fractures; a woman in her fifties had ten, eight of which were perimortem, on the arms, legs, and pelvis; and a male of the same age had twenty-three (Blakey and Rankin-Hill 2009, 450). Even adolescents were found to have fractures, some of which—especially cranial ones—were undoubtedly the cause of death. The most compelling burial is no. 25, a 20–24-year-old woman who not only had a musket ball embedded in her ribs but had had blunt trauma force applied to her face and had her arm broken through simultaneous twisting and pulling. She appears to have lived for a few days after the beating (Blakey and Rankin-Hill 2009, 458). These bodies bear especially compelling witness to the violence endemic in slave societies.

But just as important as the information that the excavation provided about the population of Africans in eighteenth-century New York was simply the discovery of the burial ground itself. Its presence made it clear once and for all that slavery had existed in New York. Although scholars, of course, were aware of the long-term African presence in the city, before the discovery of the burial ground, the conventional wisdom had been that slavery was a southern phenomenon, to be found in the plantation South, but not in the North. Slavery in New York and even in the North as a whole had been "forgotten." Many have noted that one of the important roles that archaeology can play is that it can bring back to living memory things that have been forgotten, either purposely or not, in the highly selective process of constructing history. The materiality of the burial ground in the shadow of New York's City Hall offered incontrovertible proof of the historically deep presence of the African population there; as African American New York City mayor David Dinkins put it, "We were here" (quoted in Cantwell and Wall 2001, 294).

The African Burial Ground project was also the first instance where members of a descendant community (people who identify as the descendants— either real or metaphorical—of the people who formed an archaeological site under study) took control of a historical archaeology project and affected its outcome. In fact, it has been referred to as "one of the most highly contested archaeological sites in American history" (LaRoche 2011, 628). Many members of the African American communities in New York City became very involved with this project. Although there were diverse opinions as to how work should proceed, what kinds of research should be conducted, and how the human remains should be treated, there was a general consensus that the scholars in charge of the project should preferably be African Americans who had expertise in the study of the African diaspora, so that the study would address issues that were of interest to the descendant community (see LaRoche and Blakey 1997 for background). But even after Blakey, a bioarchaeologist who is African American, took over as project director, there continued to be considerable disagreement between the General Services Administration (GSA, the overseeing government agency) and members of the descendant community as to the details of the methods used on the project. It was a very stressful situation for all concerned: members of the descendant community, the government representatives, and the archaeologists. No one had anticipated such a large mortuary population, and the excavation was a very long, slow, and expensive process for the GSA. On the community's side, the disturbance of their ancestral dead was of great concern, and they protested both in demonstrations and at hearings. And the historical and forensic archaeologists who were originally involved in the project had had no experience in dealing with descendant communities.

Finally, after eight months of protest, the descendant community won, when the House Appropriations Committee threatened to cut off funds to the GSA if the digging did not stop.[2] No more human remains were removed from the site. Those already excavated were analyzed at Howard University, a historically black college, under Blakey's direction, and then in 2003 reinterred with great ceremony, just adjacent to the area from which they had been disinterred. The site is now a National Monument, administered by the National Park Service, with a memorial outside on the site (in the area which protestors saved from development) and an interpretive center inside the adjacent federal office building.[3] The African Burial Ground is the only instance that we know of where a development project in a dense urban area was severely curtailed because of intervention in the form of protests and demonstrations on the part of the public. And this was in a place where real estate values are among the highest in the world.

The Past in the Present

In the decades since the excavation of the African Burial Ground, the descendants of the people who formed the sites in the past that archaeologists study today have taught the latter again and again that the discipline is not simply about the past—it is about the present, too. And archaeologists are learning this lesson. Many archaeologists have begun to be involved in civic engagement and to specialize in this kind of archaeology—referred to variously as public archaeology, community archaeology, and heritage archaeology[4]—working with contemporary peoples in exploring and interpreting the past, particularly the pasts of subaltern groups who are often left out of the grand narrative that forms the history of the country. Archaeological excavation can do several things to help bring their stories into the forefront of historical consciousness. In many cases where there is not enough historical information available about these groups to write their stories, the information gleaned from excavations can provide the material for constructing narratives. Additionally, the simple act of excavation elevates the visibility of not only the site itself but of the group who created it, lending that group legitimacy and authenticity. In fact, we can even say that the act of excavation is in itself a form of commemoration (Shackel 2004, 14, citing McGuire and Shanks). Projects involving archaeologists working with descendant communities and community activists allow for a form of public inclusion and civic engagement that has been often advocated and is only now beginning to be regularly practiced (La Roche 2011).

Over the years, many archaeologists have learned to let go and abandon their role as cultural brokers and to let modern-day communities provide direction regarding the development of their own heritage. Archaeologists have worked with many modern groups who live in urban areas, including Chinese Americans in California, where archaeologists have worked with local community members and historical societies (e.g., Voss and Allen 2008; Greenwood 1996); members of the middle class in what had been a working-class neighborhood (e.g., Gadsby and Chidester's 2007 work in Hampden in Baltimore); and African Americans (e.g., LaRoche 2011; LaRoche and Blakey 1997; Leone 2005; McDavid 2007; Mullins 2007; Praetzellis et al. 2007).[5] In the United States the subaltern group that has been most active in reclaiming its past through archaeology is made up of African Americans. African American archaeologist Cheryl LaRoche has noted that "archaeology has allowed [her] . . . to experience black history, to walk with the ancestors," and she is able to convey that experience to others (2011). These acts of inclusion in the construction of the past can be initiated either by the archaeologists or by members of descendant or local communities. To date, there have been two instances where African American activists have taken charge of the archaeological process. In one case, the African Burial Ground, discussed above, the goal of the activism was to stop the excavations, while in the other, the President's House, described below, excavation was the goal. (The latter site is also discussed in other contexts in chapters 3 and 6.)

The activism and excavations at the President's House in Philadelphia took place earlier in this century in conjunction with the redevelopment of Independence National Park. In 1790, the federal government moved from New York City to Philadelphia and rented a house there to serve as the home of the president of the new nation; it was located in today's park. Over the following decade, first George Washington and then John Adams lived there, until the government moved to Washington in 1800.

Emancipation had come to Pennsylvania relatively early, in 1790, but slave owners from other states were still permitted to bring captives into the state and to keep them enslaved there for six months; after that time, the captives established residency in the state and became free. Throughout his tenure at the President's House, George Washington kept a number of captives there, rotating them back to Mount Vernon, his plantation in Virginia, every six months so that they would not be able to gain their freedom. The idea that the most venerable of our "founding fathers," the figure at the heart of nation's creation narrative as our leader in the fight for freedom, kept enslaved people in the President's House is shocking to most modern-day Americans. Even more shocking is the idea that he was deceitful: his letters make it clear that he did not want the enslaved to know that he was sending them back specifically so they could not be emancipated. But of course they did know (there was a large free-black community in Philadelphia at the time), and in fact two of them escaped while the Washingtons lived there.

Long after the capital moved to Washington, the house and its outbuildings were demolished and the land was redeveloped, leaving only a possible archaeological site behind. Today the President's House site is located in Independence National Park, just a block from Independence Hall. As many schoolchildren know, Independence Hall (formerly the Pennsylvania State House) is the place where the Second Continental Congress met, where Washington was appointed commander in chief of the Continental Army, where the Declaration of Independence was adopted, and where the Constitution was drafted. (The origins of the park itself are discussed in chapter 2.) Today the Liberty Bell is on view at the new Liberty Bell Center, which is on the same block as the President's House site; it was originally the official bell of the Pennsylvania State House, but has long been a separate icon in its own right. It was first called the Liberty Bell in the 1830s, when it became a symbol of the abolitionist cause.

Figure 7.2. The President's House exhibit, 2012; the Liberty Bell Center is on the far left. (Photo by Diana Wall.)

The story of the excavation of the President's House begins in the 1990s, when the Park Service was making plans to redesign the park in an effort to enrich the heritage tourism experience there (Levin 2011, 605). A main attraction for the new park was to be the new Liberty Bell Center. As the center was being built, historian Edward Lawler wrote an article on the President's House, focusing mainly on its architecture (2002). He pinpointed the location and footprint of the house and assembled data to construct a convincing floor plan. He underlined the fact that Washington had brought enslaved Africans from Mount Vernon to Philadelphia and rotated them so that they could not establish their freedom. He further pointed out that as part of Washington's preparations for moving into the house, he had an existing smoke house renovated into housing for his "stablepeople," whom Lawler interpreted to be the enslaved Africans who worked in the stable (Levin 2011, 606; Lawler 2002).[6] Most resonantly, Lawler noted the irony that in order to see the Liberty Bell, that "powerful rallying symbol of the struggle to end slavery in America" in the nineteenth century, "the last thing that a visitor will walk across or pass . . . will be the slave quarters that George Washington ordered added to the President's House" in 1790 (Lawler 2002; partly quoted also in Levin 2011, 606; Figure 7.2).[7]

Well-known historian Gary Nash read Lawler's article and in an interview on a local radio program mentioned the presence of enslaved Africans in George Washington's household in the President's House. He expressed the hope that the Park Service would not "perpetuate the historical amnesia about the founding fathers and slavery" at this site (Nash 2006, 79; quoted in Levin 2011).

The controversy first began around the exhibits that would be featured at the Liberty Bell Center. As originally designed, the interpretation steered away from any mention of slavery, which, it was feared, would "confuse the public" and take attention away from the bell itself (Levin 2011, 207; Nash 2006, 80). Two groups of African American activists—the Avenging the Ancestors Coalition (ATAC) and Generations Unlimited—formed to protest this whitewashing of the nation's history; they soon joined forces with Nash and the Ad Hoc Historians. On July 4, 2002, several thousand members of "the Avenging the Ancestors Coalition descended on the Liberty Bell site . . . to insist that their people be remembered" (Nash 2006, 328). Soon thereafter, with the support of Congressman Robert Brady and the Park Service's chief historian, who pointed out that the juxtaposition of slavery in the President's House and the Liberty Bell was an "interpretive gift" (Nash 2006, 86), as well as members of the press, Park Service personnel were persuaded. The exhibit was redesigned to present the bell within the larger context of associating liberty with the institution of slavery and the troubles the nation has had and still has in living up to the bell's symbolic promise of liberty for all.

But the protestors were not satisfied. They did not want to lose the opportunity offered by this important "teachable moment," and so they switched their focus to the President's House Site, which lay under and adjacent to the doorway of the Liberty Bell Center. They wanted a memorial acknowledging the institution of slavery and particularly the nine people whom Washington held captive in the house when he lived there, including the two who escaped. Along with demonstrations, a letter-writing campaign, and a petition, Congressman Chaka Fattah introduced an amendment to the 2003 budget for the Department of the Interior stipulating that the Park Service report to Congress about the memorial to slavery and the slaves who lived at the President's House.[8] These efforts were effective, and as the city of Philadelphia and the Park Service held a design competition for a memorial at the President's House, they also announced that an agreement had been reached among the interested parties and that an archaeological study would take place on the site before the construction of the memorial. The rationale for this project, as presented in a briefing paper by Jed Levin, the Park Service archaeologist who oversaw the excavation, was that if any archaeological trace of the president's occupation of the site survived, "it would have the potential to teach us about the birth of our nation and the intertwined themes of slavery and freedom" (Levin 2011, 610). Excavations began in March 2007, with only a modest expectation that anything of archaeological significance would be found.

The President's House excavation was extraordinary for two reasons: the archaeological discoveries that were made and the public's enormous interest in the project. The excavations revealed new information about the house itself and the lives of the enslaved people who lived there. Before he moved in, Washington had ordered that a fashionable bow window be added to the house to make its reception rooms larger and more imposing, but there was no evidence that it had actually been built. The excavations revealed the foundation for that window, showing that it had in fact been added. It is thought that this window is a precursor to the design of the Oval Office in today's White House (Levin 2011, 599).

But most importantly, the excavations uncovered the foundation walls of a previously unknown kitchen basement as well as an underground passage leading from the kitchen basement to the basement under the main house. These are the actual spaces where enslaved Africans labored and which they traversed, alongside free and indentured servants, out of sight of the family, their guests, and official visitors. The materiality of these architectural features gives enormous authenticity to the African presence in the President's House.

But the four-month excavation was extremely important in another way as well; it excited great interest on the part of the public, particularly among African Americans. At the ceremony marking the groundbreaking for the excavation, for example, after the speeches and the backhoe's first, symbolic scoop of earth, members of the crowd (which totaled in the hundreds) surged forward to touch the soil, take photos of it, and even to take a handful of it home as a memento (Levin 2011, 611). They did not care when they were told that the soil was twentieth-century landfill, not related to the President's House at all. What was important was that the soil was from that place. It was, as Levin put it, "the stuff of history," as well as, perhaps, emblematic of a political victory (2011, 612–13) and the public ownership of the site.

As the excavations progressed, the Park Service built a wooden structure to serve as a viewing platform, so the public could watch the excavations proceed. But in fact it became a "platform for dialogue on race" (Levin 2011, 614), with people ardently discussing slavery and freedom, in the contexts of the founding of the country and conditions today. During the four-month excavation, about

300,000 people (Jeppson 2010) stood on that platform and engaged with the past and present, and tens of thousands visited the publicly accessible archaeology laboratory, where artifacts from many of the Park Service's Philadelphia sites were being processed.

Although the reviews of the resulting open-air exhibit at the President's House are mixed, the exhibit tries to interweave the themes of the founding fathers and the enslaved Africans who toiled there, the contradictions of freedom and slavery, and racism, which all form important elements in the nation's roots (see Figure 7.2).[9] Made up of fragments of brick walls that outline the footprint of the building, the centerpiece of the exhibit is a large "glass box," in which the exposed archeological features are on view: the foundation walls of the kitchen basement and the underground passage—the slaves' space—and of the bow window—Washington's ceremonial space.

All in all, the excavations at the African Burial Ground and the President's House are representative of the new "public archaeology," a growing subdiscipline whereby archaeologists work with communities in uncovering the past. The examples of the African Burial Ground and the President's House show how effective archaeology can be at revealing the process of forgetting (Shackel 2004) that has taken place in the construction of our national history. These sites, in urban areas, are extremely powerful "as vehicles that communities can draw on as they struggle to understand and communicate who they are and where they came from. . . . [Furthermore, they serve as] an important tool and, sometimes, a weapon to wield in struggles for power" (Levin 2011, 597).

Conclusion

A S WE NOTED IN THE PREFACE, when we first excavated in lower Manhattan over thirty years ago, we were concerned about whether the results from that and other urban projects would be worth the substantial amounts of money and effort the excavations involved. However, in writing this book we have looked back at the results and learned that the findings from urban projects have been important. They have allowed the creation of the new field of urban archaeology, which is based on its particular ability to consider the sequential, layered growth and development of cities through its focus on space and materiality. In this book we have relied for interpretation both on how people arrange themselves across space and through time and on the materiality of urban lives, where excavation reveals the complex and often surprising ways that people mobilize objects in their homes and create their cuisines. We used two scales of analysis to look at cities, both of which are very appropriate for archaeology: the macro (where we examined the city as a whole), and the micro (where we looked at the patterns found in urban components such as households, neighborhoods, and cemeteries). And historic documents were and are as essential to the process of analysis as the artifacts: both are cornerstones of historical archaeology in urban contexts as well as in rural ones. As Kathleen Deagan noted so long ago, one of archaeology's strengths is its ability to examine those whose lives are not recorded in written records: the poor, those without property, and the hidden (1998), and we have been able to do this here.

Modern American cities are different from European cities in that they developed *de novo* with European settlement. Large, possibly urban pre-Columbian sites existed prior to colonization (for example, in Cahokia and the Southwest), but these settlements had passed their zenith by the time of the European arrivals. European colonists often placed their cities on a coast or river outlet to facilitate the transfer of goods or to protect a crucial resource from other European powers.

American cities are diverse, but share certain basic attributes. Some of their most significant distinctive qualities reference their period of development, whether they date from preindustrial or industrial times. Cities from these two periods are quite different entities in many respects, especially in the spatial separation of socially defined units. We can read much of urban social structure from its inscription in urban geography (Smith 2008, xv), revealing the reiterative connections between spatial and sociocultural attributes, such as race, ethnicity, class, and gender. Landscape formation, both within cities and in a larger regional context is influenced by several factors, including the type of transportation systems that linked the city both overseas and to its hinterland, with the city as a central place in such networks.

In our brief history of urban archaeology, we noted the importance of several factors which contributed to its creation and growth but which initially seemed to be only tangentially related to the new field. They include the historic preservation movement, as realized both privately and through the National Park Service, and the Cultural Resource Management legislation, which ultimately mandated so much urban historical archaeology and defined its staged process. It was this legislation which required that archaeologists look in cities in the first place, even when they might have preferred to look elsewhere.

On the Macro Level: Patterns of Urban Growth

Archaeological projects, we discovered, reveal both the commonalities in urban development as well as the distinctive attributes derived from particular historical circumstances. Using the framework of the city as artifact and considering the whole urban space, there were some patterns that we see over and over again. We have noted the ubiquity of the grid as a base plan throughout much of the country. But we have also seen the ways in which time after time the practicalities of politics and topography have subverted this plan (for example, in Denver or Santa Fe) and have also observed the persistent reliance on the grid in seemingly irrational settings, such as San Francisco. Other urban plans, such as the baroque, seen in cities such as St. Mary's City, Annapolis, and Washington, D.C., emerged from the Enlightenment and highlight other urban priorities. And the nineteenth-century "City Beautiful" movement had a strong influence on other cities, such as Chicago.

We also looked inside the preindustrial "walking cities," where people lived and worked together, often spatially integrated by class but clustered in terms of ethnicity (Rothschild 1990). Later, in the early industrial city, those with property underwent the long-term process of separating their homes from their workplaces (Wall 1994) and created neighborhoods that were segregated by class, gender, and race or ethnicity. We have considered the links between spatial and social elements, how space is arranged, who lives where in cities, and how the spatial and social are recursively integrated and formed. One of the dominant elements of urban growth is the reconfiguration of space over time, often controlled by forces of the political economy which rearrange the access of individuals and institutions to spatial and other resources and connect urban form to process. A common pattern comes with industrial development. A factory moves into what was a middle-class residential neighborhood, and those residents move elsewhere. Housing deteriorates in value and upkeep, and gradually what had been single-family homes become multi-tenant housing, home to a succession of the poor and socially marginal. Then city developers and politicians might call for urban renewal or support for gentrification. This forms part of the pattern whereby communities of African Americans and other disenfranchised groups, as well as members of the working class, have been displaced time and time again.

Patterns of changes in urban infrastructure also resulted in patterns of changing landscapes. Making land by claiming it from shorelines and marshes is the culmination of the commodification of land, a process which has characterized the growth of the capitalist system. Landfilling, begun in the United States in the seventeenth century and continuing to the present, has been associated with urban growth in cities located on waterways throughout the country, turning beaches, river shores, and saltmarshes into valuable real estate and creating some of the best ports in the world. We have also seen the modern ramifications of this process: with rising sea levels, much of the land in New York City that was recently flooded by the surge associated with Hurricane Sandy was originally underwater and was created by landfill.

Urban archaeology has also informed us about the materiality of public health, concerns that emerged throughout the nineteenth and early twentieth centuries and which resulted in access to clean water and sewage systems to remove waste. Archaeological studies have recorded the transformation of the private backyard privy/cistern system to public utilities and have shown that this process occurred in different cities at different times, with access in each city structured by class. While this change went a long way toward controlling some diseases, there were also what some see as heavy prices to pay: the growth in the apparatus of government along with the commodification of water and even of bodily waste. Privies and similar features are famously important to historical archaeologists as repositories of "treasure troves" of artifacts; some of the most significant data from urban sites have come from them.

On Both the Macro and Micro Levels

The study of cemeteries has proved to be extremely important in urban archaeology. Over and over again, on the macro level we have seen a pattern of urban growth whereby land-intensive features like cemeteries are placed on the peripheries of cities, which, as the latter expand, encompass them. Burials were supposed to have been removed before the land was redeveloped, but it has repeatedly turned out that they had not been moved, and there they are, still in the ground, to be uncovered by archaeologists. Then a decision has to be made about what to do with them—to stop the development, to excavate them archaeologically, or simply to move them. It is at this point, using best practices, that archaeologists and the representatives of government agencies overseeing the project consult with the descendants of those interred.

Early cemeteries tended to be open to all residents of the city, but with urban expansion, various kinds of stratification developed, both by class and race or ethnicity. From an archaeological perspective, the large populations interred in urban cemeteries provide substantial samples that can be used to construct credible interpretations about the people buried there. The study of the eighteenth-century African Burial Ground in New York City has proved to be one of the most important sources of information about the experience of enslaved Africans there (Blakey and Rankin-Hill 2009). A recent analysis of a large, multiethnic nineteenth-century cemetery in Tucson provided invaluable insights into the composition, lifeways, and burial customs of that heterogeneous population (Heilen and Gray 2011). Other cemetery analyses reveal information on cultural change in the treatment of the dead, primarily among the middle class, as the ideal of a "Good Death" was replaced by the concept of the "Beautification of Death," which developed alongside the funerary industry. The information that comes from burial populations is of a very primary kind, revealing disease and physical stress, including mistreatment, inscribed on bodies, but also showing the love and attention paid by the living to the dead (cf. Howson 2013).

On the Micro Level: Neighborhoods and Households

Operating on the micro level, urban archaeologists have also looked at the way materiality is mobilized among different ethnic and racial groups, especially in their preferences in selecting particular objects for their homes and in preparing foods to eat. A number of patterns have emerged in these analyses, including the presence or absence of matched sets of dishes and preferences for particular kinds and cuts of meats. But these studies have also shown how inappropriate it is to stereotype the behavior of the members of these various groups. Researchers examining the experience of African Americans have shown that there is no single "African American community," but rather that African Americans are members of many classes and subcultures. Others have discovered that, while European American outsiders have perceived "Chinatowns" as monolithic wholes, people within those communities discern greater social and cultural complexity, often based on class or occupation.

Archaeologists themselves have differed in the ways they have approached the study of these two groups, focusing on the cultural similarities between African Americans and whites, but emphasizing cultural differences between Chinese and European Americans, as seen in material culture. These differences may relate to racial attitudes among members of the dominant culture, which most archaeologists represent. And of course European immigrants from different countries have also been stereotyped in terms of behavior and other attributes. For these latter groups, most only developed identities in terms of their nation-state of origin after they had arrived in the United States; at home they identified themselves as denizens of particular towns and/or provinces. Furthermore, members of all of these groups arrived in America at particular points in time, from particular places, and under specific circumstances. Some emigrated by choice, while others arrived involuntarily. Some imagined themselves here for a short time, others came with the promise of a new and better permanent life, and still others had only the bleak prospect of enslavement for themselves and their children. And most of these groups were subjected to negative stereotypic prejudice and discrimination at some point in their history. Archaeological study allows us to see their changing identities as they undergo the process of Americanization (see Camp 2013). Questions of creolization and ethnogenesis are prominent here. There is amazing variability in the ways that supposedly distinct groups merged or did not and the materiality resulting from these formations. Although we are able to identify objects and we can often identify the people who owned them, it is much more difficult to understand why particular people chose particular objects to express their connections with particular groups.

Archaeologists have also examined class development in American cities. It is within the contexts of merchant and industrial capitalism that class formation and negotiation took place. Research has revealed the materiality associated with aspects of both of these forms of political economy and how they were expressed in urban contexts and processes. In exploring merchant capitalism during the colonial and early federalist era, archaeologists have looked at the merchant elites who expressed their status through consumption as well as by demonstrating their control over nature. They also have explored the experience of artisan middling folk of that period and showed some of the ways in which they responded to the impact of the transformation of their position from that of master craftsman to entrepreneur, retailer, or factory manager. Similarly, a significant transition was experienced by former apprentices or journeymen as they became members of a permanent working class, which was augmented by Africans who had formerly been enslaved but were gradually emancipated throughout this period. Case studies in many cities demonstrate the symbolic references associated with specific class positions at particular localized historical moments, in treatments for disease as well as choices for their homes. The ways in which some people actively chose objects that were considered "appropriate" for members of a different class, thus blurring class "boundaries," is also clarified through these urban projects.

Other patterns that we have seen concern gender. Material culture has helped to elucidate the importance of the role of indigenous women in creolization in Spanish colonial cities. It also has provided insights into the long-term process of the separation of the home and workplace and corresponding changes in the gender roles of the men and women of the middle class in the late eighteenth and early nineteenth centuries. And archaeologists working in urban areas are beginning to look at the roles of men and the construction of masculinity. Analyses of ceramics have helped to tell the story of the changing construction of gender among the members of different ethnic groups and classes. Archaeological excavations in socially marginal settings such as almshouses or houses of prostitution have been amazingly informative. Projects in these settings reveal details of the lifeways of their residents, their hygiene, and, among the prostitutes, differences between the foods and accouterments that they used themselves and those they offered their clients.

Some projects have required that historical archaeologists work with descendant communities, a process that has contributed to producing a new subfield within the discipline, referred to as community or public archaeology. We described two projects here that exemplify this kind of archaeology, although there are many more. One involved the excavation of an African American cemetery—New York's African Burial Ground—while the other concerned a site that challenged the country's creation narrative. It juxtaposed one of the country's icons of liberty—the Liberty Bell—with enslavement as practiced by one of its founding fathers—George Washington—at the President's House in Philadelphia. In one case, the goal of public protest was to excavate, while in the other it was to stop excavations.

Future Research

All in all, we think it is a very exciting time to engage in the archaeological study of the modern cities of the United States and of cities throughout the modern world. Archaeologists have accumulated a great deal of roughly comparable data from different places, and more and more of those data are becoming widely available, either online or on CDs that archaeologists are more than happy to share. For example, the reports and data from the Praetzellises' work in California, particularly in the Bay Area (1992, 2004, 2009)[1] and reports from New York City projects[2] are all available online, and several states are putting their reports online as well. And there are international data sets also available from urban excavations in Australia and the United Kingdom[3] (and probably from other places that we are unaware of).

With access to such large databases, we can begin to think about big questions: How did the development of industrial capitalism affect the standard of living among the working class in different places and at different times? Is there/was there a working class identity in the United States? If so, what roles did race, gender, and ethnicity play in the development of working-class consciousness in the eighteenth through early twentieth centuries (cf. McGuire and Reckner 2002, 2005). Was the materiality of class consciousness among the members of the working class embedded in its own aesthetic, or did they look to the middle class (cf. Mrozowski 2006)? What did it mean to members of different ethnic or racial groups to be assigned to (or elect) a specific identity? Is there a consistent "look" to the phenomenon of Americanization, or does it vary from group to group and from time to time? How did any of these behaviors differ throughout the country, or, if we want to look internationally, how did expressions of class, racial, and ethnic identity differ throughout the world? How do the dimensions of race, ethnicity, and class intersect? Examining the materiality of these various experiences through an archaeological lens will enable us to address these and many other questions and allow us to write about the construction of inequality both today and in the past. And we can explore one of the outcomes of spatial control by those in power, namely, the phenomenon visible today in large American cities such as Los Angeles or New York that produces increasing spatial segregation by race, class, and ethnicity.

Several of those who write about cities (from Lewis Mumford to Edward Soja and Mike Davis) are rather pessimistic about their viability—Mumford describes them as the last stage in the cycle of civilization, expressing its ultimate decline (1961). And both Davis (2002) and Soja (2000) find the class- and race-based separation just mentioned untenable in the long run. On the other hand, others find cities valuable in their ability to increase contact among their residents, stimulating creativity and both social and technological innovation. Cities are becoming increasingly important as greater numbers of people are living in them; the U.S. population is presently 82 percent urban. And in 2009 President Barack Obama established a new Office of Urban Affairs with the goal of developing a "policy agenda for urban America."[4]

Whichever of these perspectives is supported over time, cities represent fascinating places for archaeological study. They accommodate many kinds of interest. The archaeological perspective, grounded within anthropology, can analyze data over the sweep of time from both macro and micro perspectives, providing an important and distinctive set of insights into urban life and culture and a richly nuanced picture of life in the city.

As we said above, cities attract attention and are appealing places to live. They are arguably the most significant of human inventions. We have learned and will, we assume, continue to learn a great deal about them and their contribution to the American experience through the study of urban historical archaeology.

Notes

Chapter 2. Urbanization and Its Archaeological Study in the United States

1. As Wallace notes, Rockefeller's insistence on architectural accuracy was not matched by a similar insistence on cultural accuracy on the most basic level. Williamsburg originally portrayed the lives only of Virginia's planter elites; its interpretations did not even mention the fact that half of the city's population consisted of enslaved Africans (1986, 148).

2. See www.urscorp.com/About_URS/index.php.

3. See www.aia.umd.edu, accessed Sept 19, 2012.

4. Unfortunately the archaeologists have no way to know how productive in terms of artifacts any particular shaft feature may be when they are making this decision. They will know that only when they have excavated it.

Chapter 3. Landscape, Planning, and Infrastructure

1. See www.greekworks.com.

2. Archaeologists working in Santa Fe with considerable frequency include David Snow, Cordelia Snow, Cherie Scheick, James Ivey, Stephen Post, Tim Maxwell, Glenda Deyloff, and Frances Levine.

3. It is the lack of agreement at the intersections of these incongruent individual and idiosyncratic grids that make the West Village in New York City so difficult to navigate for newcomers and natives alike.

4. See www.denvergov.org.

5. http://cityroom.blogs.nytimes.com/2010/09/12/the-gudgeon-did-it-a-small-detail-settles-a-maritime-mystery/?action=click&module=Search&region=search Results&mabReward=relbias%3As&url=http%3A%2F%2Fquery.nytimes.com%2Fs earch%2Fsitesearch%2F%3Faction%3Dclick%26region%3DMasthead%26pgtype%3 DHomepage%26module%3DSearchSubmit%26contentCollection%3DHomepage% 26t%3Dqry336%23%2Fworld%2Btrade%2Bcenter%2Bship%2F.

6. We thank Charles Cheek for bringing the Chapin reference to our attention.

7. This explanation opens the door to the idea that the artifacts found in a privy or other shaft feature may not have originated in the house or building adjacent to that feature—an assumption upon which a great deal of archaeological interpretation now rests. The rationale for questioning this assumption is that the quantities of material that are used suggest that they did not come from a single domestic source, but rather from many (see Cotter et al. 1992, 306–307, McCarthy and Ward 2000, and Stottman 1996 for discussions of this problem).

Chapter 4. Trade, Manufacture, and Services in the City

1. See http://research.history.org/Files/Archaeo/MajorStudies/Shields%20Tavern .pdf.

2. See www.uri.edu/mua.

Chapter 5. Race and Ethnicity in the City

1. Of course, in any structure jointly occupied by African Americans and whites, we cannot be certain who is responsible for any particular part of the material culture associated with the structure, although it does seem clear that material from caches associated with specific locations in white homes where African Americans, either enslaved or free, worked and/or lived, such as kitchens, etc., has been affirmatively linked to African Americans.

2. We also note Mullins's observation that many people at lower income levels chose to purchase national brands so as not to be cheated by shopkeepers (1999, 173–75).

3. With thanks to Meredith Linn.

4. Which is a reminder of the significance of education to middle-class African Americans, also noted in Seneca Village (Wall et al. 2008).

5. See www.slavenorth.com/massemancip.htm.

6. Acculturation models were applied in the 1960s and 1970s to many groups, including African Americans and Native Americans as well as Chinese. The model of agency is a newer anthropological concept.

7. See www.nytimes.com/2013/12/19/nyregion/chinese-diaspora-transforms-new-yorks-immigrant-population-report-finds.html?_r=0.

Chapter 6. Class and Gender in the City

1. Historical archaeologists have tended to examine gender relationships in four different settings: under colonialism (beginning with Deagan 1974), as part of the separation of the spheres in Victorian America (Wall 1994), as part of the African diaspora (Wilkie 2003), and as part of the study of women in institutional settings,

be they utopian or correctional (Spencer-Wood 1991; De Cunzo 1995; after Voss 2006).

2. See Voss (2006) and Wilkie and Hayes (2006) for overviews of gender studies in historical archaeology.

3. The biological determination of sex is not straightforward, as we have been reminded recently by the story of Caster Semenya, the South African runner (New York Times passim, 2009–12).

Chapter 7. Cemeteries and Commemoration in the City

1. See http://shpo.sc.gov/tech/Pages/Cemsymbol.aspx.

2. Congressman Gus Savage, chair of the Committee on Public Works and Transportation's Subcommittee on Public Buildings and Grounds, held a public hearing on the Burial Ground in New York City, where he told the GSA representatives, "Don't waste your time asking this subcommittee for anything else as long as I'm chairman." Savage had been alerted to the situation by Alton Maddox, a New York civil rights lawyer and activist; members of the congressional Black Caucus had also been putting pressure on the GSA to stop the excavations (Cantwell and Wall 2001, 287, 330n25).

3. The site was composed of two areas, one where the main office building was planned, and the other where a smaller "pavilion" was planned. The area of the pavilion was not excavated and is today the site of a memorial, while all of the burials were removed from the main office area, and that building was built.

4. All of these subdisciplines have slightly different meanings.

5. Patrice Jeppson approached the issue of inclusion from a different angle and did a study of "the archaeology of archaeology" in examining the story of the excavators who worked at Franklin Court in Philadelphia (also discussed in chapter 2). She discovered that the original field crew for the excavation of the site in the 1950s were African Americans and that one of the archaeologists, Barbara Liggett, who worked there in the 1970s, was gay. Obviously the inclusion of this information in the National Park Service's interpretation of Franklin Court would make the site more relevant and accessible to African Americans and members of gay communities, respectively, today (Jeppson 2006, 2007). Unfortunately, as of this writing, neither has been incorporated into the interpretation of the site.

6. See www.ushistory.org/presidentshouse/plans/pmhb/ph1.htm.

7. See www.ushistory.org/presidentshouse/plans/pmhb/ph2.htm.

8. It is not simply a coincidence that in the case of both the African Burial Ground and the President's House, protests became effective only when they were reinforced by threatening agency funding through congressional action, in each case initiated by an African American congressman.

9. See, e.g., Julia M. Klein, "All the President's Men," *Wall Street Journal*, 2011, http://

online.wsj.com/article/SB10001424052748704774604576035873775375418.html and Edward Rothstein, "Reopening a House That's Still Divided," *New York Times*, 2010, http://www.nytimes.com/2010/12/15/arts/design/15museum.html?pagewanted=all& action=click&module=Search&region=searchResults&mabReward=relbias%3Ar&url =http%3A%2F%2Fquery.nytimes.com%2Fsearch%2Fsitesearch%2F%3Faction%3Dclic k%26contentCollection%3Dundefined%26region%3DTopBar%26module%3DSearch Submit%26pgtype%3DTopic%23%2FREOPENING%2520A%2520HOUSE%2520TH AT%2527S%2520STILL%2520DIVI.

Conclusion

1. See www.sonoma.edu/asc/publications/index.html.

2. See www.nyc.gov/html/lpc/html/publications/archaeology_reports.shtml.

3. See Tim Murray's Archaeology of the Modern City project (www.latrobe.edu.au/ humanities/research/research-projects/past-projects/archaeology-of-the-modern-city/databases/eamc-archaeology-database), which includes much of the data from the excavations in Sydney and Melbourne in Australia, and archaeologists in the UK are also now looking at the nineteenth century—a period they used to ignore. Projects include those in London, Sheffield, and Manchester, as well as at Hungate in York (Orser 2011).

4. See www.nytimes.com/2010/12/19/magazine/19Urban_West-t.html?page wanted=all.

References

Abbott, Carl. 2007. Urbanization. In *Encyclopedia of American Urban History*, ed. D. Goldfield, 2:851–55. Sage, Thousand Oaks, CA.

Agbe-Davies, Anna S. 2008. Public Archaeology and the Continuing Legacy of Uplift and Female Empowerment at the Phyllis Wheatley Home for Girls, Chicago. Paper presented at the 14th Annual Berkshire Conference on the History of Women, Minneapolis.

Alonso, Ana Maria. 1994. The Politics of Space, Time, and Substance: State Formation, Nationalism, and Ethnicity. *Annual Review of Anthropology* 23(1): 379–405.

Appiah, Kwame Anthony. 1990. Racisms. In *Anatomy of Racism*, ed. D. T. Goldberg, 3–17. University of Minnesota Press, Minneapolis.

Baldwin-Jones, Alice. 1995. Historical Archaeology and the African American Experience. Paper submitted to fulfill the course requirements for Historical Archaeology, Program in Anthropology. Paper on file, CUNY Graduate Center, New York.

Balicki, Joseph F. 1998. Wharves, Privies, and the Pewterer: Two Colonial Period Sites on the Shawmut Peninsula, Boston. *Historical Archaeology* 32(3): 99–120.

Barrett, Jared Lee. 2002. *The Urban Landscape of Health, Hygiene, and Social Control: The Development of Municipal Services in Battle Creek, Michigan.* Western Michigan University, Kalamazoo.

Basso, Keith H. 1996. *Wisdom Sits in Places: Landscape and Language among the Western Apache.* University of New Mexico Press, Albuquerque.

Baugher, Sherene. 2001. Visible Charity: The Archaeology, Material Culture, and Landscape Design of New York City's Municipal Almshouse Complex, 1736–1797. *International Journal of Historical Archaeology* 5(2): 175–202.

Baumont, Catherine, Hubert Beguin, and Jean-Marie Hurlot. 1998. An Economic Definition of the City. In *Econometric Advances in Spatial Modeling and Methodology: Essays in Honour of Jean Paelinck*, ed. J.H.P. Paelinck, D. A. Griffith, C. G. Amrhein, and J.-M. Huriot, 15–25. Kluwer Academic, Dordrecht.

Beaudry, Mary C., Lauren J. Cook, and Stephen A. Mrozowski. 1991. Artifacts and Active Voices: Material Culture as Social Discourse. In *The Archaeology of Inequality*, ed. R. H. McGuire and R. Paynter, 150–91. Blackwell, Oxford.

Bell, Edward L. 1990. The Historical Archaeology of Mortuary Behavior: Coffin Hardware from Uxbridge, Massachusetts. *Historical Archaeology* 24(3): 54–78.

Benedict, Tod L. 2003. Privy Construction and Sanitation Practices in Wheeling and the Ohio Valley. In *Middle-Class Life in Victorian Wheeling: Phase IB/II and III Archaeological Investigations: New Annex, United States Federal Building and Courthouse Site, West Virginia*, ed. R. Yamin, 64–71. HLM Design, West Chester, PA.

——. 2004. Appendix B: Bricklayers, Well Diggers, Hod Carriers, Privy Cleaners, and Carters: The Construction and Maintenance of Brick-Lined Shafts in Philadelphia to 1850. *After the Revolution—Two Shops on South Sixth Street: Archaeological Data Recovery on Block 1 of Independence Mall*. Philadelphia: Prepared for National Park Service, Denver Service Center.

Berry, Brian J. L. 1967. *Geography of Market Centers and Retail Distribution*. Prentice-Hall, Englewood Cliffs, NJ.

Binford, Lewis Robert. 1962. Archaeology as Anthropology. *American Antiquity* 28(2): 217–25.

Blackmar, Elizabeth. 1979. Rewalking the "Walking City": Housing and Property Relations in New York City, 1780–1840. *Radical History Review* 21: 131–48.

——. 1989. *Manhattan for Rent: 1785–1850*. Cornell University Press, Ithaca, NY.

Blakey, Michael L., and Lesley M. Rankin-Hill. 2009. *Unearthing the African Presence in Colonial New York: The Skeletal Biology of the New York African Burial Ground, Part 1. The New York African Burial Ground: United States. General Services, Administration* (Vol. 1). Howard University Press, in association with the General Services Administration, Washington, DC.

Bourdieu, Pierre. 1977. *Outline of a Theory of Practice*. Translated by Richard Nice. Cambridge University Press, New York.

——. 1984. *Distinction: A Social Critique of the Judgement of Taste*. Translated by Richard Nice. Harvard University Press, Cambridge.

Bower, Beth Anne. 1986. *The African Meeting House, Boston, Massachusetts: Summary Report of Archaeological Excavations, 1975–1986*. Museum of Afro-American History, Boston.

Bower, Bruce. 2008. Dawn of the City: Excavations Prompt a Revolution in Thinking about the Earliest Cities. *Science News* 173(6): 90–92.

Bradley, James W. 2007. Before Albany: An Archaeology of Native-Dutch Relations in the Capital Region, 1600–1664. *New York State Museum, Bulletin 509*. State Education Department, SUNY, Albany.

Branstner, Mark C., and Terrance J. Martin. 1987. Working-Class Detroit: Late Victorian Consumer Choices and Status. In *Consumer Choice in Historical Archaeology*, ed. S. M. Spencer-Wood, 301–20. Plenum Press, New York.

Brashler, Janet G. 1991. When Daddy Was a Shanty Boy: The Role of Gender in the Logging Industry in Highland West Virginia. *Historical Archaeology* 25(4): 54–68.

Bridges, William. 1811a. *Map of the City of New-York and Island of Manhattan with Explanatory Remarks and References*. New York: Printed for the author by T. and J. Swords.

——. 1811b. *Remarks of the Commissioners for Laying Out Streets and Roads in the City of New York, under the Act of April 3, 1807*. Retrieved from www.library.cornell.edu/Reps/DOCS/nyc1811.html.

Brighton, Stephen A. 2001. Prices That Suit the Times. *Historical Archaeology* 35(3): 18–30.

——. 2005. An Historical Archaeology of the Irish Proletarian Diaspora: The Material

Manifestations of Irish Identity in America, 1850–1910. PhD diss., Boston University, Boston.

———. 2009. *Historical Archaeology of the Irish Diaspora: A Transnational Approach*. University of Tennessee, Nashville.

Bromberg, Francine Weiss. 2000. *"To Find Rest from All Trouble": The Archaeology of the Quaker Burying Ground, Alexandria, Virginia*. Alexandria Archaeology, Office of Historic Alexandria, Alexandria.

Bromberg, Francine Weiss, and Steven J. Shephard. 2006. The Quaker Burying Ground in Alexandria, Virginia: A Study of Burial Practices of the Religious Society of Friends. *Historical Archaeology* 40(1): 57–88.

Brown, Gregory J., Thomas F. Higgins III, David F. Muraca, S. Kathleen Pepper, and Roni H. Polk. 1990 (reissued 2001). *Archaeological Investigations of the Shields Tavern Site, Williamsburg, Virginia*. Colonial Williamsburg Archaeological Report, Williamsburg. Colonial Williamsburg Foundation. http://research.history.org/Files/Archaeo/MajorStudies/Shields%20Tavern.pdf.

Burrows, Ian, and Richard Hunter. 1996. Pretty Village to Urban Place: Eighteenth-Century Trenton and Its Archaeology. *New Jersey History* 114(2–3): 32–52.

Bustamante, Adrian. 1991. "The Matter Was Never Resolved": The Casta System in Colonial New Mexico, 1693–1823. *Historical Review* 66(2): 143–63.

Camp, Stacey Lynn. 2013. *The Archaeology of Citizenship*. University Press of Florida, Gainesville.

Cantwell, Anne-Marie E., and Diana diZerega Wall. 2001. *Unearthing Gotham: The Archaeology of New York City*. Yale University Press, New Haven.

———. 2010. New Amsterdam: The Subordination of Native Space. In *Soldiers, Cities, and Landscapes: Essays in Honor of Charles L. Fisher*, ed. P. B. Drooker and J. P. Hart, 199–212. New York State Museum, Albany.

Certeau, Michel de. 1984. *The Practice of Everyday Life*. Translated by S. F. Rendall. University of California Press, Berkeley.

Chapin, Charles Value. 1901. *Municipal Sanitation in the United States*. Snow and Farnham, Providence, RI.

Childe, V. Gordon. 1950. The Urban Revolution. *Town Planning Review* 21(1): 3–17

Cohen, Lizabeth A. 1986. Embellishing a Life of Labor: An Interpretation of the Material Culture of American Working-Class Homes, 1885–1915. In *Common Places: Readings in American Vernacular Architecture*, ed. D. Upton and J. M. Vlach, 261–78. University of Georgia Press, Athens.

Conkey, Margaret Wright, and Christine Ann Hastorf. 1990. *The Uses of Style in Archaeology*. Cambridge University Press, New York.

Conkey, Margaret W., and Janet D. Spector. 1984. Archaeology and the Study of Gender. *Advances in Archaeological Method and Theory* 7: 1–32.

Costello, Julia G., Kevin Hallaran, Keith Warren, and Margie Akin. 2008. The Luck of Third Street: Archaeology of Chinatown, San Bernardino, California. *Historical Archaeology* 42(3): 136–51.

Cotter, John L., Daniel G. Roberts, and Michael Parrington. 1992. *The Buried Past: An Archaeological History of Philadelphia*. University of Pennsylvania Press, Philadelphia.

Crabtree, Pam, and Claudia Milne. 2000. Revealing Meals: Ethnicity, Economic Status, and Diet at Five Points. In *Tales of Five Points: Working-Class Life in Nineteenth-Century New York,* ed. R. Yamin, 2:130–96. John Milner Associates, West Chester, PA.

Crane, Brian D. 2000. Filth, Garbage, and Rubbish: Refuse Disposal, Sanitary Reform, and Nineteenth-Century Yard Deposits in Washington, D.C. *Historical Archaeology* 34(1): 20–38.

Crist, Thomas A. 2005. Babies in the Privy: Prostitution, Infanticide, and Abortion in New York City's Five Points District. *Historical Archaeology* 39(1): 19–46.

Dallal, Diane. 2013. Anthony Van Ardsdale Winans, New York Merchant, and His Daughter, *Canary of Lago Maggiore.* In *Tales of Gotham: Historical Archaeology, Ethnohistory, and Microhistory of New York City,* ed. D. Dallal and M. Janowitz, 27–48. Springer, New York.

Dallal, Diane, Meta Janowitz, and Linda Stone. 2012. *South Ferry Terminal Project, Final Report.* Prepared as part of NYCT-WO-41—Implementation of the Mitigation Plan for Analysis, Curation, Report Preparation, and Public Outreach for the South Ferry Terminal Project for Metropolitan Transportation Authority, New York City Transit Capital Construction.

Davidson, James Michael. 2004. Mediating Race and Class through the Death Experience: Power Relations and Resistance Strategies of an African American Community, Dallas, Texas (1869–1907). PhD diss., University of Texas.

Davis, Mike. 2002. *Dead Cities and Other Tales.* New Press, New York.

Dawdy, Shannon L. 2000. Understanding Cultural Change through the Vernacular: Creolization in Louisiana. *Historical Archaeology* 34: 107–23.

———. 2006. Thinker-Tinkers, Race, and the Archaeological Critique of Modernity. *Archaeological Dialogues* 12(2): 143–64.

———. 2008. *Building the Devil's Empire: French Colonial New Orleans.* University of Chicago Press, Chicago.

Dawdy, Shannon, and Christopher Matthews. 2010. Colonial and Early Antebellum New Orleans. In *Archaeology of Louisiana,* ed. M. A. Rees, 273–90. Louisiana State University Press, Baton Rouge.

Deagan, Kathleen A. 1974. Sex, Status, and Role in the Mestizaje of Spanish Colonial Florida. PhD diss., University of Florida, Gainesville.

———. 1983. *Spanish St. Augustine: The Archaeology of a Colonial Creole Community.* Academic Press, New York.

———. 1998. Rethinking Modern History. *Archaeology* 51(5): 54–60.

Decker, Ethan, Andrew J. Kerkhoff, and Melanie E. Moses. 2007. Global Patterns of City Size Distributions and Their Fundamental Drivers. *PLoS ONE,* 2(9): e294.

De Cunzo, Lu Ann. 1983. Economics and Ethnicity: An Archaeological Perspective on Nineteenth-Century Paterson, New Jersey. PhD diss., University of Pennsylvania, Philadelphia.

———. 1995. Reform, Respite, Ritual: An Archaeology of Institutions: The Magdalen Society of Philadelphia, 1800–1850. *Historical Archaeology* 39(1): 1–168.

———. 2001. On Reforming the "Fallen" and Beyond: Transforming Continuity at the Magdalen Society of Philadelphia, 1845–1916. *International Journal of Historical Archaeology* 5(1): 19–43.

Deetz, James. 1977. *In Small Things Forgotten: The Archaeology of Early American Life*. Anchor Press/Doubleday, Garden City, NY.

Detweiler, Susan Gray. 1982. *George Washington's Chinaware*. Harry Abrams, New York.

Domínguez, Francisco Atanasio, Eleanor B. Adams, and Angelico Chavez. 2012. *The Missions of New Mexico, 1776*. Sunstone Press, Santa Fe.

Dunlap, David W. 2011. The World Trade Center Ship, from Stem to Stern. *New York Times*, 5 August.

Epperson, Terrence V. 1990. "To Fix a Perpetual Brand": The Social Construction of Race in Virginia, 1675–1750. PhD diss., Temple University, Philadelphia.

Faust, Drew Gilpin. 2008. *This Republic of Suffering: Death and the American Civil War*. Alfred A. Knopf, New York.

Ferguson, Leland. 2011. *God's Fields: Landscape, Religion, and Race in Moravian Wachovia*. University Press of Florida, Gainesville.

Fitts, Robert K. 1999. The Archaeology of Middle-Class Domesticity and Gentility in Victorian Brooklyn. *Historical Archaeology* 33(1): 39–62.

Foner, Eric. 1976. *Tom Paine and Revolutionary America*. Oxford University Press, New York.

Gadsby, David A., and Robert C. Chidester. 2007. Heritage in Hampden: A Participatory Research Design for Public Archaeology in a Working-Class Neighborhood, Baltimore, Maryland. In *Archaeology as a Tool of Civic Engagement*, ed. B. J. Little and P. A. Shackel, 223–42. AltaMira Press, Lanham, MD.

Garman, James C. 1994. Viewing the Color Line through the Material Culture of Death. *Historical Archaeology* 28(3): 74–93.

Geismar, Joan H. 1987. Landfill and Health, a Municipal Concern, or, Telling It Like It Was. *Northeast Historical Archaeology* 16: 49–57.

———. 1993. Where Is the Night Soil? Thoughts on an Urban Privy. *Historical Archaeology* 27(2): 57–70.

———. 1996. *Saratoga Square Urban Renewal Area (SSQURA), 127 and 109 MacDougal Street (Block 1525, lots 40 and 49), 78 MacDougal (Block 1531, lot 15), and 126 Sumpter Street (Block 1524, lot 43), Brooklyn, New York Data Recovery*. New York City Department of Housing and Development, New York.

———. 1999/2003. Archaeological Evaluation. In *The Lower East Side Tenement Museum, Historic Structure Report*. Lower East Side Tenement Museum, New York.

Gibson, Campbell. 1998. *Population of the 100 Largest Cities and Other Urban Places in the United States, 1790–1990*. Bureau of the Census, Washington, DC.

Gilroy, Paul. 1990. One Nation under a Groove: The Cultural Politics of Race and Racism in Britain. In *Anatomy of Racism*, ed. D. T. Goldberg, 262–82. University of Minnesota Press, Minneapolis.

Goldberg, David Theo. 1990. The Social Formation of Racist Discourse. In *Anatomy of Racism*, ed. D. T. Goldberg, 295–318. University of Minnesota Press, Minneapolis.

Gottesman, Ruth S. 1954. The Arts and Crafts in New York, 1777–1799: Advertisements and News from New York City Newspapers. *Collections, New-York Historical Society for 1948*.

Graff, Rebecca S. 2011. Being Toured While Digging Tourism: Excavating the Familiar at

Chicago's 1893 World's Columbian Exposition. *International Journal of Historical Archaeology* 15(2): 222–35.

Gray, D. Ryan, and Jill Yakubik. 2010. Immigration and Urbanization in New Orleans. In *The Archaeology of Louisiana*, ed. M. A. Rees, 291–305. Louisiana State University Press, Baton Rouge.

Greenwood, Roberta S. 1996. *Down by the Station: Los Angeles Chinatown, 1880–1933*. Institute of Archaeology, University of California, Los Angeles.

Griggs, Heather. 1999. Gog Cuire Dia Rath Blath Ort (God Grant That You Prosper and Flourish): Social and Economic Mobility among the Irish in Nineteeth-Century New York. *Historical Archaeology* 33(1): 87–101.

———. 2001. "By Virtue of Reason and Nature": Competition and Economic Strategy in the Needletrades at New York's Five Points. *Historical Archaeology* 35(3): 76–88.

Groover, Mark D. 2008. *The Archaeology of North American Farmsteads*. University Press of Florida, Gainesville.

Grossman, Joel. 1985. *The Excavation of Augustine Heermans's Warehouse and Associated Seventeenth-Century Dutch West India Company Deposits: The Broad Financial Center Mitigation Final Report, 1985*. Report on file at the New York City Landmarks Preservation Commission and the New York State Museum, Albany.

Gums, Bonnie L., George W. Shorter, Kristen Gremillion, and Diane S. Mueller. 1998. *Archaeology at Mobile's Exploreum: Discovering the Buried Past*. University of South Alabama, Mobile.

Gutman, Herbert G., and Ira Berlin. 1987. Class Composition and the Development of the American Working Class, 1840–1890. In *Power and Culture: Essays on the American Working Class*, ed. H. G. Gutman, 380–94. Pantheon, New York.

Gutman, Marta. 2004. The Landscapes of Lodging in West Oakland. In *Putting the "There" There: Historical Archaeologies of West Oakland*, ed. Mary Praetzellis and Adrian Praetzellis, 261–77. Sonoma Archaeological Center, Sonoma, CA.

Hall, Martin. 1992. Small Things and the Mobile, Conflictual Fusion of Power, Fear, and Desire. In *The Art and Mystery of Historical Archaeology: Essays in Honor of James Deetz*, ed. A. E. Yentsch, and M. C. Beaudry, 373–99. CRC Press, Boca Raton.

———. 2000. *Archaeology and the Modern World: Colonial Transcripts in South Africa and the Chesapeake*. Routledge, New York.

Harris, Wendy, and Arnold Pickman. 2011. The Rise and Demise of the Hudson River Ice Harvesting Industry: Urban Needs and Rural Responses. In *Environmental History of the Hudson River: Human Uses That Changed the Ecology, Ecology That Changed Human Uses*, ed. R. E. Henshaw and F. F. Dunwell, 201–18. State University of New York Press, Albany.

Hartley, Michael O. 2007. Bethabara and Beyond. Paper presented at the Society for Historical Archaeology 40th Annual Conference, Williamsburg, VA.

Harvey, David. 1973. *Social Justice and the City*. Johns Hopkins University Press, Baltimore.

———. 2008. *The Condition of Postmodernity: An Enquiry into the Origins of Cultural Change*. Wiley-Blackwell, Cambridge.

Hattori, Eugene M. 2008. Native American Women on Nevada's Mining Frontier. Paper presented at the Society for Historical Archaeology 41st Annual Conference, Albuquerque.

Hayden, Dolores. 1995. *The Power of Place: Urban Landscapes as Public History*. MIT Press, Cambridge.

Heck, Dana B., and Joseph F Balicki. 1998. Katherine Naylor's "House of Office": A Seventeenth-Century Privy. *Historical Archaeology* 32(3): 24–37.

Heilen, Michael. 2012 *Uncovering Identity in Mortuary Analysis: Community-Sensitive Methods for Identifying Group Affiliation in Historical Cemeteries*. Left Coast Press, Walnut Creek, CA; SRI Press, Tucson.

Heilen, Michael, and Marlesa A. Gray, eds. 2011. *Deathways and Lifeways in the American Southwest: Tucson's Historic Alameda-Stone Cemetery and the Transformation of a Remote Outpost into an Urban City*. Statistical Research, Tucson.

Hicks, Dan. 2005. "Places for Thinking" from Annapolis to Bristol: Situations and Symmetries in "World Historical Archaeology." *World Archaeology* 37(3): 373–91.

Hodder, Ian. 1982. *Symbols in Action*. Cambridge University Press, Cambridge.

———. 2010. *Religion in the Emergence of Civilization: Catalhoyuk as a Case Study*. Cambridge University Press, New York.

Hordes, Stanley M. 2010. The History of Santa Fe Plaza, 1610–1720. In *All Trails Lead to Santa Fe: An Anthology Commemorating the 400th Anniversary of the Founding of Santa Fe, New Mexico, in 1610*, ed. J. Sanchez, 129–46. Sunstone Press, Santa Fe.

Horowitz, Judith L. 1982. Review of Judd Kahn, *Imperial San Francisco: Politics and Planning in an American City, 1897–1906. Winterthur Portfolio* 17(2/3): 156–57.

Hosmer, Charles Bridgham. 1965. *Presence of the Past: A History of the Preservation Movement in the United States before Williamsburg*. Putnam, New York.

Howson, Jean. 1992–93. The Archaeology of 19th-Century Health and Hygiene at the Sullivan Street Site, New York City. *Northeast Historical Archaeology* 21–22: 137–60.

———. 2013. HW: Epitaph for a Working Man. In *Tales of Gotham: Historical Archaeology, Ethnohistory, and Microhistory of New York City*, ed. M. F. Janowitz and D. Dallal, 159–78. Springer, New York.

Howson, Jean, and Leonard G. Bianchi. 2009. *The Archaeology of First Street, Newark, New Jersey*. Data Recovery for the University Heights Connector Project, City of Newark, Essex County, NJ. Prepared for the New Jersey Department of Transportation by the RBA Group, Cultural Resource Unit, Parsippany.

Huey, Paul. 1985. Archaeological Excavations in the Site of Fort Orange, a Dutch West India Company Trading Fort Built in 1624. New Netherland Studies, *Bulletin KNOB* 2–3: 68–79.

———. 1998. Fort Orange Archaeological Site National Historic Landmark. *Bulletin, Journal of the New York State Archaeological Association* 114: 12–23.

Ignatiev, Noel. 1995. *How the Irish Became White*. Routledge, New York.

Ingle, Marjorie, Jean Howson, and Edward S. Rutsch. 1990. *A Stage 1A Cultural Resource Survey of the Proposed Foley Square Project in the Borough of Manhattan, New York, New York*. Submitted as appendix B of the Draft Environmental Impact Statement. Foley Square Proposed Federal Courthouse and Federal Municipal Office Building, New York City. General Services Administration, Washington, DC.

Ingold, Tim. 2000. *The Perception of the Environment: Essays on Livelihood, Dwelling, and Skill*. Routledge, New York.

————. 2012. Toward an Ecology of Materials. *Annual Review of Anthropology* 41: 427–42.

Jackson, Robert H. 1999. *Race, Caste, and Status: Indians in Colonial Spanish America*. University of New Mexico Press, Albuquerque.

Jamieson, Ross W. 2008. Comment on Gender, Race, and Labor in the Archaeology of the Spanish Colonial Americas, by Barbara L. Voss. *Current Anthropology* 49(5): 880–81.

Janowitz, Meta F. 2008. New York City Stonewares from the African Burial Ground. In *Ceramics in America 2008,* ed. Robert Hunter, 41–66. Chipstone Foundation, Milwaukee.

Jeppson, Patrice. 2006. Which Benjamin Franklin—Yours or Mine? Examining Responses to a New Story from the Historical Archaeology Site of Franklin Court. *Archaeologies* 2(2): 24–51.

————. 2010. Archaeological Heritage of "We the People": Public Archaeology at Independence National Historical Park. *Anthropology News* 51(8): 5–6.

Johnson, Matthew. 1996. *An Archaeology of Capitalism*. Blackwell, Cambridge, MA.

Jones, Sian. 1997. *The Archaeology of Ethnicity: Constructing Identities in the Past and Present*. Routledge, New York.

Katkins, Mara. n.d. Down and Out in Society Hill: An Examination of Changing Attitudes in the Treatment of the Poor during Eighteenth-Century America Utilizing the First Philadelphia Almshouse Excavation. Incomplete PhD diss., Temple University.

Ketz, K. Anne, Elizabeth J. Abel, and Andrew J. Schmidt. 2005. Public Image and Private Reality: An Analysis of Differentiation in a Nineteenth-Century St. Paul Bordello. *Historical Archaeology* 39(1): 74–88.

Killion, Rachel, Elizabeth O'Brien, Stuart Fiedel, and Charles Cheek. 2001. Fort Reno Park, NW, Washington DC, Phase I Archaeological Investigation. U.S. Department of the Interior, National Park Service, JMA, West Chester, PA.

King, Thomas F., Patricia P. Hickman, and Gary Berg. 1977. *Anthropology in Historic Preservation: Caring for Culture's Clutter*. Academic Press, New York.

Kraut, Alan M. 1994. *Silent Travelers: Germs, Genes, and the "Immigrant Menace."* Basic Books, New York.

Landon, David B. n.d. *Archaeology of the African Meeting House, a Dig, and Discovery Project in Boston, MA*. Museum of African American History and the Fiske Center for Archaeological Research at the University of Massachusetts, Boston.

Landon, David B., and Teresa Dujnic. 2007. *Investigating the Heart of a Community: Archaeological Excavations at the African Meeting House, Boston, Massachusetts*. Andrew Fiske Memorial Center for Archaeological Research, University of Massachusetts, Boston.

LaRoche, Cheryl Janifer. 2011. Archaeology, the Activist Community, and the Redistribution of Power in New York City. *Archaeologies* 7(3): 619–34.

LaRoche, Cheryl, and Michael L. Blakey. 1997. Seizing Intellectual Power: The Dialogue at the New York African Burial Ground. *Historical Archaeology* 31(3): 84–106.

LaRoche, Cheryl, and Gary S. McGowan. 2000. "Material Culture" Conservation and Analysis of Textiles Recovered from Five Points. In *Tales of Five Points: Working-Class Life in Nineteenth-Century New York,* ed. Rebecca Yamin, 2:275–87. U.S. General Services Administration, New York.

Lawler, Edward, Jr. 2002. The President's House in Philadelphia: The Rediscovery of a Lost Landmark. *Pennsylvania Magazine of History and Biography* 126(1): 5–95.

LeeDecker, Charles H. 1991. Depositional Processes in Historic Privies. Paper presented at the Annual Meeting of the Mid-Atlantic Archaeological Conference, Ocean City, MD.

Lefebvre, Henri. 1991. *The Production of Space*. Translated by D. Nicholson-Smith. Blackwell, Cambridge, MA.

Leone, Mark 1984. Interpreting Ideology in Historical Archaeology: Using the Rules of Perspective in the William Paca Garden in Annapolis, Maryland. In *Ideology, Power, and Prehistory*, ed. D. Miller and C. Tilley, 25–35. Cambridge University Press, New York.

———. 2005. *The Archaeology of Liberty in an American Capital: Excavations in Annapolis*. University of California Press, Berkeley.

Leone, Mark, and Parker B. Potter, eds. 1988. *The Recovery of Meaning: Historical Archaeology in the Eastern United States*. Smithsonian Institution Press, Washington, DC.

Leone, Mark, and Paul B. Shackel. 1987. Forks, Clocks, and Power: Towards a Critical Archaeology. In *Mirror and Metaphor: Material and Social Constructions of Reality*, ed. D. Ingersoll, 45–62. University Press of America, Lanham, MD.

Lesniak, Matthew. 2003. New Evidence of Wampum Use and Production from Albany, New York. In *People, Places, and Material Things: Historical Archaeology of Albany, New York*, ed. Charles S. Fisher, 129–34. New York State Museum Bulletin 499, State Education Department, University of the State of New York, Albany.

Levin, Jed. 2011 Activism Leads to Excavation: The Power of Place and the Power of the People at the President's House in Philadelphia. *Archaeologies* 7(3): 596–618.

Lewis, Ann Eliza, ed. 2001. *Highway to the Past: The Archaeology of Boston's Big Dig*. Massachusetts Historical Commission, Boston.

Linn, Meredith B. 2008. From Typhus to Tuberculosis and Fractures in Between: A Visceral Historical Archaeology of Irish Immigrant Life in New York City, 1845–1870. PhD diss., Columbia University, New York.

———. 2010. Elixir of Emigration: Soda Water and the Making of Irish Americans in Nineteenth-Century New York City. *Historical Archaeology* 44(4): 69–109.

Little, Barbara J. 1994. People with History: An Update on Historical Archaeology in the United States. *Journal of Archaeological Method and Theory* 1(1): 5–40.

Little, Barbara J., and Nancy J. Kassner. 2001. Archaeology in the Alleys of Washington, DC. In *Archaeology of Urban Landscapes: Explorations in Slumland*, ed. A. Mayne and T. Murray, 57–68. Cambridge University Press, Cambridge.

Louis Berger and Associates, Inc. 1987. *Archaeological and Historical Investigations at the Assay Site, Block 35*. New York City Landmarks Preservation Commission, New York.

———. 1997. *Archaeological and Historical Investigation of the Metropolitan Detention Center Site (36 PH 91), Philadelphia*. Prepared for the U.S. Department of Justice, Federal Bureau of Prisons, Washington, DC.

Low, Setha M. 1999. *Theorizing the City: The New Urban Anthropology Reader*. Rutgers University Press, New Brunswick, NJ.

Maeda, Julianne. 2012. Food for the Ancestors: Faunal Analysis at Seneca Village. Senior thesis (BA), Barnard College, New York, on file at Barnard College Department of Anthropology.

Mason, Philip P., and Henry D. Brown. 1964. *Detroit, Fort Lernoult, and the American Revolution*. Wayne State University Press, Detroit.

Matthews, Christopher. 2010. *The Archaeology of American Capitalism*. University Press of Florida, Gainesville.

Matthews, Christopher, Mark Leone, and Kurt A. Jordan. 2002. The Political Economy of Archaeological Cultures: Marxism and American Historical Archaeology. *Journal of Social Archaeology* 2(1): 109–34.

Mayne, Alan. 1993. *The Imagined Slum: Newspaper Representation in Three Cities*. Leicester University Press, Leicester.

Mayne, Alan, and Tim Murray. 2001. *The Archaeology of Urban Landscapes*. Cambridge University Press, Cambridge.

McCarthy, John P., and Jeanne A. Ward. 2000. Sanitation Practices, Depositional Processes, and Interpretive Contexts of Minneapolis Privies. *Historical Archaeology* 34(1): 111–29.

McDavid, Carol. 2007. Beyond Strategy and Good Intentions: Archaeology, Race, and White Privilege. In *Archaeology as a Tool of Civic Engagement,* ed. B. J. Little and P. A. Shackel, 67–88. AltaMira Press, Lanham, MD.

———. 2011. When Is "Gone" Gone? Archaeology, Gentrification, and Conflicting Narratives about Freedmen's Town, Houston. *Historical Archaeology* 45(3): 74–88.

McDonald, Molly R. 2011. Wharves and Waterfront Retaining Structures as Vernacular Architecture. *Historical Archaeology* 45(2): 42–67.

McGuire, Randall H. 1988. Dialogues with the Dead: Ideology and the Cemetery. In *The Recovery of Meaning: Historical Archaeology in the Eastern United States,* ed. M. P. Leone and P. B. Potter, 435–80. Smithsonian Institution Press, Washington, DC.

McGuire, Randall H., and Paul Reckner. 2002. The Unromantic West: Labor, Capital, and Struggle. *Historical Archaeology* 36(3): 44–58.

———. 2005. Building a Working-Class Archaeology: The Colorado Coal Field War Project. In *Industrial Archaeology: Future Directions,* ed. E. Casella and J. Symonds, 217–41. Springer, New York.

McLaughlin, Pegeen. 2003. Painted Pearlware from the Picotte Site. In *People, Places, and Material Things: Historical Archaeology of Albany, New York,* ed. Charles S. Fisher, 135–49. Museum Bulletin 499, SUNY, Albany.

Melosi, Martin V. 2000. *The Sanitary City: Urban Infrastructure in America from Colonial Times to the Present*. Johns Hopkins University Press, Baltimore.

Merwick, Donna. 1980. Dutch Townsmen and Land Use. *William and Mary Quarterly* 37(1): 53–78.

Meskell, Lynn. 2004. *Object Worlds in Ancient Egypt: Material Biographies Past and Present*. Berg, New York.

———. 2005. Introduction. In *Archaeology of Materialities,* ed. L. Meskell, 1–18. Blackwell, Malden, MA.

Meyer, Michael D., Erica S. Gibson, and Julia G. Costello. 2005. City of Angels, City of Sin: Archaeology in the Los Angeles Red-Light District ca. 1900. *Historical Archaeology* 39(1): 89–106.

Meyer, Michael J., and David C. Austin. 2008. *Below the Surface: Excavation of the Walsh's Row Site (23SL2234), St. Louis City, Missouri: In Association with the Proposed Interstate 64 Improvements, St. Louis City, Missouri*. For the Missouri Department of Transporation, Jefferson City.

Miller, Daniel. 1987. *Material Culture and Mass Consumption*. Blackwell, New York.

Miller, Henry M. 1988. Baroque Cities in the Wilderness: Archaeology and Urban Development in the Colonial Chesapeake. *Historical Archaeology* 22(2): 57–73.

Mooney, Douglas B., Edward M. Morin, Robert G. Wiencek, and Rebecca White. 2008. *Archaeological Investigations of the Spring Street Presbyterian Church Cemetery, 244–246 Spring Street, New York, NY*. Prepared by URS Corp. for Bayrock-Sapir Organization, LLC, New York.

Mrozowski, Stephen A. 2006. *The Archaeology of Class in Urban America*. Cambridge University Press, New York.

Mrozowski, Stephen, Grace Ziesling, and Mary Beaudry. 1996. *Living on the Boott: Historical Archaeology at the Boott Mills Bordinghouses, Lowell, MA*. Lowell Historic Preservation Commission, Lowell.

Mullins, Paul R. 1999. *Race and Affluence: An Archaeology of African America and Consumer Culture*. Kluwer/Plenum, New York

———. 2007. Politics, Inequality, and Engaged Archaeology: Community Archaeology along the Color Line. In *Archaeology as a Tool of Civic Engagment*, ed. B. J. Little and P. A. Shackel, 89–108. AltaMira Press, Lanham, MD.

———. 2011. *The Archaeology of Consumer Culture*. University Press of Florida, Gainesville.

Mumford, Lewis. 1961. *The City in History: Its Origins, Its Transformations, and Its Prospects*. Harcourt Brace and World, New York.

Nash, Gary B. 2002. *First City: Philadelphia and the Forging of Historical Memory*. University of Pennsylvania Press, Philadelphia.

———. 2006. For Whom Will the Liberty Bell Toll? From Controversy to Cooperation. In *Slavery and Public History: The Tough Stuff of American Memory*, ed. J. O. Horton and L. E. Horton, 75–103. New Press, New York.

Nassaney, Michael S., and Marjorie R. Abel. 1993. The Political and Social Contexts of Cutlery Production in the Connecticut River Valley. *Dialectical Anthropology* 18: 247–89.

Nelson, Sarah M., K. Lynn Berry, Richard F. Carrillo, Bonnie J. Clark, Lorie Rhodes, and Dean Saitta. 2001. *Denver: An Archaeological History*. University of Pennsylvania Press, Philadelphia.

Noel Hume, Ivor. 1969. *Archaeology and Wetherburn's Tavern*. Colonial Williamsburg Archaeological Series No. 3. Williamsburg, VA.

Norman, Joseph Gary. 1987. Eighteenth-Century Wharf Construction in Baltimore, Maryland. MA thesis, Department of Anthropology, College of William and Mary, Williamsburg, VA.

Ogle, Maureen. 1996. *All The Modern Conveniences: American Household Plumbing, 1840–1890*. Johns Hopkins University Press, Baltimore.

Olmsted, Frederick Law, Jr. 1911. The City Beautiful. In *The Builder 101*. urbanplanning.library.cornell.edu/DOCS/olmst_11.htm.

Orser, Charles E. 2004a. *Historical Archaeology*. Pearson Prentice Hall, Upper Saddle River, NJ.

———. 2004b. *Race and Practice in Archaeological Interpretation*. University of Pennsylvania Press, Philadelphia.

———. 2007. *The Archaeology of Race and Racialization in Historic America*. University Press of Florida, Gainesville.

———. 2011. The Archaeology of Poverty and the Poverty of Archaeology. In Special Collection: Poverty in Depth: New International Perspectives. *International Journal of Historical Archaeology* 15(4): 75–103.

Palus, Matthew M. 2010. *Materialities of Government: A Historical Archeology of Infrastructure in Annapolis and Eastport*. PhD diss., Department of Anthropology, Columbia University, New York.

———. 2012. Networked Infrastructure as the Material Culture of Liberal Government. Paper presented at the 45th Annual Meeting of the Society for Historical Archaeology, Baltimore.

Pastron, Allen G. 1990. The Hoff Store Site: An Introduction. In *The Hoff Store Site and Gold Rush Merchandise from San Francisco, California*, ed. A. G. Pastron and E. Hattori, 1–3. Society for Historical Archaeology, Special Publication Series 7.

Pastron, Allen G., and Eugene M. Hattori, eds. 1990. *The Hoff Store Site and Gold Rush Merchandise from San Francisco, California*. Society for Historical Archaeology, Special Publication Series 7.

Paynter, Robert. 1982. *Models of Spatial Inequality: Settlement Patterns in Historical Archaeology*. Academic Press, New York.

Peña, Elizabeth S. 2003. Making "Money" the Old-Fashioned Way: Eighteenth-Century Wampum Production in Albany. In *People, Places, and Material Things: Historical Archaeology of Albany, New York*, ed. Charles S. Fisher, 122–27. New York State Museum Bulletin 499, New York State Education Department/University of the State of New York, Albany.

Pickman, Arnold, and Nan A. Rothschild. 1981. *64 Pearl Street: An Archaeological Excavation in 17th-Century Landfill*. Prepared for the New York Landmarks Conservancy.

Plewa, Tara Marie. 2009. A Trickle Runs through It: An Environmental History of the Santa Fe River, New Mexico. PhD diss., Department of Geography, University of South Carolina, Columbia.

Pollack, David, A. Gwynne Henderson, and Peter E. Killoran. 2009. *Frankfort's Forgotten Cemetery*. In Education Series, Kentucky Archaeological Survey, Lexington.

Praetzellis, Adrian. 1991. The Archaeology of a Victorian City: Sacramento, California. PhD diss., University of California, Berkeley.

———. 2004 Consumerism, Living Conditions, and Material Well-Being. In *Putting the "There" There: Historical Archaeologies of West Oakland: I-880 Cypress Freeway Replacement Project*, ed. M. Praetzellis and A. Praetzellis, 47–83. Anthropological Studies Center, Sonoma State University; Distributed by Dept. of Transportation, District 4, Cultural Resource Studies Office. Caltrans, Office of Cultural Resource Studies, Oakland, CA.

———. 2009. Ethnicity and Socio-Economic Status. In *South of Market: Historical Archaeology of 3 San Francisco Neighborhoods: The San Francisco–Oakland Bay Bridge West Approach Project*, ed. A. Praetzellis and M. Praetzellis, 303–22. California Dept. of Transportation, District 4, Oakland.

Praetzellis, Adrian, and Mary Praetzellis. 1992. Faces and Facades: Victorian Ideology in Early Sacramento. In *The Art and Mystery of Historical Archaeology: Essays in Honor of James Deetz*, ed. A. E. Yentsch, and M. C. Beaudry, 75–100. CRC Press, Boca Raton.

———. 2001. Mangling Symbols of Gentility in the Wild West: Case Studies in Interpretive Archaeology. *American Anthropologist* 103: 645–54.

———. 2004. Black Is Beautiful: From Porters to Panthers in West Oakland. In *Putting the "There" There: Historical Archaeologies of West Oakland: I-880 Cypress Freeway Replacement Project*, ed. M. Praetzellis and A. Praetzellis, 279–304. Anthropological Studies Center, Sonoma State University; distributed by Department of Transportation, District 4, Cultural Resource Studies Office. Caltrans, Office of Cultural Resource Studies, Oakland, CA.

———. 2009. *South of Market: Historical Archaeology of 3 San Francisco Neighborhoods: The San Francisco–Oakland Bay Bridge West Approach Project*. California Department of Transportation, District 4, Oakland.

Praetzellis, Mary. 2004. Chinese Oaklanders: Overcoming the Odds. In *Putting the "There" There: Historical Archaeologies of West Oakland: I-880 Cypress Freeway Replacement Project*, ed. M. Praetzellis and A. Praetzellis, 237–59. Anthropological Studies Center, Sonoma State University; distributed by Department of Transportation, District 4, Cultural Resource Studies Office. Caltrans, Oakland.

Praetzellis, Mary, and Adrian Praetzellis. 1992. *"We Were There, Too": Archaeology of an African-American Family in Sacramento, California*. Cultural Resources Facility, Anthropological Studies Center, Sonoma State University, Rohnert Park, CA.

———. 2004. *Putting the "There" There: Historical Archaeologies of West Oakland: I-880 Cypress Freeway Replacement Project*. Anthropological Studies Center, Sonoma State University; distributed by Department of Transportation, District 4, Cultural Resource Studies Office, Caltrans, Oakland, CA.

Praetzellis, Mary, Adrian Praetzellis, and Marley R. Brown III, eds. 1980. *Historical Archaeology at the Golden Eagle Site*. Cultural Resource Facility, Anthropological Studies Center, Sonoma State University, Sonoma, CA.

———. 1987. Artifacts as Symbols of Identity: An Example from Sacramento's Gold Rush Era Chinese Community. *Historical Archaeology*, special issue no. 5, Living in Cities, ed. E. Staski, 38–47.

———. 1988. What Happened to the Silent Majority? Research Strategies for Studying Dominant Group Material Culture in Late Nineteenth-Century California. In *Documentary Archaeology in the New World*, ed. M. Beaudry, 192–202. Cambridge University Press, New York.

Praetzellis, Mary, Adrian Praetzellis, and Thad Van Bueren. 2007. Remaking Connections: Archaeology and Community after the Loma Prieta Earthquake. In *Archaeology as a Tool of Civic Engagement*, ed. B. J. Little and P. A. Shackel, 109–30. AltaMira Press, Lanham, MD.

Psota, Sunshine, and Mary Beaudry. 2009. Needleworkers and Sewing Implements. In *South of Market: Historical Archaeology of Three San Francisco Neighborhoods*, ed. M. Praetzellis and A. Praetzellis. Sonoma Archaeological Center, Sonoma, CA.

Reckner, Paul E., and Stephen A. Brighton. 1999. "Free from All Vicious Habits": Archaeological Perspectives on Class Conflict and the Rhetoric of Temperance. *Historical Archaeology* 33(1): 63–86.

Ritchie, Neville. 1993. Form and Adaptation: 19th Century Chinese Miners' Dwellings in

New Zealand. In *Hidden Heritage: Historical Archaeology of the Overseas Chinese*, ed. P. Wegars, 335–73. Baywood, Amityville, NY.

Roberts, Daniel G., and John P. McCarthy. 1995. Descendant Community Partnering in the Archaeological and Bioanthropological Investigation of African American Skeletal Populations: Two Interrelated Case Studies from Philadelphia. In *Bodies of Evidence: Reconstructing History through Skeletal Analysis*, ed. A. L. Grauer, 19–36. Wiley-Liss, New York.

Rock, Howard B. 1979. *Artisans of the New Republic: The Tradesmen of New York City in the Age of Jefferson*. New York University Press, New York.

Rockman, Diana diZerega, and Nan A. Rothschild. 1984. City Tavern, Country Tavern: An Analysis of Four Colonial Sites. *Historical Archaeology* 18: 112–21.

Rothschild, Nan A. 1990. *New York City Neighborhoods: The 18th Century*. Academic Press, San Diego; 2008 facsimile ed., Percheron Press, Clinton Corners, NY.

———. 1992. The Development of "Rational" Markets in Historic New York City. Presented at American Anthropological Association Annual Meeting, San Francisco.

———. 2003. *Colonial Encounters in a Native American Landscape: The Spanish and Dutch in North America*. Smithsonian Books, Washington, DC.

———. 2006. Colonial and Post-Colonial New York: Issues of Size and Scale. In *Urbanism in the Preindustrial World: Cross-Cultural Approaches*, ed. G. R. Storey. University of Alabama Press, Tuscaloosa.

———. 2008. Colonized Bodies: Personal and Social. In *Past Bodies: Body-Centered Research in Archaeology*, ed. D. Boric and J. Robb, 135–44. Oxbow Books, Oxford.

Rothschild, Nan, and Arnold Pickman. 1990. *The Archaeological Investigations on the Seven Hanover Square Block*. For the New York City Landmarks Preservation Commission, New York City.

Rothschild, Nan, and Diana Rockman [Wall]. 1982. Method in Urban Archaeology: The Stadt Huys Block. In *Archaeology of Urban America*, ed. R. S. Dickens Jr., 3–18. Academic Press, New York.

Rothschild, Nan, Diana diZerega Wall, and Eugene Boesch. 1987. *The Archaeological Investigations of the Stadt Huys Block: A Final Report*. New York: New York City Landmarks Preservation Commission.

Rutsch, Edward. 1975. Salvage Archaeology in Paterson, N.J., 1973–75. *Northeast Historical Archaeology* 4(1–2): 1–16.

Sackett, James R. 1977. The Meaning of Style. *American Antiquity* 42: 369–80.

———. 1985. Style and Ethnicity in the Kalahari: A Reply to Wiessner. *American Antiquity* 50(1): 154–59.

Sacks, Karen Brodkin. 1994. How Jews Became White. In *Race*, ed. S. Gregory and R. Sanjek, 78–102. Rutgers University Press, New Brunswick.

Said, Edward. 1978. *Orientalism*. Random House, New York.

Salwen, Bert, Sarah Bridges, and Nan A. Rothschild. 1981. The Utility of Small Samples from Historic Sites. *Historical Archaeology* 15(1): 79–94.

Samford, Virginia. 1996. The Archaeology of Virginia's Urban Areas. In *The Archaeology of Eighteenth-Century Virginia*, ed. T. R. Reinhart, 35: 65–86. Archaeological Society of Virginia.

Sanchez, Joseph P. 2010. Introduction. *All Trails Lead to Santa Fe: An Anthology Commemo-*

rating the 400th Anniversary of the Founding of Santa Fe, New Mexico, in 1610, ed. J. San-chez, 19–33. Sunstone Press, Santa Fe.

Scheick, Cherie L. 2003. Final Report: Archaeological Resources of "La Otra Banda del Rio." City of Santa Fe Railroad Properties. Santa Fe City Rail Yard Project, Santa Fe.

Schuyler, Robert. 1978. *Historical Archaeology: A Guide to Substantive and Theoretical Contri-butions.* Baywood, Farmingdale, NY.

Seasholes, Nancy S. 1998. Filling Boston's Mill Pond. *Historical Archaeology* 32(3): 121–36.

———. 2003. *Gaining Ground: A History of Landmaking in Boston.* MIT Press, Cambridge.

Seifert, Donna J. 1991. Within Sight of the White House: The Archaeology of Working Women. *Historical Archaeology* 24(4): 82–108.

———. 1994. Mrs. Starr's Profession. In *Those of Little Note: Gender, Race, and Class in His-torical Archaeology,* ed. E. M. Scott, 149–73. University of Arizona Press, Tucson.

Seifert, Donna J., and Joseph Balicki. 2005. Mary Ann Hall's House. *Historical Archaeology* 39(1): 59–73.

Seifert, Donna J., Elizabeth B. O'Brien, and Joseph Balicki. 2000. Mary Ann Hall's First-Class House: The Archaeology of a Capital Brothel. In *Archaeologies of Sexuality,* ed. R. A. Schmidt and B. L. Voss, 117–28. Routledge, London.

Shackel, Paul A. 1996. *Culture Change and the New Technology: An Archaeology of the Early American Industrial Era.* Plenum Press, New York.

———. 2004. Heritage Development and Applied Archaeology. In *Places in Mind: Public Archaeology as Applied Anthropology,* ed. P. A. Shackel and E. Chambers, 1–18. Routledge, New York.

———. 2010. Identity and Collective Action in a Multiracial Community. *Historical Archae-ology* 44(1): 58.

Silliman, Stephen. 2005. Culture Contact or Colonialism? Challenges in the Archaeology of Native North America. *American Antiquity* 70(1): 55–74.

Sjoberg, Gideon. 1960. *The Preindustrial City, Past and Present.* Free Press, Glencoe, IL.

Slattery, David. 2008. Minding the Gaps (Epistemological and Modern) on Dublin's New Light-Rail System. *International Journal of Baudrillard Studies* 5(1): note 1. www.ubishops.ca/baudrillardstudies/vol5_1/v5-1-article17-slattery.html.

Smith, Neil. 2008. *Uneven Development: Nature, Capital, and the Production of Space.* Univer-sity of Georgia Press, Athens.

Smits, Nicholas J. 2008. Roots Entwined: Archaeology of an Urban Chinese American Cemetery. *Historical Archaeology* 42(3): 111.

Snow, David H. 1996. *Archaeological and Historical Investigations for the New Mexico School for the Deaf Water System Installation (Sangre de Cristo Water Co.), Santa Fe, New Mexico.* Rivers and Trails, and Suburban Districts, Santa Fe. Prepared for New Mexico School of the Deaf.

Soja, Edward W. 1989. *Postmodern Genographies: The Reassertion of Space in Critical Social Theory.* Verso, London.

———. 1996. *Thirdspace: Journeys to Los Angeles and Other Real-and-Imagined Places.* Black-well, Cambridge, MA.

———. 2000. *Postmetropolis: Critical Studies of Cities and Regions.* Blackwell, Malden, MA.

Solari, Elaine-Maryse. 2001. The Making of an Archaeological Site and the Unmaking of a

Community in West Oakland, CA. In *The Archaeology of Urban Landscapes: Explorations in Slumland,* ed. A. Mayne and T. Murray, 22–38. Cambridge University Press, Cambridge.

Spencer-Wood, Suzanne M. 1991. Toward an Historical Archaeology of Materialistic Domestic Reform. In *The Archaeology of Inequality,* ed. R. H. McGuire and R. Paynter, 231–86. Blackwell, Oxford.

Stallybrass, Peter, and Allen White. 2007. The City: The Sewer, the Gaze, and the Contaminating Touch. In *Beyond the Body Proper: Reading the Anthropology of Material Life,* ed. M. M. Lock and J. Farquhar, 266–85. Duke University Press, Durham.

Staski, Edward B. 1993. The Overseas Chinese in El Paso: Changing Goals, Changing Realities. In *Hidden Heritage: Historical Archaeology of the Overseas Chinese,* ed. P. Wegars, 125–50. Baywood, Amityville, NY.

Stewart, Pamela J., and Andrew Strathern. 2003. *Landscape, Memory, and History: Anthropological Perspectives.* Pluto, London.

Stokes, I. N. Phelps. 1915–28. *Iconography of Manhattan Island, 1498–1909.* 6 vols. Dodd, New York.

Stoler, Ann. 1997. Sexual Affronts and Racial Frontiers. In *Tensions of Empire: Colonial Cultures in a Bourgeois World,* ed. F. Cooper and A. L. Stoler, 198–237. University of California Press, Berkeley.

Stottman, M. Jay. 1996. Out of Sight, Out of Mind: An Archaeological Analysis of the Perception of Sanitation. MA thesis, Department of Anthropology, University of Kentucky, Lexington.

———. 2000. Out of Sight, Out of Mind: Privy Architecture and the Perceptions of Sanitation. *Historical Archaeology* 34(1): 39–61.

———. 2010. Landscape and Memory at Western Cemetery, Louisville, Ky. Paper presented at the 27th Annual Kentucky Heritage Council Archaeology Conference, Cumberland Falls State Park.

Stottman, M. Jay, and Lori Stahlgren. 2006. *Archaeological Investigations at the Center St Site (15WA116) and the 306 Seventh St Site (15WA117), Bowling Green, KY (ITEM NO. 3-310.00).* Kentucky Archaeological Survey, Report 110. Bowling Green.

Sutphin, Amanda. 2012. Working in the World of New York City Archaeology. Paper presented at the conference Women in Archaeology, Hunter College, New York City.

Teaford, Jon. 1998. Urbanization. In *Encyclopedia of Urban America: The Cities and the Suburbs,* ed. N. L. Shumsky, 2:841–51. ABC-CLIO, Santa Barbara.

Terrey, Paula B., and Allen G. Pastron. 1990. Chinese Export Porcelain in Gold Rush San Francisco. In *The Hoff Store Site and Gold Rush Merchandise from San Francisco, California,* ed. A. G. Pastron and E. M. Hattori, 75–81. Society for Historical Archaeology, Special Publication Series 7.

Thiel, J. Homer. 1997. *Archaeological Investigations of a Chinese Gardener's Household, Tucson, Arizona.* Center for Desert Archaeology, Tucson.

———. 1998. *Phoenix's Hidden History: Archaeological Investigations at Blocks 72 and 73.* Center for Desert Archaeology, Tucson.

———. 2005. *Down by the River: Archaeological and Historical Studies of the León Family Farmstead.* Center for Desert Archaeology, Tucson.

Thiel, J. Homer, and Jonathan B. Mabry. 2006. *Final Report: Rio Nuevo Archaeology, 2000–2003*. Technical Report 2004–11. Center for Desert Archaeology, Tucson.

Thomas, Julian. 2001. *Interpretive Archaeology: A Reader*. Continuum International, London.

———. 2007. The Trouble with Material Culture. In *Overcoming the Modern Invention of Material Culture: Proceedings of the TAG Session, Exeter 2006*, ed. V. O. Jorge and J. Thomas, special issue of *Iberian Archaeology* 9–10: 11–23. ADECAP, Porto.

Thompson, E. P. 1964. *The Making of the English Working Class*. Pantheon Books, New York.

Tigges, Linda. 1990. *Santa Fe Historic Plaza Study: With Translations from Spanish Colonial Documents*. City Planning Department, Santa Fe.

Upton, Dell. 1988. White and Black Landscapes in Eighteenth-Century Virginia. In *Material Life in America, 1600–1800*, ed. R. B. St. George, 357–69. Northeastern University Press, Boston.

———. 1996. Ethnicity, Authenticity, and Invented Traditions. *Historical Archaeology* 30(2): 1–7.

Voss, Barbara L. 2005. The Archaeology of Overseas Chinese Communities. *World Archaeology* 37(3): 424–39.

———. 2006. Engendered Archaeology: Men, Women, and Others. In *Historical Archaeology*, ed. M. Hall and S. W. Silliman, 107–27. Blackwell, Malden, MA.

———. 2008. Gender, Race, and Labor in the Archaeology of the Spanish Colonial Americas. *Current Anthropology* 49(5): 861–93.

Voss, Barbara L., and Rebecca Allen. 2008. Overseas Chinese Archaeology: Historical Foundations, Current Reflections, and New Directions. *Historical Archaeology* 42(3): 5–28.

Voss, Barbara L., and Robert A. Schmidt. 2000. Introduction to *Archaeologies of Sexuality*, ed. R. A. Schmidt and B. L. Voss, 1–32. Routledge, London.

Walker, Mark. 2004. Aristocracies of Labor: Craft Unionism, Immigration, and Working-Class Households. In *Putting the "There" There: Historical Archaeologies of West Oakland: I-880 Cypress Freeway Replacement Project*, ed. M. Praetzellis and A. Praetzellis, 207–36. For the Department of Transportation, District 4, Cultural Resource Studies Office, Federal Highway Administration, by the Anthropological Studies Center, Sonoma State University, Rohnert Park, California.

———. 2009. Maritime Workers. In *South of Market: Historical Archaeology of Three San Francisco Neighborhoods*, ed. M. Praetzellis and A. Praetzellis, 323–56. For the California Department of Transportation, District 4, Oakland, by the Sonoma Archaeological Center, Sonoma.

Wall, Diana diZerega. 1987. At Home in New York: Changing Family Life among the Propertied in the Late Eighteenth and Early Nineteenth Centuries. PhD diss., Department of Anthropology, New York University, New York.

———. 1991. Sacred Dinners and Secular Teas: Constructing Domesticity in Mid-19th-Century New York. *Historical Archaeology* 25(4): 69–81.

———. 1994. *The Archaeology of Gender: Separating the Spheres in Urban America*. Plenum, New York.

———. 1999. Examining Gender, Class, and Ethnicity in Nineteenth-Century New York City. *Historical Archaeology* 33(1): 102–17.

———. 2002. Setting the Table. Paper presented at the 35th Annual Meeting of the Society for Historical Archaeology, Mobile, AL.

———. 2008. Daniel Van Voorhis, a Dutch-American Artisan in Post-Colonial New York City. In *From De Halve Maen to KLM: 400 Years of Dutch-American Exchange,* ed. M. B. Lacy, C. Gehring, and J. Oosterhoff, 57–70. Nodus, Munster, Germany.

———. 2013. The Van Voorhis Family: Artisans in Post-Colonial New York City. In *Tales of Gotham: Historical Archaeology, Ethnohistory, and Microhistory of New York City,* ed. Diane Dallal and Meta Janowitz, 211–24. Springer, New York.

Wall, Diana diZerega, and Anne-Marie Cantwell. 2004. *Touring Gotham's Archaeological Past: Eight Self-Guided Walking Tours through New York City.* Yale University Press, New Haven.

———. 2013. Imagining the Stadt Huys. In *Opening Statements: Law, Jurisprudence, and the Legacy of Dutch New York,* ed. Albert M. Rosenblatt and Julia C. Rosenblatt, 105–116. State University of New York Press, Albany.

Wall, Diana diZerega, Nan A. Rothschild, and Cynthia Copeland. 2008. Seneca Village and Little Africa: Two African American Communities in Antebellum New York City. *Historical Archaeology* 42(1): 97–107.

———. 2010. Seneca Village and Weeksville: Two African American Communities in Antebellum New York City. Paper presented at the 43rd Annual Meeting of the Society for Historical Archaeology, Amelia Island, FL.

Wallace, Michael. 1986. Visiting the Past: History Museums in the United States. In *Presenting the Past: Essays on History and The Public,* ed. S. P. Benson, S. Brier, and R. Rosenzweig, 137–64. Temple University, Philadelphia.

Warner, Mark S. 1998. Food and the Negotiation of African American Identities in Annapolis, Maryland, and the Chesapeake. PhD diss., Department of Anthropology, University of Virginia, Charlottesville.

Warner, Mark S., and Robert A. Genheimer. 2008. "Cats Here, Cats There, Cats and Kittens Everywhere": An Urban Extermination of Cats in Nineteenth-Century Cincinnati. *Historical Archaeology* 42(1): 11–25.

Westmont, V. Camille. 2012. Rising to Meet the American Queensware Challenge: A Stratigraphic Analysis of the Lewis Pottery Site. Senior honors thesis, Department of Anthropology, University of Kentucky, Lexington.

Wheeler, Kathleen, ed. 2000a. View from the Outhouse: What We Can Learn from the Excavation of Privies. *Historical Archaeology* 34(1): 97–110.

———. 2000b. Theoretical and Methodological Considerations for Excavating Privies. *Historical Archaeology* 34(1): 3–19.

Wiessner, Polly. 1983. Style and Social Information in Kalahari San Projectile Points. *American Antiquity* 48(2): 253–76.

———. 1984. Reconsidering the Behavioral Basis for Style: A Case Study among the Kalahari San. *Journal of Anthropological Archaeology* 3(3): 190–234.

———. 1985. Style or Isochrestic Variation? A Reply to Sackett. *American Antiquity* 50(1): 160–66.

Wilkie, Laurie A. 2003. *The Archaeology of Mothering: An African-American Midwife's Tale.* Routledge, New York.

——. 2010. *The Lost Boys of Zeta Psi: A Historical Archaeology of Masculinity at a University Fraternity.* University of California Press, Berkeley.

Wilkie, Laurie A., and Katherine Howlett Hayes. 2006. Engendered and Feminist Archaeologies of the Recent and Documented Pasts. *Journal of Archaeological Research* 14: 243–64.

Wilkie, Laurie A., and George W. Shorter Jr. 2001. *Lucrecia's Well: An Archaeological Glimpse of an African-American Midwife's Household.* University of South Alabama Center for Archaeological Studies, Mobile.

Will de Chaparro, Martina. 2007. *Death and Dying in New Mexico.* University of New Mexico Press, Albuquerque.

Williams, Bryn. 2008. Chinese Masculinities and Material Culture. *Historical Archaeology* 42(3): 53–67.

Williams, Martha, Noran Sheehan, and Suzanne Sanders. 2000. *Phase I, II, and III Archaeological Investigations at the Juvenile Justice Center, Baltimore, Maryland.* Prepared for Maryland Department of General Services by R. Christopher Goodwin and Associates, Frederick.

Williams, Richard E. 1990. *Hierarchical Structures and Social Value: The Creation of Black and Irish Identities in the United States.* Cambridge University Press, New York.

Wirth, Louis. 1938. Urbanism as a Way of Life. *American Journal of Sociology* 44: 1–24.

Wobst, H. Martin. 1977. Stylistic Behavior and Information Exchange. In *For the Director: Research Essays in Honor of James B. Griffin,* ed. C. E. Cleland, Michigan Anthropological Papers 61: 317–42. Museum of Anthropology, University of Michigan, Ann Arbor.

Wurst, LouAnn, and Robert K. Fitts. 1999. Introduction: Why Confront Class? *Historical Archaeology* 33(1): 1–6.

Yamin, Rebecca. 1999. *With Hope and Labor: Everyday Life in Paterson's Dublin Neighborhood: Data Recovery on Blocks 863 and 866 within the Route 19 Connector Corridor in Paterson, New Jersey.* Prepared for New Jersey Department of Transportation by John Milner Associates, Philadelphia.

——, ed. 2000a. *Tales of Five Points: Working-Class Life in Nineteenth-Century New York.* 7 vols. Prepared for Edwards and Kelcey Engineers, Inc., and the General Services Administration by John Milner Associates, West Chester, PA.

——. 2000b. People and Their Possessions. In *Tales of Five Points,* ed. Yamin, 1: 91–148.

——. 2001. Alternative Narratives: Respectability at New York's Five Points. In *The Archaeology of Urban Landscapes: Explorations in Slumland,* ed. A. Mayne and T. Murray, 154–70. Cambridge University Press, Cambridge.

——. 2005. Wealthy, Free, and Female: Prostitution in Nineteenth-Century New York. *Historical Archaeology* 39(1): 4–18.

——. 2007. *Hudson's Square: A Place through Time. Archaeology Data Recovery on Block 2 of Independence Mall.* John Milner Associates, Philadelphia.

——. 2008. *Digging in the City of Brotherly Love: Stories from Philadelphia Archaeology.* Yale University Press, New Haven.

Yentsch, Anne E. 1994. *A Chesapeake Family and Their Slaves: A Study in Historical Archaeology.* Cambridge University Press, Cambridge.

——. 2009. Tracing Immigrant Women and Their Household Possessions in 19th-Century San Francisco. In *South of Market: Historical Archaeology of 3 San Francisco Neigh-*

borhoods: The San Francisco–Oakland Bay Bridge, ed. A. Praetzellis and M. Praetzellis, 134–87. Prepared for the California Department of Transportation, District 4, by the Anthropological Studies Center, Sonoma State, Rohnert Park, CA.

——. 2011. A Teapot, a House, or Both? The Material Possessions of Irish Women's California Assemblages. *Archaeologies* 7(1): 170–221.

Yokota, Kariann Akemi. 2011. *Unbecoming British: How Revolutionary America Became a Postcolonial Nation.* Oxford University Press, New York.

Zierden, Martha A., and Elizabeth J. Reitz. 2005. Archaeology at City Hall: Charleston's Colonial Beef Market. *Archaeological Contributions* 34. Charleston Museum, Charleston.

——. 2007. *Charleston through the 18th Century: Archaeology at the Heyward Washington House Stable.* Charleston Museum, Charleston.

Zueblin, Charles. 1905. *Decade of Civic Development.* University of Chicago Press, Chicago.

Index

Page numbers in *italics* refer to photographs or illustrations.

Arizona: Phoenix, 19, 50, 51–52; statehood, 127; Tucson, 50–51, 122, 124–26, 127–28, 163–65, 188

Art, 4

Artifact, city as: baroque cities, 48–49, 186; less formal landscapes, 47–48; nineteenth-century concerns and the ideal city, 52–54; overview, 1, 20, 38, 70; planning early urban landscapes, examples, 41–47; urban expansion, 54–69; urban plans and landscapes, 38–41; urban renewal and, 41, 69–70, 116–17; utopian landscape, 49, 53; western urban landscapes, 50–52

Artifacts. *See* Material culture

Artisan system, 87–90, 92, 96, 135, 136, 169, 190

Assay (New York City), 57, 60, 60

Auger test, 31

Australia, 120, 121, 191, 196n3; Archaeology of the Modern City project, 196n3

Avenging the Ancestors Coalition (ATAC), 182

Backyards, urban: of boardinghouses, 98, 148; of brothels, 156–57; excavation methods, 32; as mini-landscapes, 64–65; as ornamental space, 148; wells in, 61. *See also* Cisterns; Privies

Baroque cities, 48–49, 186

Basement floors, excavation, 32, 33, 80, 175

Beads, 73–74, 111, 111

Belize, 114

Beverages: alcoholic (*See* Alcoholic beverages); coffee, 80, 86; tea, 85, 86, 115, 126 (*See also* Tea ware); tonic water and soda water, 123, 129

Bias. *See* Subjectivity in archaeological research

Bioarchaeology, 160, 176, 177

Birth control, 156–57

Blacksmith, 94

Blakey, Michael, 170, 176, 177, 178

Boarding and lodging, 92, 94, 96–99, 148

Bone(s): buttons, 157; cattle, 56; dice, 124; feline, 61; human, 163, 164–65, 166, 170, 172, 176; from meals, 85, 98, 126

Boott Mills (Lowell, Mass.), 94, 98

Boston, Mass.: African Meeting House project, 117–19, 118; "Big Dig" (Central Artery/Tunnel Project), 75; landfill, 60; privies, 62–63, 118; reform movements, 157; settlement, 16, 18; as a walking city, 7; waterfront, 55

Bottles, 75–76, 80, 86, 101, 156, 164, 168

Brady, Congressman Robert, 182

Brick: Charleston Beef Market, 84; cistern, privy, and well construction, 62, 63, 65; Golden Eagle Hotel, 99; heat ducts, 137; New Orleans recon-struction, 46; President's House, 184; reuse, 68; sampling methods, 34

Bridges, 46, 53, 54

British. *See* English and English Americans

Brothels, 155–57

Buildings: of civil and religious power (*See* Structures, institutional); "ghost structure" to display, 24; historical preservation, 21–24, 26–27, 28; post-fires reconstruction, 46; post-World War I reconstruction, 22; special purpose (*See* Structures, special purpose); tenement, 65, 66, 69. *See also* Architecture

Burials. *See* Funerary industry; Human burials; Mortuary ritual

Buttons, 33, 58, 91, 111, 157, 164, 172

California: anti-immigration legislation, 122; Berkeley, 152–53; Los Angeles, 19, 155, 156, 157, 192; migrants from rural areas, 19; Oakland, 69, 85, 116, 155; Sacramento, 10, 98–99, 114–15, 126; San Bernardino, 124; San Francisco (*See* San Francisco); San Jose, 122–23, 153–54; Stockton, 100, 125; West Oakland (*See* West Oakland)

Canals: agricultural irrigation, 42, 50, 63; creation, 90, 92; Erie Canal, 80; Morris Canal, 94; transportation, 17, 41, 54; water power, 94

Candace (whaler), 78

Capitalism: colonialism to ensure materials and markets, 16, 71–72, 77; grid layout and, 40; industrial, 17, 70, 92, 101, 148, 170, 190; mercantile, merchant, or commercial, 17, 18, 48, 71–72, 80, 148, 190; rise as a worldwide system, 71, 79, 80

Caribbean, 16, 44, 46, 77, 120, 150

Castillo de San Marcos (St. Augustine, Fla.), 23

Cemeteries: Alameda-Stone Cemetery, 163–65; archaeological study of, 160, 188; common burial, 162–63, 164; composition, and the urban landscape, 160–65, 171; Freedman's Cemetery, 167–68, 174; garden-like or park-like, 163, 167, 171; Lone Fir Cemetery, 122, 170; military, 164, 165; Old Frankfort Cemetery, 162–63; property values and space for, 160; public health concerns, 166, 171; reflection of status, 170–73; segregation by race, 161, 163, 173, 188; segregation by religion, 163, 171–72; segregation by social class, 161, 163, 171, 188; Spring Street Presbyterian Church Cemetery, 172–73; vaults, 164, 172; Western Cemetery, 163. *See also* African Burial Ground

Census data, 5, 21, 30, 39, 87, 100, 112

Central business district, 10

Community archaeology, 158, 159, 174, 177–79, 181–84, 190–91, 195n4, 195n8

Conkey, Margaret, 149

Conservators, 36

Consultants, independent, 28

Consumption practices, 46, 103, 112–15, 122–23, 132, 190

Contract archaeology, 27, 28. *See also* Cultural Resource Management

Cook family (West Oakland, Calif.), 114–15

Cooking: kosher practices, 132; metal pots, 50; metate, 128; private *vs.* public cookware, 150; stone mano, 128; tortilla griddle (comale), 50, 128; as women's work, 109–10, 154

Cotton, 44, 94, 130

Cotton Men's Executive Council, 130

Counting artifacts: abacus, 100; counting boards/cloths, 73

Countinghouses, 55

Courthouses, 10, 51

Creolization, 109–10, 112, 123, 189, 190

Crolius pottery (New York City), 89, *89*

Cuba, 44

Cultural Resource Management (CRM), 27, 28, 30, 54, 186

Culture. *See* Values, cultural

Curators, 36

Currency. *See* Coins; Wampum

Customs house, 87

Databases, 191

Deagan, Kathleen, 150

Death: attitudes toward, 160, 161, 165; "Beautification of Death" movement, 160, 166–69, 171, 188; funerary industry, 167, 188; "Good Death," 160, 165–66, 188. *See also* Cemeteries; Human burial; Mortuary ritual

Delaware: New Sweden, 58

Diet. *See* Food(s); Foodways

Discrimination: class, 161, 163, 171, 188; disease and, 130; racial, 99–100, 114–15, 122, 125, 127, 161, 163, 173, 188; racism, methodologies, 105, 109, 112, 129; religious, 18, 163, 171–72; segregation, 119, 161, 163, 173, 187, 188, 192; stereotypes, 121, 132, 133, 153–54, 189; violence, 18, 99, 100, 123, 167, 172, 176; by women, 127

Disease: arthritis and osteoarthritis, 163, 168, 173, 176; bone fractures, 176; bone hypertrophy and remodeling, 176; brucellosis, 163; bubonic plague, 122; cerebral palsy, 163; cervical osteo-

phytosis, 176; cholera, 65, 66; dental caries, 164; enamel hypoplasia, 163, 164, 165, 169, 176; epidemics, 56, 65, 66, 161, 165; germ theory, 65; Harris lines on long bones, 163; joint degeneration, 165, 173; miasma theory, 56, 65–66, 161; osteomyelitis, 165; osteoporosis, 165; parasites, 52, 61, 119; periosteal new bone, 165; rickets, 163; smallpox, 166; staphylococcus infection, 163; systemic infection, 165; tuberculosis, 130, 163, 173; typhus fever, 130; venereal, 156, 157; yellow fever, 56. *See also* Health issues

Dishes. *See* Ceramics; Tableware

Display and interpretation: excavation viewing platform, 183–84; exhibits, 23, 25, 36, 182, 184; by the government, 182, 195n5; use of "ghost structure," 24

Diversity, 6, 46, 50, 102, 107–8, 109, 189

DNA. *See* Genetics

Documents. *See* Records, historical; Reports, project

Dolls, 111, *111*, 115, 131–32, 143, 168

Domesticity, the cult of, 151–52, 155

Domestic service, 99–100, 151, 155, 157

Drawings, in project report, 34

Drug use. *See* Opium

Dutch and Dutch Americans: colonial settlement by, 8, 16, 29, 72–74, 106, 108; manipulation of ethnicity, 106

Dutch West India Company, 72

East Asians, 102

Economic considerations: artifact storage and conservation, 36; burial site upkeep, 161; contract archaeology, 27–28; excavation in urbanized areas, 25–26, 28; municipal water/sewer systems, 66, 67; property values, 67–69, 160, 178; racism, 105, 115; shipbuilding, 77; unemployment, 19, 69, 115, 116; wages, 98, 99; wampum production, 74. *See also* Commodification

Economy: colonial America, 17, 72–78; Depression, 69, 115; development and function, 4–5, 8, 11–12; economic nodes, 11; migration from rural areas to find jobs, 19, 158; Panic of 1819, 88; Panic of 1837, 88. *See also* Capitalism; Labor; Trade

Education: African Americans, 115, 116, 119, 158, 194n4; Chinese Americans, 123; college-level, 106; effects at home of children in school, 151; literacy, 100–101, 119; Mexican Americans, 127–28; women, 158

Eighteenth century: African populations, 17;

172–73; ethical considerations of excavation/analysis, 169, 174, 177–78, 188; in houses, 4; practices (*See* Mortuary ritual); secondary, 161, 163, 195n3; site (*See* Cemeteries)

Hume, Ivor Noel, 23, 75

Hurricane Sandy, 187

Illinois. *See* Chicago

Immigrants: Americanization of, 22, 189, 191; construction techniques from, 58, 63; historical overview, 18, 19–20; impact of population size, 6; increase in heterogeneity due to, 7; labor, 90–91, 94, 95, 98, 99–101; legislation, 19, 20, 99, 122; nation-state of origin identity, 12, 189; percent of U.S. population, 18; relationship with dominant group, 102, 107, 121, 128, 132, 155, 189–90, 194n7. *See also specific nationalities*

Independence National Historical Park, 23–24, 179, 180

Indigenous peoples: Aztec, 150; Inka, 150; intermarriage with colonists, 51, 150; labor, 41; products provided by, 41. *See also* Native Americans

Indoor plumbing, 19, 33, 66, 148

Industrialization: effects of, 11, 13, 92, 151; factory system, 92–96, 139, 141, 187; impact of population size, 6; industrial capitalism, 17, 70, 92, 101, 148, 170; labor force needed for, 18, 92, 95. *See also* Manufacturing

Infrastructure: Chicago World's Fair, 53; as a component of cities, 10; components of, 54; municipal electrical system, 67; uneven provision due to social class, 6. *See also* Sewage disposal; Water distribution systems

Invasive *vs.* noninvasive methods, 31–32

Iraq: Ur, 1, 2, 20

Ireland, 154, 155

Irish and Irish Americans: ceramics, 91, 115, 129, 132, 155; citizenship, 129; clothing manufacture, 90–91; limitations in medical care, 130; middle-class, 131; mortuary ritual, 171, 172–73; political activity, 106; privy artifacts, 91; race/ethnicity classification, 129; railroad labor, 90, 94; relationship with African Americans, 129, 130–31; role of women, 154–55; time of immigration, 18; working-class, 68, 90–91, 94, 106, 129–30, 132, 154–55

Italianate style, 99, 144

Italians and Italian Americans, 25, 128

Jackson Park (Chicago, Ill.), 53

Jails, 10, 51, 55, 194n1 (chap. 6)

Janowitz, Meta, 79, 89

Japanese and Japanese Americans, 25

Jars, 52, 89, 89, 93, 126, 157

Jeppson, Patrice, 195n5

Jeton (token), 72–73, 73

Jewelry, 87, 124, 163, 167

Jewish Americans: in cemeteries, 164, 171–72; clothing manufacture, 91; discrimination, 108, 129; food and beverages, 129, 132; kin networks, 131; middle-class, 131–32

Jim Crow laws, 19, 130, 143

John Earthy's tavern (Pemaquid, Maine), 76, 76–77

Journeymen, 18, 87, 92, 96, 140, 142, 190

Kentucky: Bowling Green, 68, 69; Frankfort, 162–63; Louisville (*See* Louisville)

Key Corp (Albany, N.Y.), 74

Kiln, glost, 88

King's House (New York City), 76, 76–77

Knives, 95, 168

Labor: to build institutional structures, 7; children, 94, 163, 176; clothing manufacture, 90–91, 157; commuting to work, 19, 151; Cotton Men's Executive Council, 130; enslaved, 17, 77, 85, 167, 173; immigrant, 90–91, 94, 95, 98, 99–101; indigenous peoples, 41; middle-class women, 97, 114, 151–52; mining, 99; needed for industrialization, 18, 92, 95; railroads, 90, 99, 149; relationship with management (*See* Labor relations); textile manufacture, 94; unemployed workers, 19, 69, 115, 116, 158

Labor relations: acts of defiance, 95; biracial labor organization, 130; in the factory system, 92, 95; labor movement in the 1890s, 167; strikes and riots, 18; unions, 94, 116

Landfill: dikes and polders, 56; flood risk, 94, 187; historic sites preserved by, 30, 35–36, 86; New York City, 31, 35–36, 175, 187; San Francisco, 53, 54, 78, 86; scuttled ships in, 35–36, 58, 59, 77, 78; sources of fill, 56; techniques to combat settling, 58–60; urban expansion through, 38, 55–60, 94, 187; wharfing out, 56, 57, 58. *See also specific sites*

Landmarks Preservation Commission, 27, 29

Land ownership: African Americans, 112, 116; as an investment, 91; commodification of land into real estate, 55, 65, 67–68, 70, 187; to control urban space, 13; Irish Americans, 131, 154, 155; Jewish Americans, 131; women, 154, 155

99; masculinity, concepts of, 152–54, 190. *See also* Gender and gender roles

Mesopotamia, 4

Mestizo culture, 127, 128, 166

Metal: brass, 50; coffin hardware, 167, 168, 172; copper, 91; gold, 87 (*See also* Gold rush); iron, 50; lead, 34, 127, 148; pins, 91, 92, 111, 124, 157; silver, 6, 86, 87; tableware, 89, 95, 127, 128

Mexicans and Mexican Americans, 50, 124, 125, 126–28

Mexico: land which became new U.S. states, 51, 127, 145; Spanish exploration and exploitation, 71, 150; Teotihuacan, 2, 20; trade, 50, 85, 127

Michigan: Battle Creek, 67; Detroit, 23

Middle class: African Americans, 112, 114, 115, 116, 117–19, 131, 168, 194n4; boardinghouse managers, 97; colonial and federalist, 139–42, 190; food from retail shops, 94; Irish Americans, 131; Jewish Americans, 106, 131–32; masculinity, concepts of, 152–54, 190; mealtimes, 151–52; mid-nineteenth century, 142–45; residential areas, 18–19, 49; women, 28, 97, 114, 151–52, 157–58, 168

Migration within the U.S., 19–20, 158

Mills: flour, 18, 96; housing near, 69, 98; lumber, 96; textile, 44, 94, 98

Mining towns: definition of urban and, 6; Denver, 6, 52; immigrants, 99, 120, 122; Phoenix, 51; provisions from San Francisco, 85; urban landscape, 50; Virginia City, 6. *See also* Gold rush

Minnesota: Minneapolis, 18, 95–96; St. Paul, 155, 156

Missions, 11, 50

Missouri: St. Louis, 18, 39, 68, 69

Moravian immigrants, 49, 173

Mortuary ritual: "Beautification of Death" movement, 160, 166–69, 171, 188; bones to join with ancestors, 122, 170; coins on eyelids, 163; compass alignment of body, 164; embalming, 163, 167; "Good Death," 160, 165–66, 188; gravestones, 169, 170–72; items placed in graves, 163, 164, 168, 169, 172–73, 174; monuments and mausoleums, 171; overview, 159, 160, 188; shrouds, 163, 172; social class and, 168, 171. *See also* Human burials

Mount Vernon plantation (Mount Vernon, Va.), 21, 179, 180, 181

Mrozowski, Stephen, 148, 149

Multidisciplinary team approach, 24

Murray, Tim, 196n3

Museums. *See* Display and interpretation; Reconstruction and restoration

Nash, Gary, 182

Natchez Rebellion of 1729, 110

National Historic Landmarks, 49, 93

National Park Service, 23–24, 178, 181–84, 186, 195n5

National Register of Historic Places, 26, 93

Native Americans: Algonquian, 73; Apache, 50, 51; Cahokia settlement, 21, 185; in cemeteries, 164, 166, 174; ceramics, 44, 85, 110, 127; conflict with European settlers, 23, 41, 42, 50, 51, 110; Contact Period, 25; decimation of population, 74; forced assimilation, 51; funerary objects in museums, 174; fur trade, 72, 73–74; Hohokam, 50; inter-marriage with colonists, 51, 150; Iroquois, 72, 73; Natchez, 110; Paleo-Indian, 20; Pueblo Bonito settlement, 21; Tohono-O'odham, 127; Yavapai, 51. *See also* Indigenous peoples

Nature: control over, 52, 136, 137, 190; illusion of isolation from, 3

Nebraska: Lincoln, 10

Netherlands, 17, 56, 71, 73

Nevada: Virginia City, 6

New Hampshire: Portsmouth, 62

New Jersey: New Brunswick, 68; New Sweden, 58; Paterson, 93–94, 129, 130; Trenton, 47

New Mexico: Albuquerque, 18, 27, 166; burial under church floors, 160; Santa Fe (*See* Santa Fe)

New Orleans, La.: cemeteries, 162; diversity, 109–10, 130; early urban plan, 40, 44–46, 45; foodways, 109–10

New York: Albany, 29, 36, 72, 74, 79; Brooklyn, 131, 144–45; Broome County, 170–72; end of slavery, 117; New Brooklyn, 63; Newburgh, 21; New York City (*See* African Burial Ground; New York City)

New York City: almshouse, 157; Assay, 57, 60, 60; brothels, 155, 156; Chinese Americans today, 126; contract archaeology, 27; Crolius pottery, 89, 89; and the definition of a city, 3; diversity, 108; fires, 80, 86; Five Points, 36, 90–91, 129–30, 132, 146, 154; Harlem, 19; immigrants, 18; King's House, 76, 76–77; landfill, 55, 56, 58–59; Landmarks Preservation Commission, 27, 29; Manhattan, 20, 31, 47, 62, 80; markets, 81, 82, 83, 84; New Amsterdam, 8, 16, 47, 72–73, 74, 106, 107–8; patchiness of urban development, 29; politics and historical preservation, 27; Port Mobil, 20; privies, 62, 63, 64–65; Remmey pottery, 89; scuttled ship in landfill, 35–36, 58, 59; Seneca Village, 131, 194n4; South Ferry, 79; South Street Seaport Museum, 36; Spring Street Presby-

New York City—*continued*
terian Church Cemetery, 172–73; Stadt Huys
Block, *12–13*, 31, *33*; street layout, 47–48, 193n3;
Tenement Museum, 65; Trinity Church, 160;
urban renewal, 69, 131; Van Voorhis shop, 86,
87; as a walking city, 7; waterfront, 30–31, 35–36,
55; Water Street, 35–36, 58, 77; Winans grocery,
80; World Trade Center, 58, *59*, 77, 146. *See also*
African Burial Ground
New York State Museum, 36
Night soil, 61. *See also* Privies
Nineteenth century: archaeologically overlooked
until recently, 196n3; "Beautification of Death"
movement, 160, 166–69, 171, 188; cholera
epidemics, 65, 66; clothing manufacture, 90;
gender and the working class, 154–55; gold rush,
6, 52, 85, 86, 99, 120, 145; historic preservation
movement, 21–22; the ideal city, 52–54; middle
class in the, 142–45; post-Civil War, 22
Non-profit organizations, 28
North Carolina: Bethabara, 49; Bethania, 49;
Moravian immigrants, 49, 173; Old Salem, 49;
Winston, 49

Oasis towns, 50
Obama, Pres. Barack, 192
Occupational Safety and Health Administration
(OSHA), 34
Occupational safety considerations, 34, 95
Occupations, specialized, 4, 6, 7, 115. *See also*
Service industry
Office of Urban Affairs, 192
Ohio: Cincinnati, 18, 62; Zanesville, 62
Oklahoma: Oklahoma City, 19
Old Frankfort Cemetery (Frankfort, Ky.), 162–63
Olmsted, Frederick Law, 44, 53
Opium, 122, 123, 124
Oregon: Portland, 122, 170
Orientalism, 153
"Orientals," 121, 154
Ornamentation: buttons, 33, 58, 91, 111, 157, 164, 172;
home décor, 7, 52, 119, 129, 153; jewelry, 87, 124,
163, 167
Osteological analysis, 164–65, 169
Outhouses. *See* Privies

Pakistan: Harappa, 2
Paper, 91, 93
Penn, William, 46
Pennsylvania: construction techniques from im-

migrants, 58; New Sweden, 58; Philadelphia (*See*
Philadelphia); Pittsburgh, 18, 23, 62
Perryman, Lucrecia, 114
Philadelphia, Penn.: almshouse, 90; colonial settle-
ment, 17, 46–47; early urban plan, 46–47; First
African Baptist Church, 168; Franklin Court, 24,
195n5; Independence Hall, 24, 180; Independence
National Historical Park, 23–24, 179, 180; Met-
ropolitan Detention Center, 34, 35; President's
House, 174, 179–84, *180–81*, 191, 195n8; privies, 62,
63–64; reform institution, 158; shipbuilding, 77,
78; as a walking city, 7; waterfront, 55
Philadelphia City Almshouse (Philadelphia,
Penn.), 90
Photography, in project report, 34
Phyllis Wheatley Home for Girls (Chicago, Ill.), 158
Picture frames, 164
Pins, 91, 92, 111, 124, 157
Pipes, tobacco, 53, *76*, 76–77, 85, 164
Planning. *See* Urban planning
Plants: cactus fruits, 128; grass and lawn, 98; mortu-
ary rituals with, 164, 170; phytoliths, 33; pollen,
33, 98
Plumbing, indoor, 19, 33, 66, 148
Poland, 131
Politics: of annexation, 5; development and func-
tion, 4–5, 8, 11–12; feminist approach and, 150;
of historical preservation, 27; ideals and the
grid layout, 40, 45, 46; Irish Americans in, 106;
manipulation of ethnic identity, 106; policy
agenda for urban America, 192; power and city
planning, 45, 48, 49; power through uncovering
the past, 184; of racism, 105, 115; regulation and
control of space, 8, 13–14, 187, 192; regulation of
trade, 4. *See also* Government
Pollution: groundwater, 52, 63, 64 (*See also* Sewage
disposal); soil, 34, 148
Poor: in almshouses, 74, 90, 157, 190; burial, 160, 161,
167; clothing manufacture, 90; hauling water, 66;
historical archaeology on, 25, 185; purchase of
national brands, 194n2; residential area allocation (*See under* Residential area)
Population: percent living in cities, 2, 17, 20, 192;
relationship with urban landscape, 39
Population density, 5, 6, 8, 29, 67, 69
Population size, 5, 6
Port Mobil (New York City), 20
Portugal, 71
Posset pots, 75
Potter's fields, 161, 169

Pottery. *See* Ceramics

Power: electricity, 67, 96; water, 93, 94, 95–96

Preservationists, 27, 28, 49, 93

President's House (Philadelphia, Penn.), 174, 179–84, *180–81*, 191, 195n8

Private property. *See* Land ownership

Privies: above-ground, 63; artifacts from (*See* Privies, artifacts deposited in); backhoe excavation, 32; of Benjamin Franklin family, 24; construction, 61, 62–63, 64–65; double-shaft, 64; health issues, 52, 64–65, 98, 187–88; innovations in design, 64, 65

Privies, artifacts deposited in: ceramics, 79, 130; gambling, 124; garbage, 33, 61, 63; human remains, 157; information from, 61, 75, 193–94n8; overview, 188; as "percolation fill," 64; tableware, 75; textiles and sewing materials, 90, 91

Project management: analysis of artifacts and stratigraphy, 26, 30, 36; challenges with community archaeology, 177–78, 195n2; laboratory phase, 36; Phase 1, site assessment, 29–32; Phase II, field testing, 32–34, 35; Phase III, excavation, 32, 34–36 (*See also* Excavations); prioritization of tasks, 31, 35; processing the artifacts, 30; reports (*See* Publication of findings; Reports, project); research design, 31, 35, 193n4; safety considerations, 34; the unexpected, 35–36, 175, 183

Property. *See* Land ownership

Prostitution, 155–57, 158, 190

Proton magnetometry, 32

Provenience sheet, 34

Prussians and Prussian Americans, 63, 132

Public archaeology, 159, 178, 184, 191, 195n4. *See also* Community archaeology

Publication of findings: books on urban archaeology, 29; data bases, 191; government publications, 29, 195n5; "gray literature," 29; online and CDs, 191

Public health: animal issues, 63, 119, 148, 166; Chicago World's Fair, 53; development of municipal water/sewer systems, 65–66, 166, 187–88; overview, 19, 70; reform in the Southwest, 166; regulations on fill materials, 56; regulations on garbage disposal, 52, 56, 63, 166. *See also* Disease

Public participation, 27, 183–84. *See also* Community archaeology; Tourism

Public spaces: ornamental space, 148; playgrounds and parks, 52, 53, 69, 117, 163; urban planning, 70. *See also* Central places; Meeting places

Pueblo Revolt of 1680, 41

Puerto Ricans, 19

Quakers, 46, 169

Quality of life, 6, 66, 140

Race and ethnicity: *casta* system, 109, 110; challenges to classification by scientists, 129, 133; change in artifacts with change in demographics, 44; definition of "black," 112; definition of ethnicity, 105–6; definition of race, 104–5; diversity, 6, 46, 50, 102, 107–8, 109, 112, 189; ethnic "signifiers," 107; intersection (*See* Race and ethnicity, intersection between); manipulation for political advantage, 106; material culture and group identity, 103, 107, 121–22, 129–30; meat in diet, 124, 126, 132; "melting pot" or acculturation model, 121, 194n7; mixed, 108, 112, 127, 162; model of agency, 121, 194n7; neighborhood development, 107–8; privy construction and, 63; residential area allocation (*See under* Residential area); "whiteness," 106, 129. *See also* Discrimination; Immigrants; *specific groups*

Race and ethnicity, intersection between: African Americans, 110–19; Chinese, 120–26; French settlements, 108–10; Irish Americans, 129–31; Mexican household, 126–28; overview, 106; Spanish settlements, 108–9, 127–28

Racism: methodologies for justification, 105, 109, 112, 129

Railroads: development after the Civil War, 17–18, 54; effects on property value, 68–69; elevated railway, 53; impact in Arizona, 50, 51, 127; impact in Colorado, 52; impact in West Oakland/Oakland, 69, 85, 149; labor force, 90, 99, 120, 122, 124–25; manufacture, 93–94; porters, 115, 116, 143; Victorian Pullman cars, 115; wooden railway, 78

Ranching, 50

Real estate. *See* Land ownership

Reconstruction and restoration: after World War I, 22; Bethabara, 49; Bethania, 49; Old Salem, 49; waterfronts, 55; Williamsburg, 22–23, 193n1

Reconstruction Era, 167

Records, historical: background research for site assessment, 30; census, 21, 30, 39, 112; city directories, 30; of construction and destruction, 39; deeds, 30; diaries, 21, 98; government documents, 30; hospital, 130; land ownership, 112; local histories, 30; lost, 54; maps, 5, 7, 10, 14, 21, 30, 39; newspapers, 101; quantity available, and degree of urbanization, 29, 31; tax, 21, 30, 31, 39, 112; written, 21, 30, 98, 111

35–36, 58, 59, 77; *Ronson* (merchant vessel), 77; ship breaking yard, 78; shipbuilding, 77–78, 116

Shoes and boots, 18, 86, 168, 171

Shoreline, regularized. *See* Waterfront

Shovel test, 31, 32

Shrouds, 163, 172

Sixteenth century, 48, 71, 153

Slayton House (Annapolis, Md.), 111, *111*

Slums, 11, 18, 49, 116–17, 146. *See also* Urban renewal

Social class: artifacts reflecting, 52, 128, 135, 140, 168; *casta* system, 109, 110; cemeteries reflecting, 161, 163, 170–73, 188; effects of the factory system, 92, 148, 187; funeral services and, 168; overview, 135–36; relationship with gender, 134, 151–57; residential area allocation (*See under* Residential area); stratification and formation of cities, 4; transition from merchant to industrial capitalism, 148–49, 190; use of municipal systems, 6, 66–67. *See also* Elite class; Middle class; Poor; Working class

Social injustice, 6

Social landscape, 107–8

Social relationships: in boardinghouses, 97; connections by water-delivery ditches, 42; in crowded conditions, 7; gatherings (*See* Central places; Meeting places); between labor and management (*See* Labor relations); relationship between archeologist and community, 158, 159, 174, 177–79, 181–84; sense of community, 40, 42, 74, 97, 103, 158; tea parties, 144, 145

Society for the Establishment of Useful Manufactures, 93

Society of Friends, 169

Soil: contaminated, 34, 127, 148; coring and stratigraphy, 31, 32, 34, 36; "night soil," 61; as "the stuff of history," 183

South Carolina: Charleston, 7, 16–17, 81, 84–85

South Ferry (New York City), 79

South Street Seaport Museum, 36

Spain: exploration and exploitation by, 71, 150; grid layout, 40; Spanish Caribbean, 44, 150

Spanish and Spanish Americans: attitude toward death, 165; colonial settlement by, 8, 12, 16, 23, 41–42, 44, 108–9, 128, 150–51; immigration to Cuba, 44; majolica ceramics, 44, 110; mission settlement, 50

Spatial elements, 7–9, 13–14, 107, 185, 187

Spector, Janet, 149

Spring Street Presbyterian Church Cemetery (New York City), 172–73

Stadt Herberg (New Amsterdam, N.Y.), 74

Stadt Huys Block (New York City), *12–13*, 31, *33*, 74

Statehouse, 74

St. Augustine, Fla.: Castillo de San Marcos, 23; engendered analysis study, 150–51; excavation, 29; formation and Spanish colonialism, 16, 150; indigenous foodway, 109–10

Stone: grave construction, 163; limestone, 62, 163; manos, 128; privy and well construction, 62; quartz, 111, *111*; slab over coffin, 163

Storage of artifacts or repository, 26, 30, 36

Stores and shopkeepers: city markets, 81, *82*, *83*, 84–86; Hoff store, 86; unethical, 194n2; Van Voorhis shop, 86, 87; Winans grocery, 80

St. Peter Street Cemetery (New Orleans, La.), 109

Stratigraphy: analysis, 2–3, 36; excavation in complex sites, 26, 34, 36; maps, 34; soil coring methods, 32

Street layout: alternative to the grid, the baroque city, 48–49, 186; as a component of cities, 10, 12; curvilinear, 48; grid (*See* Grid layout); irregular or organic, 47

Street paving, 52

Structures, institutional: analysis by urban archaeology, 10; as an attribute of cities, 4, 6, 7, 39, 186; churches, 106, 117–19, *118*, 164, 166, 168; city planning and placement of, 40, 41, 45, 48, 49, 126; courthouses, 10, 51; statehouse, 74

Structures, special purpose: adaptive reuse of, 9–11, 74; as an attribute of cities, 6; in the factory system, 92–96, 139, 141, 187. *See also specific types of structure*

Subjectivity in archaeological research: in analysis of material culture, 112, 121, 154; bias in exhibitions and displays, 193n1; bias in sampling strategy, 35; challenges to racial/ethnic classification, 129, 133; gender bias in focus of studies, 149–50, 152; gender bias in written record, 134; interpretation of cultural segregation or assimilation, 100, 120–22, 133

Sullivan, Louis Henry, 53

Swedish and Swedish Americans, 12, 16, 58

Swiss and Swiss Americans, 58

Syria: Tell Brak, 7

Tableware: bowls, 89, 118, 126, 143, 146, 168; cutlery, 75, 95, 168; drinking vessels, 75, 85, 89, 110, 126, 127; glassware, 97, 129–30, 146; metal, 89, 95, 127, 128; plates, 79, 97, 118, 126, 127, 143, 156, 172; platters, 79, 98, 129; porringers, 89; wooden trenchers, 75. *See also* Tea ware

Values, cultural: authentication of self by material goods, 75; ethnicity and, 106, 131; expressed by architecture, 7; expressed by grid layout, 40, 45, 46; expressed by utopian landscape, 49, 53; gender, 149; individuality, 113–14; temperance, 119; time is money, 92; use of municipal water/sewer systems, 66–67; Victorian, 142–43

Van Voorhis, Daniel, 87

Van Voorhis shop (New York City), 86, 87

Vases, 119, 129, 132

Venereal disease, 156

Victorian America: "Beautification of Death" movement, 160, 166–69, 171, 188; "civilized man," 152; in gender relationships research, 194n1 (chap. 6); ornate design aesthetic, 147; Pullman car practices, 115; values, 142–43

Violence: inflicted on slaves, 176; racial, 100, 123, 167, 172; riots, 18, 172

Virginia: Alexandria, 27, 169; Jamestown, 76, 76–77; Manassas, 169; Mount Vernon, 21, 179, 180, 181; Williamsburg, 22–23, 75–76, 193n1

Vitruvius, 40

Walker, Mark, 149

Wall, Diana, 80, 113, 149, 151

Wampum, 73–74

Warehouses, 45, 55, 69, 72–73, 73

Washington, D.C.: baroque plan, 48–49, 186; brothels, 155; privies, 63; Reno suburb, 116

Washington, Pres. George, 179, 180, 181, 182, 191

Washington, Martha, 87, 139

Water distribution systems: agricultural irrigation, 4, 42, 50, 63; indoor plumbing, 19, 33, 66, 148; municipal, 52, 54–55, 61, 65–67, 70, 187; storage (See Cisterns; Wells); water-delivery ditches, 42

Waterfront: Chicago, 53; New York City, 81, 82, 83; real estate development, 55, 70; regularized shoreline, 55, 70; restoration as tourist attraction, 55; San Francisco, 54, 86; shipyards, 77–78, 116

Water power, 93, 94, 95–96

Water resources: groundwater contamination, 52, 63, 64; hauling water, 66; oasis communities, 50; settlement along, 42, 50, 52, 185–86; territorial defense of, 50; water as a commodity, 67

Water Street (New York City), 35–36, 58, 77

Wellfleet Tavern (Wellfleet, Mass.), 76, 76–77

Wells, 32, 33, 61–62

Welsh and Welsh Americans, 172–73

West Africa, 172

West Coast, 85, 102, 120

Western Cemetery (Louisville, Ky.), 163

West Oakland, Calif.: African Americans, 115, 116; boarding and lodging, 96–97; Chinese Americans, 123–24; Jewish Americans, 132; privies, 62, 115; railroad, 69, 85, 149; shipyards, 116; urban renewal, 69–70, 116–17

West Virginia: Harpers Ferry, 62, 140; Wheeling, 62, 63

Wetherburn Tavern (Williamsburg, Va.), 75–76

Winans, Anthony, 80

Winans grocery (New York City), 80

Wisconsin: Milwaukee, 18

Women: arrival in Tucson, 51; birth control, 156–57; boardinghouse managers, 97; childbirth and midwives, 114, 166, 173; clothing manufacture, 90–91, 157; cooking as women's work, 109–10, 154; domesticity, cult of, 151–52, 155; domestic service, 99–100, 151, 155, 157; historical archaeology on, 25, 149, 151–52, 154–58; institutions and, 157–58, 194n1 (chap. 6); laundry as women's work, 123, 154; middle-class, 28, 97, 114, 151–52, 157–58, 168; prostitution, 155–57, 158, 190; "race women," 116; strong or assertive, 114, 154; textile manufacture by, 94; in urban archaeology, 28, 150–51; women-owned businesses, 28, 97, 151; women's movement, 149; working-class, 90–91, 94, 97, 148, 154–55, 157–58. See also Gender and gender roles

Wood: barrels, 61, 77, 80, 86; beams, to combat landfill settling, 58–60; coffins, 162, 163, 164, 172; pilings, 60; railway, 78; tree-ring study, 77; trenchers, 75

Working class: cemetery, 172–73; in factory system, 92–96, 139, 141, 187; gender and the, 154–55; hauling water, 66; historical archaeology on, 25, 154–55; in industrial land use areas, 69; mealtimes, 154–55; overview, 145–47, 190; public transportation for the, 19; residential area allocation (See under Residential area)

Workplace, separation of home and, 18–19, 96, 140, 141, 151, 187, 190

World Trade Center (New York City), 58, 59, 77, 146

World War I, 22, 116

World War II, 24, 69, 116

Writing tools, 73, 100–101, 119, 127

Zane family (Louisville, Ky.), 88

NAN A. ROTHSCHILD is director of museum studies at Columbia University and research professor at Barnard College. She is interested in urban issues, colonialism, and other social archaeological questions.

DIANA DIZEREGA WALL is professor of anthropology at the City College of New York and the CUNY Graduate Center. She is an archaeologist who studies aspects of American culture in New York City.

The University Press of Florida is the scholarly publishing agency for the State University System of Florida, comprising Florida A&M University, Florida Atlantic University, Florida Gulf Coast University, Florida International University, Florida State University, New College of Florida, University of Central Florida, University of Florida, University of North Florida, University of South Florida, and University of West Florida.

The American Experience in Archaeological Perspective

EDITED BY MICHAEL S. NASSANEY

The books in this series explore events, processes, settings, or institutions that were significant in the formative experience of contemporary America. Each volume frames the topic beyond an individual site and attempts to give the reader a flavor of the theoretical, methodological, and substantive issues that researchers face in their examination of that topic or theme. These books are comprehensive overviews that allow serious students and scholars to get a good sense of contemporary and past inquiries on broad themes in American history and culture.

The Archaeology of Collective Action, by Dean J. Saitta (2007)

The Archaeology of Institutional Confinement, by Eleanor Conlin Casella (2007)

The Archaeology of Race and Racialization in Historic America, by Charles E. Orser Jr. (2007)

The Archaeology of North American Farmsteads, by Mark D. Groover (2008)

The Archaeology of Alcohol and Drinking, by Frederick H. Smith (2008)

The Archaeology of American Labor and Working-Class Life, by Paul A. Shackel (2009; first paperback edition, 2011)

The Archaeology of Clothing and Bodily Adornment in Colonial America, by Diana DiPaolo Loren (2010; first paperback edition, 2011)

The Archaeology of American Capitalism, by Christopher N. Matthews (2010; first paperback edition, 2012)

The Archaeology of Forts and Battlefields, by David R. Starbuck (2011; first paperback edition, 2012)

The Archaeology of Consumer Culture, by Paul R. Mullins (2011; first paperback edition, 2012)

The Archaeology of Antislavery Resistance, by Terrance M. Weik (2012; first paperback edition, 2013)

The Archaeology of Citizenship, by Stacey Lynn Camp (2013)

The Archaeology of American Cities, by Nan A. Rothschild and Diana diZerega Wall (2014; first paperback edition, 2015)

The Archaeology of American Cemeteries and Gravemarkers, by Sherene Baugher and Richard F. Veit (2014; first paperback edition, 2015)

The Archaeology of Tobacco and Smoking, by Georgia L. Fox (2015)

The Archaeology of Gender in Historic America, by Deborah L. Rotman (2015)

The Archaeology of the North American Fur Trade, by Michael S. Nassaney (2015)

The Archaeology of the Cold War, by Todd A. Hanson (2016)